The Civic Imagination

The Civic Imagination

Making a Difference in American Political Life

Gianpaolo Baiocchi, Elizabeth A. Bennett,
Alissa Cordner, Peter Taylor Klein, and
Stephanie Savell

Paradigm Publishers
Boulder • London

Copyright © 2014 Paradigm Publishers

Published in the United States by Paradigm Publishers, 5589 Arapahoe Avenue, Boulder, CO 80303 USA.

Paradigm Publishers is the trade name of Birkenkamp & Company, LLC,
Dean Birkenkamp, President and Publisher.

Library of Congress Cataloging-in-Publication Data
Baiocchi, Gianpaolo, 1971–
  The civic imagination : making a difference in American political life / Gianpaolo Baiocchi,
Elizabeth A. Bennett, Alissa Cordner, Peter Taylor Klein, and Stephanie Savell.
    pages cm
  Includes bibliographical references and index.
  ISBN 978-1-61205-305-9 (pbk. : alk. paper)
  ISBN 978-1-61205-314-1 (library eBook)
  1. Civics. 2. Political participation—United States. 3. Political culture—United States.
4. Social change—United States. I. Title.
  JK1764.B35 2013
  306.20973—dc23
                                                                                    2013022330

Printed and bound in the United States of America on acid-free paper that meets the standards of the American National Standard for Permanence of Paper for Printed Library Materials.

18 17 16 15 14   1 2 3 4 5

Contents

Preface and Acknowledgments

A few short months after we concluded the fieldwork for this book, the Occupy movement burst on the scene and captured Americans' collective imagination. For our research team, the idea of a movement for the 99 percent was intriguing, not only because we had been thinking and writing about creative forms of engagement but also because inequality resonated as one of our greatest concerns. Occupy, as the movement came to be called, was not unique; other such spontaneous democratic protests arose elsewhere in the world, from the Spanish Indignados, to Real Democracy Now! in England, to the Arab Spring. It felt, in some ways, that a common thread of hope, outrage, tenacity, and creativity was beginning to weave together populations that had previously seemed worlds apart. Despite—or perhaps *because of*—Occupy's lack of a clear ideology, a specified platform, or a direct relationship with existing movements, "occupy" quickly became a one-word moniker for fighting structural injustice. Public encampments—literally, "occupations"—sprang up nearly everywhere in the United States, as did symbolic and metaphorical iterations, like Occupy Rosh Hashanah and the more recent Occupy Sandy.[1] Despite some early derision from members of the Democratic Party, and outright hostility from commentators on the political Right, Occupy appeared to capture Americans' need to have a more meaningful experience of democracy.

We were struck by how many of the issues raised by the Occupy movement resonated with our findings about contemporary political culture in America. In Providence, the site of our research, Occupy arrived a bit late, though a small cluster of tents remained in a city park for months, reminding passersby of the "99 percent." The city eventually deemed the occupation "unsafe" and "illegal." The city court mediated negotiations with the activists, who eventually agreed to disband

---

1. Occupy Rosh Hashanah first took place on September 16, 2011, when a thousand people gathered in New York City to reflect on the relationship between the Jewish holiday and the values of Occupy. The Occupy Sandy movement was born in late October 2012. It offered disaster relief and drew attention to issues of inequality in response to Hurricane Sandy, a "superstorm" that ravaged the East coast, particularly low-lying neighborhoods in and around New York City.

the camp in exchange for a new day shelter for the homeless to be sponsored and hosted by a local Catholic church. Though controversial and complicated for the activists, the mayor's office dubbed the agreement a "peaceful end of Occupy Providence's encampment" (Taveras 2012). Indeed, Occupy activity soon dwindled, and attention returned to Rhode Island's severe economic recession and high rates of unemployment.

The sudden appearance of Occupy in Providence connects with several of the themes that were apparent throughout our fieldwork, and that we discuss in this book. In particular, we found that dissatisfaction with the political system is at the core of how Americans experience democracy, and that creative imagining of new futures is central to how they work to rebuild it. Americans' frequent—and vehement—disavowal of politics is not necessarily a route to thin commitments or to avoid important issues. Instead, it creates space to rescue a sense of democratic possibility and renewal. That Occupy turned its back on traditional politics while creating a movement centered on addressing inequality and reinventing democracy should put to rest any notion that widespread disavowal of politics necessarily signals that democratic values have been lost.[2]

Occupy's manifesto includes a stated mistrust of "the political elites of both parties that run this country." In this book we describe many activists who assert, "What I do isn't political," and that "politics is dirty and broken." Occupy may not see eye to eye on all things political with the neighborhood association leaders, tech-savvy entrepreneurs, or education activists we describe in this book, but this commonality should not be underestimated. Indeed, these shared sentiments hold unique possibilities in the current moment for unusual and unexpected alliances. As many a commentator has noted, Occupy's broad appeal won over sympathizers from beyond the usual suspects of movement activists.[3] Even the business-oriented magazine *Wired* hired a writer to embed with Occupy camps around the country and file gritty (if mostly complementary) stories on the movement, its activists, and their clashes with the police (Norton 2012).

Occupy also shows that the relationship between citizens and the state is complicated, that inequality is hard to talk about, and that, even with the best of intentions, people can be blind to some aspects of social life—all issues we examine

---

2. Ruth Milkman, Stephanie Luce, and Penny Lewis, faculty researchers at the City University of New York, surveyed 729 protesters at a May 1, 2011, Occupy march and rally in New York City and conducted extensive interviews with twenty-five people who were core activists in the Occupy movement. They found that "most OWS [Occupy Wall Street] Activists and supporters were deeply skeptical of the mainstream political system as an effective vehicle for social change." However, "despite being disillusioned with mainstream politics, many OWS activists and supporters remain politically active and civically engaged" (2013, 4).

3. As Milkman, Luce, and Lewis report, Occupy "was able to attract supporters with a wide variety of specific concerns, many of whom had not worked together before" (2013, 5).

in this book. The debates that have plagued and divided Occupy are similar to the stories that fill these pages. Does Occupy support progressive politicians or unions? Should Occupiers vote in the next election? What can Occupy do to avoid reinforcing race, class, and gender power imbalances? The ideas and ideologies, tactics and tendencies that divide and unite civic groups are fuzzy, complicated, and far from self-evident. And taking on inequality only amplifies the challenges. If Occupy came about because of the need to address inequality, its trajectory is marked by the challenge that naming inequality poses. It is easier to talk abstractly (albeit creatively!) about the richest 1 percent than to address, concretely, inequalities within the 99 percent. Likewise, it is more straightforward to use a "progressive stack" in assemblies—allowing women and people of color to talk first—than to bring marginalized groups into the fore of leadership, visibility, and power and sustain those roles over time. No doubt, Occupy has thus far been challenged by its limited ability to transform itself from a movement organized around "demanding the impossible"—to use Judith Butler's words—to a movement organizing to propose and pursue the possible (Butler 2011).[4]

Our goal in writing this book has been to contribute to ongoing efforts to reinvigorate civic and political life, and to do so with attention to, and normative preference for, activism that begets greater equality. Many of our stylistic and analytic choices were underwritten by these greater intentions. We hope that the civic imaginations we describe will be fodder for debates in cultural sociology; yet we wish them to be even more consequential for engaged citizens and students trying to understand the potentials and limits of certain ways of seeing, judging, and imagining the world. Another one of the choices we made, which was somewhat at odds with our academic reflexes, was to rely on a mode of critique that literary theorist Eve Sedgwick (2003) calls "reparative." Both "reparative critique" and its more typical counterpart, "paranoid critique," unmask power and unveil domination. However, paranoid critique stops there—blinding us to possibility and impoverishing our ability to see agency. Paranoid modes are important and powerful, but Sedgwick invites us to also think about what the knowledge we produce *can do* and urges us to question the steadfastness of power that paranoid critiques assume. Our writing has rested, instead, on the assumption that a text may seek to unearth surprises, draw attention to creativity and agency, richly describe the world, and point to renewed possibilities and avenues for change. Finally, following in the path of normative philosophers and critical sociologists, we are unapologetic for injecting the value of equality into our analysis of what it means to *revive* and to live in a democracy *revived by* civic engagement.

The need to address the social problems of our time—and the need to do so without relying exclusively on government—has captured the American imagination, and we, in turn, are captured by how Americans have put their imaginations to work. These are the stories that fill the pages of this book. Of course, another

---

4. For Butler's comments, and those of other writers who "support Occupy Wall Street and the Occupy Movement around the world," see http://occupywriters.com.

headline-grabbing movement in recent years, the Tea Party movement, is also founded on mistrust of political institutions, though their focus is not promoting the reduction of inequality (Williamson, Skocpol, and Coggin 2011). Understanding democratic possibilities, or alternatively, the contractions of democracy, in any one moment or context calls for the kind of careful analysis we have done here. As the saying goes, the politics is in the details.

*   *   *

This book, as we describe in Appendix A, was born from an experiment, itself hatched in a classroom. We began as a group of students and a professor at Brown University and ended the journey as a group of friends and colleagues, all professors or nearly so, and most of us no longer at Brown. Along the way we have incurred innumerable debts, big and small, that made the research, and the book, possible. We cannot list everyone who helped, though we must mention a few.

First, our partners and families put up with more talk of our project—which we came to refer to as "Project" (see Methodological Appendix A)—than they deserved, and for their support we are endlessly indebted and grateful. Special thanks to our hosts in Maine, who provided a serene environment for fieldnote coding.

Second, we thank our host institution of Brown University. While we did not receive direct funding from Brown for any of this work, the university provided a lively intellectual context that, in many ways, shaped our conversations. Stephanie received an Integrative Graduate Education and Research Traineeship/National Science Foundation (IGERT/NSF) fellowship from the Graduate Program for Development that supported two years of research and writing. Gianpaolo had a one-semester fellowship from the Pembroke Center for Teaching and Research on Women as research started, and a one-semester fellowship from the Cogut Center for the Humanities during the writing process; both opportunities reduced teaching loads and provided intellectual conversation. During the formative moments of the research, we received invaluable advice from our "research board": Marcy Brink-Danan, Sharon Krause, Catherine Lutz, Keith Morton, and Corey Walker. At Brown, we are also grateful for the insights and encouragement of Tatiana Andia, Diana Graizbord, and Michael Rodríguez Muñiz.

Many thanks to Paradigm Publishers; Dean Birkenkamp's willingness to take a gamble with us was crucial for our group process, as was his generosity with deadlines, thoughtful feedback, and consistent encouragement. Our afternoon visit and work with Javier Auyero was invaluable, as was critical but affirming feedback from Claudio Bezencry, as we were deciding on putting together a book. Our writing benefited tremendously from suggestions gathered in two workshops, one at the University of Georgia Political Ethnography Workshop, where we received feedback from Becca Hanson, Pablo Lapegna, and David Smilde; the other at the University of São Paulo working group on political society and collective action, where we received feedback from Domitila Caires, Adrian Gurza Lavalle, and José Swazko. Similarly, the manuscript was improved by the questions and comments gathered at meetings of the American Sociological Association, Eastern Sociological Society, and Western Political Science Association. In this regard, special thanks are due to Caroline Lee and Edward Walker. We are also extremely indebted to the readers of the manuscript whose insights were critical to the final version: Claudio Bezencry, Nina Eliasoph, Pablo Lapegna, Peter Levine, and Michael Schudson. Naturally, the standard disclaimer applies: all errors and omissions are our own responsibility.

Finally, our greatest debt is to the people who allowed us into their meeting spaces and living rooms, making time in their busy schedules and hectic lives to share with us their dreams, ideas, activism, and knowledge. If they felt skeptical of our curiosity or tired of our intrusions, then they were infinitely more patient and generous, continuing to allow us, and thus our readers, into their experience of bringing forth new visions of a better city and a better civic life. We do not mention them by name in this book, but we hope they find their yearnings well represented, their words and actions accurately described, and our analysis meaningful. It is to them this book is warmly dedicated.

*   *   *

A note on citing this work: While we understand that standard citation practices would limit an in-text citation to the first of the five authors of this book, as in "(Baiocchi et al. 2014)," we respectfully ask you to avoid this custom when referring to the book if at all possible. It is our preference that you cite all of our names, as in "(Baiocchi, Bennett, Cordner, Klein, and Savell 2014)," or refer to us in alternative fashion, such as "the authors of *The Civic Imagination.*"

Chapter 1

American Civic and Political Life

Americans hate politics. They are skeptical of elected officials, and they suspect that special, elite interests trump the needs of the average Joe. The political system is broken, unfair, and corrupt—on *that*, everyone agrees, even America's leaders. In the 2008 presidential election, two US senators argued over who was the *least* like "politics as usual," and was therefore the better candidate.[1] By 2010, the wake of the financial crisis had exacerbated this wave of distrust, which was marked by low approval of Congress and lack of confidence in public officials (ANES 2010; Pew 2010). Disdain for elected representatives continued to hit all-time lows, with Americans reporting that they have a higher opinion of root canals, head lice, traffic jams, and colonoscopies than Congress (Public Policy Polling 2013).[2] And in today's context of increasing inequality and decreasing state service provision, the political climate has only worsened. In short, *Americans have come to distrust their democracy.*

---

1. Barack Obama, then-senator of Illinois and winner of the election, notably exclaimed, "Change doesn't come *from* Washington. Change comes *to* Washington" (speech at the Democratic National Convention on August 28, 2008). His opponent, Senator John McCain of Arizona, similarly asserted that if you ask Americans "what frustrates them most about Washington, they will tell you they don't think we're capable of serving the public interest before our personal and partisan ambitions; that we fight for ourselves and not for them. Americans are sick of it, and they have every right to be" (speech in Columbus, Ohio, on May 15, 2008).

2. For data on these comparisons with Congress, see Public Policy Polling's press release "Congress Less Popular Than Cockroaches, Traffic Jams" from January 8, 2013. Public Policy Polling surveyed 830 American voters via automated telephone interviews between January 3 and 6, 2013, asking questions like, "What do you have a higher opinion of: Congress or ebola?"

The city of Providence, Rhode Island, and the sentiments of the people whose stories fill the pages of this book are no different. In 2010, when we set out to study civic engagement and political culture, the city was in economic and political turmoil. The two-term mayor of Providence, David Cicilline, had just announced that he would seek a US Congress seat, leaving the mayor's office open—and hotly contested. The winning mayoral candidate, Angel Taveras, reflected the contemporary moment of distrust in government, noting in an op-ed that "sometimes, the best thing City Hall can do is get out of the way" (Taveras 2010).

As the city's first Latino mayor, Taveras was celebrated: "Out with the old, in with the new," one headline cheered (Fitzpatrick 2010). But the 2008 global financial meltdown and subsequent recession had hit the state hard. In January 2010, Rhode Island's unemployment rate climbed to 11.9 percent, a full 2 percentage points higher than the national average (US Bureau of Labor Statistics 2013). And by early 2011, the city was so close to economic collapse that the mayor described it as a "category five financial hurricane." Mayor Taveras proposed closing several schools and argued that pensions for city employees would have to be renegotiated. His popularity nosedived.

Amid this turbulence, citizens in Providence and elsewhere were engaged in a flurry of activity, suggesting that it is possible to work for positive changes in American political life, even in times of great economic and political stress. As we began our fieldwork, we were bombarded with a bewildering variety of ways to "participate" and "get involved": Sign a petition to bring US troops home from Afghanistan! Attend a meeting about rezoning local schools! Contribute to the annual food drive! Finding opportunities to "make a difference" was easy, but what was difficult was making sense of it all. Why are there so many different groups working on a single issue? How do people decide which activities are worth their time? For activists of all different stripes, what determines the right way to work for change?

To learn more about the current landscape of civic engagement and political culture in America, we joined civic groups in Providence, attended their events, worked alongside activists, and interviewed both extraordinary leaders and everyday members. What struck us immediately was how inventive people are in thinking about and working toward making change. We attended a "listening party" during the mayoral campaign, where the classic format of *voters* questioning *candidates* was reversed: instead, mayoral *candidates* posed questions to an audience of *voters*. The organizing group, we later discovered, thought that one important way to influence electoral politics was to be sure that candidates listened to their constituents. We also attended a neighborhood association Halloween event that involved launching pumpkins with a trebuchet (a medieval-style catapult) in the local park. As we helped to clean up pounds of pumpkin guts, the organizers commented that the way to make Providence a better place was to bring neighbors together—first to socialize, then to collectively organize. And flying pumpkins did just that! Throughout the year, we canvassed, protested, and organized with activists of all kinds. No two individuals described political participation—others' or their own—in the same way. However, collectively, their stories and actions share some similarities that help us understand why people try to make a difference in the ways they do.

The Civic Imagination is a report of our findings, a snapshot of civic life in America, and a discussion of contemporary political culture, based on our experiences in Providence. We recount a year in the lives of activists striving to make their city a better place. Those activists are part of seven civic groups, chosen for their diversity of interests, constituencies, tactics, and organizational forms, that allowed us into their work and lives. The book is motivated by the themes that emerged in this field research. Most significantly, where we expected to find cynicism, apathy, and individualistic commitments, we instead encountered reflective, sober, and tremendously *hopeful* citizens.[3] On the one hand, we heard repeatedly that the political system is broken, and we grew accustomed to the common refrains, "I'm not political" and "I don't see my work as political." On the other hand, we learned that these discourses were not necessarily signals of political disengagement, but instead part of a more complicated relationship with political life. Another theme that emerged was a difference in how groups paid attention to inequality, both as a social problem to be solved and as an issue that plagues civic groups themselves. While inequality was central to the work of some organizations, it was more commonly a blind spot—something removed from the forefront of attention and readily overlooked.

Our goal is to explore the contours of these complex relations—between citizens and their democracy, skepticism and engagement, and inequality and activism. Upon closer inspection, it is evident that while skepticism of politics is indeed widespread, as many have reported, a critique of politics is not incompatible with civic engagement. Public officials say, "I'm a nonpolitical guy," to endear themselves to their audiences. Civic leaders say, "Government won't solve problems," while working on political campaigns. And activists say, "I don't like *politricks*," despite their engagement with city government. Citizens are adamant that they and their activism not be associated with the dirty, corrupt, self-interested, combative sphere of politics. This "disavowal" of the polluted sphere of politics allows people to creatively constitute, and engage in, what they imagine to be appropriate and desirable forms of political engagement. As people envision a future that goes beyond what they see as the contemporary problems of politics, they develop and modify working theories of civic life. These cognitive roadmaps or moral compasses help people make sense of their place in the political world. We call this concept "the civic imagination" and illustrate it in the following example.

In February 2011, Providence residents erupted in protest when Mayor Taveras proposed closing several schools as a partial solution to the city's budget crisis. Randi Weingarten, president of the American Federation of Teachers, called it an "unprecedented power play" (Goodnough 2011). At public meetings, citizens waved

---

3. A note on our usage of "citizens" and "Americans": we use "citizen" in the broadest sense, as a member of a political community or resident of a city, not in the more restrictive sense having to do with legal status or realization of rights. Thus, in describing the "citizens of Providence," we include undocumented immigrants, children, and international students as well as legalized or US-born citizens. Similarly, by "Americans" we mean people living in the United States or otherwise identifying as American.

banners proclaiming, "It's not about the $; it's about the kids," and children wore nametags that read, "My name is ___. I am a good investment." Parents and teachers organized the Save Our Schools Coalition, which accused the board of "assassinating schools." When the city announced *which* schools were under consideration for closure, an activist called the selection "geographical genocide," asserting the targeted neighborhoods were primarily inhabited by people of color.

In the subsequent months, parents, teachers, ordinary citizens, and public officials came together to debate the future of the city's schools in a series of public forums. During these meetings, we witnessed many different ways in which Americans imagine making a difference in political life. In other words, we observed how people's theories of civic life shape their diagnoses of political problems and guide their prospective thinking about possible solutions. Some people were concerned that the school closings primarily affected students from poor and racial minority neighborhoods; others focused on the opportunity for neighbors and city residents to come together to voice their opinions. Even the simple notion of holding public forums elicited diverse reactions. Cynics said the meetings were a formality—window dressing for decisions already made. Optimists understood the meetings to be a genuine opportunity—a chance to "sit down and talk about our differences" and to generate "productive" and "concrete" ideas as a community. As one citizen put it to the school board, "We will find a solution you haven't."

Our observation is that these diverse civic imaginations organize into three clusters, each with a unique focus and inspiration, a particular conception of success, and a set of blind spots—issues and problems rendered out of focus by the blinders of its own logic.[4] Each family of imaginations makes different tradeoffs: for example, some groups value making decisions quickly, while others prefer the slower process of consensus-building; some activists employ anger and conflict as tactical strategies, while others use strategies less likely to upset or offend. The plurality of understandings of how political life "works" sometimes creates ambiguities or misunderstandings, as common words come to mean very different things in practice. In Providence, "transparency," for example, was defined in diverse ways: as an innovative technology, as openness about funding sources, or as government's accountability to citizens. Civic imaginations guide action and thus have important consequences not just for a school debate but for civic life in its broadest sense: civic imaginations can both foster democratic values and limit democratic possibilities.

We pay particularly close attention to the connections between these civic imaginations and inequality, something that is both a defining characteristic of the present moment and an aspect of social and political life that is often overlooked. Socioeconomic inequality has been on the rise since the 1970s and was exacerbated by the 2008 financial crisis and subsequent recession. However, some of the ways in which Americans organize themselves in civic life pay little attention to this

---

4. As we will describe in Chapter 4, people within and outside of civic groups have fluid relationships with these practical philosophies, relationships that can change over time, between contexts, or even at two points within the same conversation.

fact—something we examine in depth in Chapter 6. We believe that greater equality is good for society as a whole, and so we cannot help but see—and feel concerned about—the glaring omissions of inequality in many discourses, processes, and practices of contemporary civil society.[5] The consequences are serious, we argue, and include a threat to the democratic value of equal opportunity for all. Thus, while we have a hopeful perspective on the agency of people in working toward positive change, we join other critics in worrying that some current trends in civic life are entrenching or even exacerbating existing inequalities.

CONTOURS OF POLITICS AND CIVIC LIFE IN AMERICA

"Politics" is a term central to our argument, and one marked by a wide range of connotations and uses in everyday life. Conventionally, the "political" includes the diverse array of institutions, processes, and actors affiliated with the state, such as politicians and government employees.[6] In this book, we use the term loosely, in accordance with the myriad meanings attributed by people in our study. Often these uses of the term share a sense that the political system is broken, and that the "political process" is an obstacle to the ideal functioning of democratic principles. Thus, we hear "politics" used as a moniker for the unsavory and undesirable aspects of democracy: corruption on behalf of public officials, deadlocked bipartisan battling, the promotion of elite-based special interests, anger and contention in public protests, the obscuring of discrimination against marginalized populations ... the list goes on.

As we describe in more detail in the next chapter, our research in Providence employed an ethnographic method: we participated in the lives and activities of particular individuals active in civic life, using our position as (almost) "insiders" to observe and analyze as "outsiders." While we rely on these close encounters for definitions of key terms such as "politics," and indeed, for our findings, we turn first to large-scale survey data in order to set the scene and describe the broader context of our research.

Skepticism

Our research year was marked by a dismal economy, bitter partisan-based backlash, and epic discontent with Congress and elected officials. The Pew Research Center, an

---

5. We recognize that "civil society" is a complex and problematic term. Conceptually and in practice, it can be used to marginalize groups, negate their demands on the state, and perpetuate inequalities (Paley 2002). Here, however, we use the term to mean all forms of associational life—both those reproducing and those challenging structures of power.

6. Here, "the state" is an institution that includes all branches of government (legislative, executive, and judicial) at all levels (local, state, and national), as well as police and military.

independent, nonpartisan research organization that studies attitudes toward politics, argues that these events, taken together, have created the "perfect storm" for distrust of government (Pew 2010, 1). At the most basic level, Pew defines "trust" as a conviction that the government will do what is "right." According to this measure, between 10 percent and 22 percent of Americans trust the federal government in Washington.[7] This is a low point for skepticism among Americans. Answers to this question were first systematically recorded in 1958. At that time, 73 percent of Americans trusted the government to do what is right "just about always" or "most of the time." Since then, trust has only plummeted to today's extremely low level on two occasions: around 1980 and around 1994 (Pew 2010, 13). If you complicate the measure of trust, the news gets even worse. The American National Election Service measures trust in government by creating an index that combines the answers to several questions: Do you trust the federal government? Is the government run for the benefit of all the people, or does it look out for narrow interests? Does government waste taxes? Are the people who run the government crooked? The indexed responses give an annual sense of where politics stands in the eyes of the public. The years 1994 and 2008 have the lowest scores *in half a century* (ANES 2010, Table 5A.5).[8]

In the mid-1990s, confidence was at an unprecedented low in the United States, and scholars engaged in a broad conversation over whether American culture could become—or already was—too skeptical for the health of its democracy.[9] Record numbers of Americans felt "alienated." They even disapproved of the House of Representatives, the institution "designed to represent the public will" (Ansolabehere and Iyengar 1995, 2). A particular concern was that young Americans were more cynical than the previous generation: they had a visceral dislike of politics, did not trust politicians, considered government unresponsive, believed average people did not have any political clout, and saw special interest groups as reigning supreme (S. Bennett 1997). Both within and outside of academic circles, people wondered: What becomes of democracy in times of distrust? In particular, what becomes of civic and political participation?

Civic Engagement and Political Participation

The concepts of "civic engagement" and "political participation" are defined and put into practice in myriad ways. In our analysis, "civic" activities commonly include the following: (1) political action—such as voting, campaign participation,

---

7. Figures from NYT/CBS (2011) and Pew (2010, 13), respectively.

8. For a discussion of the merits and challenges of measuring public attitudes toward the government, see Norris (2011).

9. Among the scholars who examined disenchantment of politics are Craig (1993); Tolchin (1996); Nye, Zelikow, and King (1997); and Pharr and Putnam (2000). Popular titles included *The Culture of Cynicism: American Morality in Decline* (Stivers 1994); *Spiral of Cynicism: The Press and the Public Good* (Capella and Jamieson 1997); *Everybody Knows: Cynicism in America* (Chaloupka 1999); and *For Common Things: Irony, Trust, and Commitment in America Today* (Purdy 1999).

and lobbying elected officials; (2) community building—such as membership in voluntary associations, hobby groups, and social affairs; and (3) values, morals, knowledge, and skills—such as reading the news and volunteering (following the work of Berger 2009). Throughout this book, "civic engagement" and "civic participation" are used interchangeably and refer to any or all of these activities. References to "political engagement" or "political participation" are more specific, referring to activities intended to influence the state, either directly, by affecting the making or implementation of public policy, or indirectly, by influencing the selection of people who make those policies (drawing on Zukin et al. 2006, 6).[10]

In the 1990s, not only did Americans' unprecedented political skepticism and cynicism attract attention, but so did changes in how Americans engaged in civic life. In a country that had long enjoyed a reputation as a nation of joiners (de Tocqueville 2003 [1840]), the surprising consensus was that adult participation in voluntary associations was on the decline (ANES 2010). Some argued that these data indicated a broader trend: an overall withdrawal from civic and political life. They pointed out that Americans were consuming less politically oriented media (Pew 2010), engaging in fewer political conversations (HERI 1999), and failing to vote (ANES 2010). In a well-known argument, Robert Putnam claimed that American participation in civic and associational life was on the decline (2000).

Other scholars argued that the overall trend was not so clear—that although the era was marked by declining membership in *some* types of organizations, it also saw the emergence of others. Social scientist Theda Skocpol (2004) calls this a "reorganization" of civic life. Business associations, professional groups, trade unions, and fellowship federations had all grown tremendously in the post–World War II period, but saw memberships wane significantly by the 1990s. In contrast, thematically organized groups focused on issues of social welfare and public affairs became more popular in the same decade. These new groups diversified both the types of causes that civic groups engaged in and the demographic makeup of their constituencies (Hayes 1986; Berry 1999). Many of the new groups had professional staffs (Smith 1992; Putnam 2000); others were informal and flexible, offering participants the opportunity to engage in ad hoc volunteering rather than making formal, regular commitments (Wuthnow 1994, 2002). Finally, by the turn of the century, online media had begun to fundamentally alter how Americans participate in civic life, learn about news and events, and connect with each other (Kahn and Kellner 2004; Castells 2012). What is important here is that not only do levels of civic engagement wax and wane, but engagement itself changes shape, and the demographics of participation shift.

Taken together, this literature on American civic life helps us identify what to look for, what we might expect, and what may have changed or stayed the same since the 1990s debates over skepticism and civic engagement. Like other scholars

---

10. For examples of defining and measuring civic engagement, see the Center for Information and Research on Civic Learning and Engagement (CIRCLE) website on "Survey Measures of Civic Engagement" (2011). For a discussion on the problems of defining and measuring civic engagement, see Berger 2009.

before us, we aim to contribute a new snapshot of civic life in the present moment. Our fieldwork experiences of American civic life in 2010 and 2011 were certainly not defined by withdrawal, apathy, or disengagement. It was easy to get involved, and we got the sense that many people were engaged in some way. We were not surprised to learn that, nationally, Americans today are breaking records for their widespread participation in civic and political life. Volunteering is at a thirty-year high (CNCS 2006, 2012), and electoral campaigning and voter registration are both on the rise, as is voter turnout (ANES 2010). In 2012, over 57 percent of the voting age population cast their ballot in the presidential election, up from a low of 50.3 percent in 1988 (US Census Bureau 2012).

These data, coupled with unequivocal data on public skepticism, sketch a unique moment in American civic life: Americans hate politics, yet they work—*and work hard*—to make their communities better places to live, work, and play.

Inequality

The backdrop against which these trends in political attitudes and engagement take place has also been changing. If mid-twentieth-century America was defined by a rising middle class, economic prosperity, the civil rights movement, and movement toward gender equity, the 1980s and 1990s were marked by rising inequality, a retrenchment of the welfare state, increased privatization, and transition from a manufacturing-based economy to a globalized "knowledge economy" that favored well-educated, highly skilled professionals. These changes were informed and supported by "neoliberal" thinking, which, in simplest terms, advocates limited government intervention in social and economic affairs.[11] It was within this neoliberal context that the 2008 financial crisis and subsequent economic recession struck. These events ushered in astronomical rates of unemployment, poverty, mortgage default, and demands for welfare assistance—all of which continued to plague both Providence and the nation during our research.[12]

---

11. Neoliberalism is vehemently (though not universally) criticized for driving a wedge into an already widening income gap. See, for example, Duggan 2003.

12. The year 2010 in numbers: The national unemployment rate was 9.6 percent. With the exception of 1982 (9.7 percent) and 1983 (9.6 percent), this is the highest rate since systematic data collection began in 1942 (US Bureau of Labor Statistics 2013). Americans reported nearly 4 million foreclosure filings, default notices, scheduled auctions, and bank repossessions in 2010, a 23 percent increase over 2008 (RealtyTrac 2011). Enrollment in the Supplemental Nutritional Assistance Program (formerly the Food Stamp Program) soared: in 2010, over 40 million individuals, or about 12 percent of Americans, received aid. Until 2008, that number had never topped 28 million, and typically hovered around 20 million (US Department of Agriculture 2013). Finally, the poverty rate soared from 11.3 percent to 15.1 percent of the population between 2000 to 2010 (US Department of Health and Human Services 2011).

America's economy is always changing, but the pace of change has become increasingly pronounced in recent decades . Middle-income jobs were once provided in abundance by secure manufacturing positions or entry-level civil service positions, but income distribution now has more of a hollow middle, wedged between the low-earning masses on one side and the wealthy few on the other. The greatest growth in jobs has been in the low-skill and high-skill ends of the service sector, now the dominant sector of the economy. The bulk of jobs created in recent years are low-skill, low-wage positions that have become more insecure and offer fewer benefits than in previous years. At the same time, the barrier to enter highly paid jobs has grown higher, as even entry-level jobs require more skills (US Bureau of Labor Statistics 2012).[13]

Of course, these economic transitions have not been experienced in the same way by all Americans. The restructuring of jobs has been spatially and demographically stratified, with disastrous consequences for racial equality. Inner-city urban areas have been the hardest hit by these changes and such incidents as the mortgage crisis, leaving many Black and Latino neighborhoods with concentrated unemployment (Chakravartty and Silva 2012). Since the 1970s, racial inequality has worsened by many measures, despite modest gains by some middle-class families of color (Taylor et al. 2011). Patterns of segregation between economic and racial groups persist as well (Fischer 2003; Reardon and Bischoff 2011; Quillian 2012). Black Americans are still more likely to live in minority neighborhoods and to be close to concentrated poverty, whatever their income levels (Pattillo-McCoy 1999; Logan and Zhang 2010). Inequality has been further confounded by a rhetoric of "color-blind racism," the idea that we are living in a post-racial society, and therefore provisions to address racism are no longer needed (Bonilla-Silva 2010).[14]

All of this has been accompanied by a retrenchment of the welfare state and the rise of a new consensus that the state must shrink in order to allow for the free operation of the market (Holland et al. 2007). Under both the Democratic and Republican Parties, the provisions of the safety net have steadily eroded since the 1980s. In fulfilling a campaign promise to bring about the "end of welfare as we

---

13. For example, of the three fastest growing occupations in 2010, two were personal care aides and home health aides, each with a median income of roughly $20,000 (the poverty line for a family of four in 2010 was $22,000). The third fastest was biomedical engineer, with a median income of $82,000. In 2010, over 1.2 million jobs were created for personal care and home health aides, while only 9,000 jobs were created for biomedical engineers. Since 2008, over 70 percent of jobs created have paid less than $28,000 per year (US Bureau of Labor Statistics 2012).

14. Economic and racial inequity also diminishes quality of life. For example, health inequalities along lines of gender, race, and class are persisting and, in many cases, increasing (Bleich et al. 2012). For example, African American children have higher rates of child mortality and higher odds of being in poor or fair health than White children, yet have access to lower-quality health care (Flores 2010).

know it," Bill Clinton's 1996 welfare reform was one of the significant moments in the "breaking of the American social compact" (Piven and Cloward 1997).[15] Ever since, social policy has moved away from providing a safety net and toward increasing emphasis on individual responsibility, incentivizing work and market mechanisms. In comparison to three decades ago, Americans have many fewer social provisions, less spending on social programs, and tightened eligibility requirements for assistance. The private sector has come to play a much larger role in welfare provision, with the growth of for-profit health care, for-profit charter schools, and infrastructure projects funded by "public-private partnerships." Responsibility for social provision has been increasingly devolved to states and municipalities, giving rise to what Jamie Peck (2012) calls "austerity urbanism," a comment on the reality that blighted municipalities can hardly afford to pay for these services. One of the many symptoms of the new inequality is that today's public schools face vast differences in funding and other resources between urban/poor and suburban/rich areas, leading to dramatically different levels of educational achievement (Hochschild and Scovronick 2003). In perverse contrast, tax rates for the wealthiest Americans have dramatically declined from 91 percent in 1960 to 38 percent in 2012 (Tax Foundation 2013).

In short, for myriad economic, policy, and ideological reasons, inequality in America has been increasing since the 1970s (Uslaner and Brown 2005). By a variety of measures, the United States is one of the most unequal of all industrialized countries (OECD 2012).[16] The income gap between the richest 1 percent and the rest of Americans has more than tripled since the 1980s (Sherman and Stone 2010). In 2010, while Americans were struggling to bounce back from the recession and when our research began, the incomes of the top 1 percent of earners grew by 11.6 percent while the incomes of the bottom 99 percent grew only by 0.2 percent. In other words, *the top 1 percent of income earners captured 93 percent of the income gains* (Saez 2012, 1). In this time of immense, increasing, and multifaceted inequality, civic engagement is especially important.

---

15. The notion of a "social compact" was developed by seventeenth-century political philosophers Thomas Hobbes and John Locke and made popular by eighteenth-century thinker Jacques Rousseau. The idea is that when individuals agree to surrender the "natural liberties" they would enjoy in an anarchic world and accept the safety, order, and protection of the organized state, this state must in turn reflect the will of the people. For a state to break the social compact, then, is to stray from public will and the duty to protect.

16. For example, the pretax Gini coefficient increased from 40.6 in the 1970s to 48.6 in the 2000s. The Gini index is a common indicator of how wealth is distributed within a population. On this scale, a score of zero indicates that wealth is evenly distributed among all members of society—*perfect equality*. As the distribution of wealth becomes more inequitable, the score increases. A score of 100 indicates that all of a society's wealth is held by only one person—*perfect inequality*. Thus, a rise in the Gini coefficient indicates increasing inequality (OECD 2012).

SKEPTICISM, PARTICIPATION, AND INEQUALITY: IMPLICATIONS FOR DEMOCRACY?

Until this point, we have described the contemporary moment in terms of political attitudes, civic participation, and (in)equality. Now, we turn our attention to the question: *So what?* In particular: *So what for democracy?* How are widespread skepticism, shifting textures of participation, and exacerbated inequality related to the democratic health of our country?

As we noted earlier in this chapter, folk uses of the word "politics" draw attention to the pathologies of public life—corruption, special interests, and inefficiency, to name a few. "Civic" or "community" life, on the other hand, connotes working together and serving broad interests. Scholars call this turn *away* from politics and *toward* community the "post-political condition," meaning the political has become passé, while public life remains important. This could be the result of Americans losing faith in their public institutions and underappreciating the power of the political sphere (Calhoun 1998). Alternatively, it could be part and parcel of the broader neoliberal era (Rose 1999). Scholars critical of the post-political argue that by turning their back on politics, citizens in advanced democracies are ignoring the central struggles of democratic life, especially inequality and belonging, in their expectation that romantic notions of "community" and technocratic solutions will replace needed political discourse (Žižek 1999; Mouffe 2000). A post-political culture could undermine democracy for several reasons: first, it romanticizes and overestimates the power of local associations (Herbert 2005, 851–852); second, community organizing does not necessarily promote democratic values, institutions, and practices (Macedo 2005); third, it ignores inequalities in associational membership (Verba, Schlozman, and Brady 1995); and fourth, it generates benefits that are disproportionately distributed among those members (Miller 2010).

Putnam, the author of *Bowling Alone*, argues that under conditions of disaffection, narrow and disgruntled forms of participation emerge, and that these replacements are counter to the public interest (2000). Many agree that cynical sentiments make for thin, privatist, or selfish kinds of citizen engagements (Goldfarb 1991; Wuthnow 2002; Bellah et al. 2008 [1985]). For nineteenth-century political theorist Alexis de Tocqueville, despotism—absolute power belonging to only one or a few—emerges when individuals in a democracy turn their back on the common good, and begin to think of fulfilling their political duties as "a troublesome annoyance" (2003 [1840], 627). In this way of thinking, modern democratic states require the appropriate set of political attitudes among their citizens in order for democracy to function properly (Almond and Verba 1963; Inglehart 1988). Perhaps cynicism blocks productive social relations and erodes social capital in ways that are damaging to political life (Berman 1997). If citizens conclude that government is damaged beyond repair, then they may have little incentive to engage with the political system (Jackson, Mondak, and Huckfeldt 2009). Some even argue that skepticism can lead to regime failure (Keane 2009).

Inequality is also widely believed to undermine democracy and to dampen participation in civic and political life (Beramendi and Anderson 2008; Stiglitz 2012). Thus, high levels of inequality in the United States are of concern not only because they lead to unequal life outcomes for the population[17] but also because they may decrease democratic participation. Supporting this perspective are studies that show how Whites and individuals with high socioeconomic status are more likely to be politically and civically active in political campaigns, protesting, and civil society organizations, largely due to differences in educational attainment (Schlozman et al. 2004). Higher levels of inequality may lead to lower levels of civic trust, and lower levels of civic trust can be associated with dampened participation (Uslaner and Brown 2005). For these reasons, some conclude that greater equality is not only a desirable outcome, but also a precondition for building the community and social relations necessary for a strong society (Wilkinson and Picket 2010).[18]

Overall, these arguments about the relationships between skepticism, participation, inequality, and democracy are pessimistic about today's democratic health. Our approach, however, follows some alternative perspectives. As other scholars have shown, we see that skepticism of politics may spur unconventional forms of engagement (Cain, Dalton, and Scarrow 2003) and lead to high rates of participation in both conventional and alternative political arenas (Booth and Seligson 2009). We also find evidence that supports findings that citizens in advanced industrial countries maintain their commitments to democratic principles in times of distrust and doubt (Dalton 2004). Even in times of widespread skepticism, democratic aspirations can—and do—bolster citizens' interest and activism in public life (Norris 2011).[19]

Like these interpretations of today's political culture, we neither lament skepticism nor idealize engagement. Instead, we interrogate the meanings people give to their skepticism and their participation, and we highlight the themes and issues that surface in those meanings.

INTERROGATING THE CONTEMPORARY MOMENT

Surveys and other broad-scale social science research have highlighted findings similar to our own observations: that people both distrust politics and engage in civic

---

17. For example, countries with higher levels of inequality experience more social and health problems, even among the richest and most developed countries of the world (Wilkinson and Picket 2010).

18. Other scholars suggest that inequality may be inherent to society (e.g., Ong 2006), in which case achieving equality in practice may be unrealistic. Gutmann (2002), for example, asks whether the concept of equal citizenship is an illusion, because society is founded on inequalities.

19. For example, research in cultural sociology has found that "local-only" activism aiming to solve local problems rather than address broader political concerns allows Americans to become civically engaged despite feelings of powerlessness about complex political problems (Eliasoph 1998).

life, and that inequality is at once a central social problem and an issue of uncertain focus among today's activists. Our ethnography allowed us to gain insight into these tensions in ways that go beyond what survey data or structured interview responses can tell us. Observing and listening to practices and discourses on the ground helped us answer important questions about the forms, meanings, and consequences of contemporary civic life, and speculate about the expansions and contractions of today's democracy. Here we describe these motivating questions and our approach to uncovering answers.

How do Americans engage? Put differently, what is the shape of contemporary civic life? To answer this question, we studied a diverse array of civic groups, ranging from wealthy neighborhood homeowner interest groups to organizations allied with the needs of marginalized communities. The several dozen activists we followed are representative of many other engaged citizens in the ways they think about politics or relate to the political sphere. The activists we sat next to in meetings, marched with at protests, and ate with in local diners can be cynical about government, angry with politicians, and frustrated with possibilities for change. Yet, simultaneously, they generate the many opportunities for participation that bombard citizens every day—inviting us to "listening parties" and asking us to come together on Halloween to watch pumpkins fly. Although we see them as leaders in terms of engagement, they are typical in their skepticism.

Given Americans' disappointment in politics, how and why do they engage in civic life? In the words of one citizen, "Politics is a negative word. Ultimately, I think that's why [people] don't want to think of themselves as political. Civic engagement . . . it's the new politics, right?" The boundary between civic activity and politics is constantly redefined, as people act out their value of active citizenship and community-mindedness. In a related question, w*hat does that participation mean, and how is it understood in relation to the political system?* As the school debates highlighted in the opening pages reveal, people have many different understandings of what engagement is, what purpose it serves, and whether and how it works.

What are the expressions of civic life that are particularly salient in the imaginations of contemporary Americans? The past several years have highlighted a unique set of local, national, and transnational social movements and organizing tactics that have galvanized citizens across the globe. In the United States, the rise of the Tea Party, the growth of social media activism, and, several months after our fieldwork concluded, the development of the Occupy movement are in many ways *new* forms of civic life, as are the Arab Spring uprisings that took hold in the Middle East. In Providence, we observed citizens' attraction to civic innovation, a style of civic engagement that applies the ideas and values of the business sector to the goals of bolstering civic participation and improving politics. Civic innovation opens the possibility of engaging more people in the political lives of their neighborhoods and cities.

In a period of unprecedented inequality, how is inequality understood, framed, and discussed (or not) within activist settings? In Providence, the present moment's persistent and increasing inequality is reflected in political culture and patterns of civic engagement in diverse ways. Inequality can be openly discussed or never mentioned, addressed head-on through organizational priorities or seen as something that will resolve itself naturally if policy makers pay attention to citizens. We saw these and other orientations to inequality in our fieldwork.

Underlying the answers to these questions are our ideas about how researchers can come to know and understand others. We attempt to take the individuals and groups in our study seriously, meaning that we refrain from judging their knowledge, visions, experiences, values, strategies, theories, and objectives around making a difference in American life. This book does not determine what kinds of activism are right or wrong, effective or inadequate. Rather, we treat the diverse ways people imagine a better world as equally valid spheres of political action, each with strengths and weaknesses.[20] Although we studied people of different classes, races, cultures, and political views, we aimed to treat them "symmetrically"—that is to say, to the best of our ability, we refused to indulge in preset assumptions or comparisons.[21] *The Civic Imagination* is thus both a theoretical contribution and a practical roadmap, an analysis of stories of American civic life, and a guide for thinking critically about one's own participation.[22]

PREVIEW OF SUBSEQUENT CHAPTERS

Chapter 2: Joining Groups and Following Activists

Within studies of political culture, we are not the first to examine activists' understandings of politics, or to think about the influence of imagination on action. Here we show how contemporary studies of civic engagement can be informed by political philosophy. We discuss how imaginations help us consider others' points of view, and how imaginations are constrained, in some ways, by larger sociopolitical

---

20. We do suggest that different ways of seeing and being in the world are more popular, or resonate more strongly with a population, at different times. On this topic, see Michael Schudson's book *The Good Citizen: A History of American Civic Life* (1998) or his more recent article "New Technologies and Not-So-New Democracies" (2006).

21. We tried to shed common scholarly presuppositions such as "elites use political engagement to seek personal power and material benefits," or "marginalized groups are duped into forms of participation only meant to appease and silence their grievances," and instead identify what we observed and experienced in our research.

22. Two stylistic notes are worth mentioning. First, we have relegated many renowned scholars and award-winning books to footnotes in order to enhance readability for those unfamiliar with or disinterested in the minutiae of "who said what, when." We hope such questions are answered at the bottom of each page. Second, we have done away with many of the shortcuts for presenting information—there are no charts, graphs, text boxes, or highlighted definitions. Instead, we have left our insights entangled with the words and stories of the people from whom we learned. We hope this helps our reader flesh out, critique, and play with the arguments we present.

contexts. We also highlight how theories of "prospective thinking"—the ways in which people consider the future—help us understand how civic imaginations have consequences for actions.

Chapter 2 describes our research methodology of political ethnography, and places it within the traditions of our various disciplines—sociology, anthropology, and political science. We used *multi-sited collective ethnography*, a method in which each of five researchers followed each of seven fieldsites. By deploying our attention in this way, we expanded our capacity to identify cross-group similarities and differences, and increased our ability to recognize our own biases and prejudices. Providence is an ideal place to examine the issues that face much of America today. The city is large enough to encounter diverse approaches to civic engagement, yet small enough to facilitate an intimate knowledge of the civic landscape and its actors.

Chapter 3: "I Am Not Political": Making Sense of Skeptical Engagement

The phenomenon of "skeptical engagement" captures the paradox of Americans' simultaneous frustration with politics and desire to participate in civic life. To make sense of how people reject the political while engaging it, we introduce the concept of "disavowal of politics." Disavowal is not a mere statement of dislike, but instead a forceful separation—a shove away—from the political. Americans want to *distinguish themselves* from politics. We found that people do this because they understand politics to be polluted—to be muddied and contaminated by unsavory things. They do not see themselves and their work as unbecoming in these ways— instead they see it as honest and genuine. Some scholars and public intellectuals think this turning away from politics is narrow cynicism, or a gateway to apathy, but we disagree. Disavowal of the political expresses a yearning for a more autonomous and democratic civic engagement, and also makes certain alliances and engagements possible. In this way, the disavowal of politics provides an avenue for Americans to "rescue" their democracy.

Chapter 4: The Civic Imagination

We were struck by the observation that people across the political spectrum are continuously, actively engaged in prospective thinking about a better society and political system. We capture this dynamic meaning-making process with our concept of the "civic imagination," or the ways in which people individually and collectively envision better political, social, and civic environments and work toward achieving those futures. This chapter uses the story of a heated controversy around the closing of several Providence schools in order to analyze the civic imagination in the contemporary United States, showing how imaginations shape understandings and action. Civic imaginations are formed at once "in the thick of social life" and in people's processes of reflection and constant reevaluation, as they seek out their version of good democratic engagement. We make sense of the variability in civic imaginations by observing that they seem to cluster around three strong sets of discourses: concern with power and inequality, prioritizing solidarity, and collective thinking to solve social problems. Finally, we examine the consequences of each of these dialects of civic life.

Chapter 5: Participation 2.0: The Politics of Civic Innovation

If "civic imaginations" are mental maps and moral compasses that guide how people think about engagement with public life, then "expressions" of civic imagination are how those ideas are translated into action. Expressions are what people *do* as they seek to make a difference. One trend that marks civic life today is that of "civic innovation." Civic innovators are oriented toward using reason to create pragmatic solutions to social problems. They often argue that communities can and should solve their own problems—independently of government. In this chapter, we show how civic innovators use business language, adopt market logics, and deploy trendy technologies to create new forms of engagement, and we highlight connections between previous generations of political reformers. We also point to some of the tradeoffs that innovators are prone to make, emphasizing developing the "right process" over the outcome of that process, and their reflexivity (or lack thereof) around the exclusionary consequences of their outreach methods.

Chapter 6: Inequality: A Difficult Conversation

In this chapter, we focus explicitly on how groups orient themselves toward issues of inequality. Some groups choose to tackle the issue head-on while others seem to side-step inequality at every opportunity. This chapter tells the story of how civic groups approached the idea of bringing participatory budgeting, a process by which citizens are given the authority to collectively decide how an allocated pool of municipal funds will be spent, to Providence. Some groups saw it as a civic innovation, others imagined it as a tool to build community solidarity, and still others saw it as a way to tackle long-entrenched inequalities. We show how different groups interpreted the goals of participatory budgeting, used different strategies in their organizing efforts, and expressed different concerns about how participatory budgeting might play out. This chapter also examines how groups engage with issues of inequality—explicitly or implicitly—through their actions, campaigns, dominant discourses, and group styles. While for some activists inequality is best tackled head-on and discussed directly, for others it is something to be ignored, danced around, or discussed only through the use of euphemisms. We find that attention to inequality is a particularly prevalent blind spot in American civic life. We explore some of the forms this blind spot takes. In particular, how does each type of imagination understand and act, or fail to act, on issues of inequality? We also show how inequality surfaces in civic groups' relationships to each other. We argue that this blind spot to inequality threatens the potential of civic groups to do what they intend, which is benefit their communities.

Chapter 7: Making a Difference in American Political Life

In the concluding chapter, we highlight what students, engaged citizens, and scholars have to gain by identifying and understanding the diversity of civic imaginations and the various ways these imaginations are expressed as Americans work to improve their communities and deepen democratic engagement. We argue that the contemporary democratic conversation too often overlooks inequality and avoids conflict in favor of polite conversation. Instead, we urge citizens to use their civic imaginations to "go visiting"—to put themselves in other people's shoes—in order to better understand and collaborate with people whose imaginations differ. This process demands a reflexive look at the limitations, blind spots, and tradeoffs of one's own civic imagination and an acceptance of conflicts that will inevitably arise during frank discussions of inequality.

Methodological Appendixes

Methodological Appendix A, "How Many Scholars Does It Take to Answer a Question?" is a detailed description of our methodological approach. We provide a chronological account of methodological decisions such as fieldsite selection, fieldnote protocol, and coding process, and discuss how we employed technological tools for managing shared electronic files. We also share our concerns about, and solutions to, the ethical dilemmas of ethnographic research, especially reciprocity—how do you give back to the people who allow you into their lives, homes, thoughts, and activities? This appendix candidly describes the merits and challenges of our methodological approach and offers suggestions and advice to those who may adopt it for their own research.

In Methodological Appendix B, we depart somewhat from convention to offer a glimpse of our work process as seen by an outside ethnographer. In the spirit of opening up the black box of the research process, fellow sociologist Tatiana Andia actively researched our process by attending our meetings, interviewing us, and analyzing our fieldnotes and internal documents. In this "ethnography of an ethnography," which includes some of her fieldnotes and reflections, she discusses the rituals, meanings, and boundaries that animated our group work over the year. This appendix helps make the point that the research process itself does not escape the logic of the social worlds we observed. It gives the inquisitive reader additional information with which to evaluate our findings and provides fellow researchers who are considering collective work some points to consider about group process.

* * *

Finally, a note about the perspectives that underlie our research: Each of the authors of this book values democracy and cares deeply about the democratic health of the United States and other countries around the world. We are seriously concerned about the well-being and empowerment of marginalized populations within our country, and are thus forthcoming about our desire to move Americans to create a more equitable society. These themes are central to this collective endeavor as well as much of our individual work.[23] In writing this book, we aimed to be objective about the values and objectives that activists pursue, yet particularly attentive to the ways activists address or reify inequalities. In this way, our discussion about inequality as a dimension of political culture is somewhat overrepresented. We hope the reader forgives, and perhaps even appreciates, this aspect of the book.

---

23. See, for example, Baiocchi and Corrado (2010) and E. Bennett (2012).

Chapter 2

Joining Groups and Following Activists

The stories we tell in this book take place in public spaces—parks, schools, government offices, and the steps of the capitol building—as well as in the spaces of voluntary groups—headquarters, organizers' cars, around kitchen tables, and in backyards. The offices of civil society organizations are often both unremarkable and profoundly alike: dated computers, repurposed and mismatched furniture, and stacks of brochures everywhere. But what often sets these spaces apart are the walls: taped to the walls of nonprofit groups are posters, slogans, meeting agendas, and advertisements for events passed. At a social justice organization introduced later in the chapter, what stands out is the slogan of the World Social Forum, "Another World Is Possible"; a list of principles for justice-oriented development in Providence; and a Black Power poster of Angela Davis. At a neighborhood association, on the walls are the "ten principles of our neighborhood"; the stenciled words "diversity," "environmentalism," and "preservation"; and taped up pieces of butcher paper with the results of a long-concluded community visioning exercise. For one of our organizations that has no formal office, their most visible "walls" are online: their Facebook page not only shares city council meeting times and news stories about development but also invites conversation about city funding priorities.

These images are familiar to anyone who has ever been to a community meeting or a social movement gathering, and they reflect something fundamental about what happens when activists get together to work on common goals: people imagine possibilities for themselves, their organizations, and their communities. Imagined futures are a central feature of civic life. Behind the meetings, protests, visits to city hall, community celebrations, and infinite other ways people engage with their communities, people are actively thinking about the future and often questioning what can be done to make that future a reality. How can my community be improved? How will political decisions made today affect me, my neighbors, and my children? What can I, or we, do to make this a better place to live and work? The backdrop that informs those questions is an imagined vision of a better future.

As we discuss below, two mid-century philosophers (Hannah Arendt and Cornelius Castoriadis) have clearly articulated the idea that the capacity for people to act publicly in a democracy is predicated on their *ability to imagine*. As people engage with each other in purposive ways, they create and recreate worlds in words and with deeds that are, in part, imagined. This collective imagining may set the standard against which actions are judged. The act of imagining takes place at the nexus between what exists and what we desire to exist. Our imagining is informed by the world around us—by what we understand to be reasonable and possible, by our circumstances, by other ideas—but it is also something creative, unique, and *new*. One of the central arguments of this book is that these imaginations matter, and that to understand the state of democracy it is important we listen to them, and watch closely as people try to bring them to life.

What we call "civic imaginations"—the ways in which people individually and collectively envision a better political, social, and civic environment, and work toward achieving that future—are a central aspect of civic involvement and demand a close, thoughtful examination if we are to understand the nature of modern-day engagement in the United States. As we have shown in our introductory chapter, scholars, public intellectuals, and citizens have come to a near consensus that contemporary US politics is in disarray. Between political skepticism, fears of a failing democracy, declining public services, poor access to government officials, and increasing inequality, it should not be surprising that disaffection is rampant. But given that scenario, what do Americans think they are doing when they engage (which they continue to do)? What visions animate that engagement? As useful as opinion polls or macro-political analyses have been, a central premise of this book is that there is something to be learned from paying attention to popular definitions of politics and democracy as they emerge in day-to-day interactions and then investigating how these definitions, in turn, shape action. We seek a fine-grained sense of how civically engaged Americans understand their engagement and how they choose to act as a result.

To pay attention to the imagination may not at first blush seem the proper province of a group of sociologists, anthropologists, and political scientists. After all, to examine the imagination is to partially refer to things that do not exist. We have resisted the powerful disciplinary reflex to ignore these phantoms and look *behind* them for something more real. In contrast to readings that see power and conspiracy behind societal practices, ours was a "reparative approach," seeking to be fair to people's intentions while simultaneously critical, in the sense of providing insights about the nature of society (see our discussion of Sedgwick 2003, below).

IMAGINATION, THE FUTURE, AND MORAL JUDGMENT

"Imagination is the prerequisite of understanding."
—Hannah Arendt

The civic imagination refers to acts of inventive, prospective thinking about a better society. We use "civic" because we are interested in imaginations that are concerned with society and collective futures. We use "imagination" because we are attentive to its creative dimension; imagination implies thinking of things that do not exist, and imagining is an act of bringing forth something new. Until recently, philosophers more than social scientists were the ones who spent time conceptualizing this crucial human activity. Aristotle and Immanuel Kant, for example, concerned themselves with the human capacity to imagine alternative futures. Likewise, early twentieth-century thinkers, such as George Herbert Mead and John Dewey, considered forward thinking a central part of human agency.

It is the work, though, of two mid-twentieth-century political philosophers that most informs our understanding: Cornelius Castoriadis and Hannah Arendt. Castoriadis, whose name and philosophy are often associated with the new social movements of the 1960s, was a former economist who became interested in the capacity of groups to imagine new futures and new norms of self-regulation.[1] For Castoriadis, the creative imagination is universal and involves a combination of individual and social processes. The individual's ability to imagine new worlds has the potential to enter public life and go beyond existing patterns of thought and behavior, but the social world we inherit and the norms that guide social action form the imagination in the first place and limit the potential of imagination to institute new worlds (K. Tucker 2005). Castoriadis conceives of social movements as social phenomena that bring about "new ways of thinking and acting, that have their origin in the individual and collective imaginary" (Wallace 2000, 111). He calls this creative and collective ability the "social instituting imaginary," highlighting that political activity involves both *imagining* new worlds and *instituting* them, or bringing them to life (Castoriadis 1994, 136; see also 1998). We follow Castoriadis in seeing the imagination as creative and intentional, though not boundless. The activists in this book actively work to bring their visions to life in new practices, institutions, and rules, but these visions emerge out of particular material and social circumstances. That is, people actively imagine, but not in conditions of their own choosing. There are unthinkable ideas, and among those that are thinkable, there are those that seem

---

1. Scholarship examining "new social movements" considers the relationship between the rise of contemporary social movements, the larger sociopolitical environment, and issues of identity and personal behavior. New social movements include the environment, women's and gay liberation, and urban social struggles (Pichardo 1997). For a discussion about how this research agenda relates to more general theories of politics and culture, see Buechler (1995, especially Table 1).

less feasible. There are silences and gaps, and the imaginations people have about others not present can be strikingly impoverished and narrow.

Political theorist Hannah Arendt is also centrally concerned with the role of the imagination in political activity. For her, imagination brings about "the ability to begin anew through words and deeds, to think in unanticipated ways about recent events, to make sense of their multiple meanings with others" (Wedeen 2007, 67). Imagination cultivates and makes possible "human capacities for action," one of which is the ability to talk together about collective futures. This is possible because of the imagination's close relation to *understanding* and *judgment*. For Arendt, imagination brings about the ability "to see things in their proper perspective, to be strong enough to put that which is too close at a certain distance so that we can see and understand it without bias and prejudice, to be generous enough to bridge abysses of remoteness until we can see and understand everything that is too far away from us as though it were our own affair" (Arendt 1994, 323). Thus, the imagination allows people to separate themselves from a situation in order to make a more impartial "judgment," or evaluation, while also remaining close enough to understand. To be able to imagine, in other words, also makes possible another crucial democratic capacity: "enlarged thinking." When people view their democracy as failing and imagine an alternate future, they are making a judgment about the political system they inhabit. To think in this way is to imagine different futures but also to imagine *the point of view of others*. Considering others' views, for Arendt, requires imagination, to put yourself in someone else's position is to employ your imagination "to go visiting" in their world, since it is not actually possible to know another's experience (Arendt 1992, 43).

Taken together, the insights about collective imagination from Castoriadis and Arendt—that imagination is creative but also constrained by circumstance, and that imagination is closely bound up with understanding and judgment—are central to our own conceptualization of the civic imagination and build a foundation for this book. The civic imagination is not only important for thinking about seemingly distant and perhaps abstract futures (such as a government without corruption, or a city without poverty) but also comes into play when people consider others around them, make evaluations about civic life, and act on those evaluations in ways that affect public life. A discussion of whether a school should be closed, or whether a highway should pass through a neighborhood, *necessarily calls for acts of civic imagination*.

Civic imaginations provide a conceptual grid through which individuals imagine a future against which they judge the present they inhabit. An imagination emerges and is informed by specific interactions and experiences; it is nourished by cultural traditions, inspired by familiar symbols. Our fieldwork did not support the notion that there is a White civic imagination or a working-class civic imagination, or that people can be mapped a priori onto any one civic imagination. However, civic imaginations are *informed by* and *filtered through* individual, socially located experiences. Imaginations are working theories: individuals constantly adjust and change them as their experiences confirm or contradict them.[2] Moreover, civic imaginations come alive in groups. Voluntary groups are often explicitly inspired by the shared civic imaginations of their founders, and their mission statements, rules, and norms are themselves direct expressions of these imaginations.[3]

Our attention to the civic imagination resonates with the recent resurgence of social science literature on the role of *future-oriented*, or projective, thinking on present social events.[4] In arguing for increased theoretical and empirical examination of "the impact of the imagined future on social events" (Mische 2009, 695), scholars point out that all action and interaction, while informed and structured by the past and present, is oriented toward and has a relationship with the future. In other words, aspirations and expectations of what has yet to come deeply inform everyday social practices, personal identity, and creative action. These "imagined futures" are "the first step in actively and creatively responding to a situation" (Frye 2012). Recent sociological scholarship points to how the ways in which people orient themselves to the future have an impact on social processes. For example, Margaret Frye (2012) shows how aspirations and expectations affect educational outcomes in Malawian women, and David Gibson (2011) examines how "foretalk," or talk about possible futures, impacted decision making during the Cuban missile crisis.[5] Sociologist Ann Mische, borrowing from sociologist W. I. Thomas, notes that these imagined futures are "real in their consequences" even if those consequences "are quite different than the imagined future that motivated the action" (2009, 696). Our focus on the civic realm of social life builds upon this growing body of empirical research to suggest that the *imagined* civic world has particular and important consequences on *real* democratic discourses and practices.

If Castoriadis and Arendt help us develop foundational elements of "imagination" as a concept, and scholars who write about imagined futures and prospective thinking confirm that imaginations have consequences, then pragmatist thinkers

---

2. Here we are indebted to Andreas Glaeser's (2011) proposal for a "sociology of understanding" (9–17). The sociology of understanding is one that places the actors and their understandings of the world at the forefront. People's experiences of the world validate (or disprove) these understandings, which are dynamic. When extended, Glaeser's framework can account for many things, such as the trajectory of political institutions.

3. Again, we refer interested readers to Glaeser (2011). Drawing on philosopher Ludwig Wittgenstein, Glaeser argues that institutions emerge from repeated interactions based on aligned understandings.

4. Emirbayer and Mische eloquently define projectivity as "the imaginative generation by actors of possible future trajectories of action, in which received structures of thought and action may be creatively reconfigured in relation to actors' hopes, fears, and desires for the future" (1998, 971). Alfred Schutz, for example, argues in a classic essay, "Unable to control what is imposed upon us, we are mere observers of what is going to happen, but we are observers governed by *hopes* and *fears*" (1959, 87–88).

5. See also Robin Wagner-Pacifici (2009), who explores how research on future-oriented thought can be applied in the context of violent events.

provide inspiration on how to investigate imaginations. The "pragmatic turn" in sociology is often associated with French scholars such as Laurent Thévenot, Luc Boltanski, and Daniel Cefaï, whose work engages the intersection of the moral and the political. Pragmatism assumes that people are primarily moral, reflexive agents who are constantly engaging with the world to bring about their version of "the good." This school of thought is attentive to the *justifications* people use to make claims about how they are working for change and to what end (Boltanski and Thévenot 2006), and brings our attention to the "reflective, creative moments of agency" that occur in political contexts (Smilde 2006, 52).[6] We are guided by pragmatists' call to *take people seriously* as moral beings who are seeking to instantiate their version of the good, and who must constantly readjust in the face of disagreements and of a world that does not quite measure up. Importantly, this perspective allows us to accept that people have different versions of what is "good," to respect these differences, and then to interrogate how the differences matter for the ways people evaluate society and choose to engage their communities. By closely considering what actually makes up a particular culture, the pragmatic approach helps us to unpack people's moral evaluations in order to see, in Thévenot's words, how "the good and reality are jointly engaged" (2001, 68).

POLITICS, CULTURE, AND THE EVERYDAY

As Paul Lichterman and Daniel Cefaï (2006) remind us, "Political action requires meaning-making" (392). From Almond and Verba's (1963) *The Civic Culture*, a classic study of democratic culture in five countries, to more recent accounts like Jeffrey Alexander's (2006) *The Civil Sphere*, scholars across the social sciences have explored the fruitful concept of "political culture," looking to the way that inherited patterns of meaning—culture—have shaped political outcomes. In contemporary usage, and as we deploy it here, political culture implies shared practices, symbols, discourses, and meanings, and how they enable and constrain political action. More specifically, we seek to understand "how, through shared inter-subjective meanings, actors understand and act in their daily worlds" in relation to politics (Ross 1997, 73).[7]

In exploring the meaning of politics in the day-to-day, we connect with a rich tradition of studies, particularly in the sociology of culture, that have explored the

---

6. For the purposes of this chapter we are treating pragmatism as one theoretical program, while there are meaningful distinctions between the French authors above, the early twentieth-century American school (e.g., Dewey 1954), and contemporary pragmatists (e.g., Joas 1996; Emirbayer and Mische 1998).

7. Ross (1997) argues that culture contributes to the study of politics in at least five ways: (1) framing the context in which politics occurs by defining interests and identifying how they are pursued; (2) linking individual and collective identities; (3) defining groups and the patterns of associations within and between them; (4) providing a framework for interpreting action and motives; and (5) providing resources to leaders and groups that allow them to engage in organization and mobilization.

contours of American political culture since the 1980s.[8] Like other scholars, we focus on "civil society"—the realm of voluntary activity, or the place where an "I turns into a We" (Putnam 2000). Through their work fashioning and refashioning the symbols and traditions of US civic culture, participants in civil society make meaningful a commitment to the public good. Despite the long line of literature that has sought to articulate a common cultural vocabulary of civil society in the United States— beginning with Alexis de Tocqueville (2003 [1840]) and including scholars such as Jeffrey Alexander (2006), Robert Wuthnow (2002), and the authors of *Habits of the Heart* (Bellah et al. 2008 [1985])—it is clear that American political life is not simply one monolithic political culture. A central insight has been that civil society is at once a terrain of shared meanings and also of *multiplicities of interpretations.*[9] We depart somewhat from the view that these differences are a matter of different civic groups' styles (e.g., Eliasoph and Lichterman 2003). While that view argues that group style is a primary determinant of differences in the visions and actions of members of civil society, for us various group styles are *consequences* of particular moral grammars that are put into play in these interactions. Our perspective is closer to the view articulated by Andreas Glaeser (2011), who argues that certain ways of knowing and understanding can become routinized into something like a group style. There are distinct, competing models of good citizenship and political cultures in US political and civic life, as described by Michael Schudson (1998). As Stephen Hart (2001) suggests, "Discursive rules and the grounds for them, in sum, represent a political ethic. They are about the right way to be a citizen activist. And as we have seen, Americans have varied understandings of what that way might be" (16).

Like these scholars, we look at democracy not at the level of the nation-state but "as people encounter it in their workplaces and schools, in volunteering and mobilizing," and in how people experience the gap between their ideals and how democracy is actually lived (Polletta 2013, 50). Thus, we set out to explore the diversity of political cultures, recognizing that these cultures are all at once distinct and identifiable, and overlapping and interdependent. Across the diverse spectrum of ideas and actions, we saw a constant simmering of forward thinking and read-justing. The activists and leaders with whom we worked did not hold a static view of the world but rather were constantly reimagining what the future civic and political world could look like, based on the problems they saw as most pressing, the solutions they developed, and the ways they reflected on these potential solutions. In what follows, we support our epistemological argument that no political culture or civic imagination acts in a vacuum, and that we as researchers can seek to understand the breadth and depth of civic imaginations as well as the ways that imaginations impact one another. In order to examine these dynamics, we required

---

8. See, for example, Wuthnow 1994; Lichterman 1996, 2008; Eliasoph 1998; Jacobs 2000; Wood 2002; Perrin 2005, 2006; Edgell, Gerteis, and Hartmann 2006; Lee 2007; Bellah et al. 2008 [1985]; and Macgregor 2010.

9. This theme of multiplicity within US civil society is present in the work of many scholars. See, for example, Lichterman 1996; Hart 2001; Jacobs 2000; and Polletta 2006.

a methodological approach that pays close attention to actors' discourses, practices, symbols, and meanings—the civic and political culture in which they operate—and takes these cultures seriously. That is why, like many pragmatic scholars and cultural sociologists, we focus on the ordinary conversations and practices that take place in everyday moments, at a wide variety of group meetings, rallies, and social events.[10]

OUR ETHNOGRAPHIC APPROACH

The research presented in this book relies primarily on ethnography, a method of inquiry in which a researcher pays attention to what people say and do by standing shoulder to shoulder with them. The attraction of ethnography to researchers like us lies not only in its power to evoke distinct social worlds to readers but also in how it allows us to grapple with the realms and questions that are of interest; in our case, these are the connections between individuals and their communities, civil society and the state, and modes of engagement and political structures (see Baiocchi and Connor 2008). By being physically present as interactions take place and stories unfold in settings and with people we visited frequently enough to feel comfortable, we were able to gather information about how people communicate, how they organize civil spaces, and how they evoke ideas and experiences to help guide their actions.[11] We saw how boundaries between people are constructed and maintained, how discourse is connected to behaviors and decision making, and how cultural logics empower or constrain action.

We are not alone in studying meaning-making and political culture through an ethnographic lens. Political ethnographers have long used participant observation and semistructured (rather than formally structured, survey-style) interviews to examine and explain political practices, the meanings that animate action in civil society, and the day-to-day expressions of political life.[12] This methodology has shed light on many interesting and important aspects of civic life. Taken together, the collective "anthropology of democracy" draws on "relationships with people outside of formal and elite political institutions," with specific attention to "local meanings, circulating discourses, multiple contestations, and changing forms of power" (Paley

---

10. Other scholars have studied political culture by measuring observable indicators, such as newspaper subscriptions (e.g., Putnam 1993), or by using surveys to collect data on knowledge, feelings, and judgments about structures, incumbents, policies, and one's place in the system (e.g., Almond and Verba 1963).

11. Ethnographer Paul Lichterman describes how being present allows the researcher to pay attention to what is *unsaid* and *awkwardly said*, and to witness the "interactional 'mistakes'" and "irreconcilable misunderstandings" occurring in a specific context (2005a, 275).

12. See, for example, Eliasoph and Lichterman 2003; Auyero 2006; and Baiocchi and Connor 2008.

2002, 469–470). Our work closely reflects the questions and methods that define this literature.

Multi-Sited Collective Ethnography

Ethnographies come in many shapes and sizes, from the lone researcher spending years in a place and culture far away from home (e.g., Scott 1985, 1990), to a group of scholars who are geographically dispersed, each looking at the same issue in their own particular location (e.g., Holland et al. 2007). We call our particular approach "multi-sited collective ethnography." It is *multi-sited* because we studied seven different civic organizations; it is *collective* in that all five of us investigated all seven groups, pooled our data, and collaborated in the analysis and writing; and it is *ethnographic* in that we used participant observation and thoughtful conversations (sometimes ad hoc, sometimes semistructured interviews) to gather data. This constellation of methodological choices is somewhat unusual, and so we have included an in-depth (or, more accurately, a downright nitty-gritty) description of our research practices in Methodological Appendix A, at the end of the book.[13]

Working collectively was an important part of our research design. The five of us spanned three social science disciplines, had lived in many different countries, and had engaged American politics in vigorous but different ways. This allowed us to draw on diverse literatures and experiences as we followed people from across the social, political, economic, and cultural spectrums represented in our Providence fieldsites. Instead of divvying up research sites—one or two sites per researcher—each of us rotated among all seven fieldsites. Our goal was for each of us to feel comfortable and be recognized if showing up unannounced at any fieldsite. Whenever possible, multiple researchers attended the same event, each contributing to a single, collaborative fieldnote document. Conducting research in this way allowed us to observe events through multiple lenses, increasing the reliability of our data and improving our ability to capture and describe social worlds (May and Pattillo-McCoy 2000). To write up our findings, we collectively analyzed our fieldnotes and other documents. We also wrote together, rather than assigning specific chapters to particular authors. Unlike most collective ethnographies, ours was a communal effort at every step of the process—from the initial idea to final edits.[14]

---

13. Methodological Appendix A includes the following topics: becoming a research team, working across disciplines, the civic landscape of Providence, selecting fieldsites, collecting data, managing fieldnotes, coding, moving between theory and evidence, writing as a group, soliciting feedback, being reflexive, creating reciprocal relationships with research subjects, and reflecting on the process as a whole. We also offer suggestions here for scholars considering adopting or adapting multi-sited collective ethnography for their own research.

14. Other co-researched and/or co-written ethnographic studies served as examples and roadmaps as we crafted our own approach. See, for example, Holland et al. 2007; Auyero and Swistun 2008; and Hirsch et al. 2009.

Symmetrical Approach to Diverse Groups

A typical approach to conducting research at several fieldsites would have been to create a comparative research design, identifying how the sites were similar or different, and deciding which similarities or differences were important, before beginning analysis.[15] Instead, we found inspiration in the notion of "generalized symmetry," put forth by actor-network theory (ANT).[16] This approach is, to use Ilana Silber's words, "a way of deliberately counteracting the perennial tendency of individual agents themselves to promote one principle of evaluation against other possible ones" (2003, 432). In our case, the tendency would be to promote our principles of evaluation, as social scientists, over and above those of the people in our study. To the best of our ability, we refrained from making these types of evaluations. Actor-network theory aims to understand different social actors in the same terms (Callon 1986), "suspending judgments about what is natural or social, true or false, right or wrong, and looking at how judgments are made when entities are brought into particular relations in an actor-network" (Clarke 2002, 113). In other words, ANT places primacy on the ways ordinary people generate their own theories of the world, calling for social scientists to take these theories as seriously as their own.

For us, a symmetrical approach meant selecting groups that outwardly appeared to have very different missions and socioeconomic profiles, yet refraining from assuming from the outset of our research why they might be similar or different, or what the consequences of these differences might be. We tried—and tried hard—to employ a uniform and evenly agnostic theoretical and analytic framework to each case and actor, even to those that differ so dramatically in their political and social orientations that they would typically not be studied together (e.g., a radical grassroots group and an elite technology-oriented network). In conducting the ethnographic research, being symmetrical meant being open to discussing and participating in whatever it was that the group found meaningful, and what counted as meaningful varied greatly from group to group.

Taking People Seriously

We aimed to be open to all of the wildly different ideas and assertions put forth by the people in our fieldsites. That is to say, we took people seriously by not beginning with the presumption that people are either dupes or out to dupe others (Boltanski

---

15. See, on this, Adam Przeworski and Henry Teune's (1970) *The Logic of Comparative Social Inquiry*.

16. We selectively appropriate from ANT. While we are inspired by the call for symmetry, we do not assume that the "world is flat" (Latour 2005, 172). In other words, we believe, in contrast to strict interpretations of ANT, that there are important power relations at stake in any given societal interaction. Likewise, we do not follow the ANT call to treat humans and nonhumans equally, as objects do not play a significant role in our account.

2011). This is a departure from much critical social science, which often relies on the assumption of widespread misrecognition of the social world—a misrecognition that we, as social scientists, are duty-bound to see through and expose for what it really is.[17] The problem with that assumption is that it can quickly lead to a self-confirming framework populated by amoral elites and deluded subalterns, empty denunciations that ultimately do not contribute much to the public conversation on democracy. An alternative route, which we have taken, is to concern ourselves with people's own descriptions of their circumstances and to avoid distorting these views (Silber 2003).

In practice, this meant reining in our own skepticisms, judgments, comparisons, and the urge to ask doubtful questions.[18] Thus, we began our work with the assumption that the activists with whom we worked are aware, moral, reflexive, and forward-thinking actors capable of making Providence a better place to live. At times, it was challenging to accept activists' descriptions of social situations: our tendency, as is common among progressive academics, was to be more sympathetic to grassroots groups advocating for social justice and skeptical of groups with more elite-oriented objectives. As the concept of civic imagination emerged, however, our symmetrical orientation became more natural, since what mattered in our data collection was how citizens thought, theorized, prospected, and strategized around making a difference—not whether we believed these imaginations mapped onto reality as we perceive it. In taking people seriously, we did not forfeit the possibility of critique. Indeed, we offer a critique of the democratic conversation around the contemporary political moment, and we point to the limits, silences, or gaps we find in civic life. In doing so, however, we start not from a position of suspecting people's motives, but instead from a position of believing in people's capacity to act according to their own quest for the "good."

Reparative Critique

Our understanding of critique draws from Eve Sedgwick, a literary theorist whose critical writings helped create the field of queer studies. As a starting place, we follow her advice to think about what knowledge *does,* or, more accurately, what we *hope*

---

17. Pierre Bourdieu is most associated with this view. According to him, by penetrating the "darkness of misrecognition," "sociology unmasks 'self deception,' that collectively entertain[s] and encourage[s] forms of lying to oneself, which in every society, is at the basis of most sacred values, and thereby, of all social existence" (1990, 183). For a trenchant rejoinder, and general criticism of what he calls "sociologist as killjoy," see Rancière 2012. Much as we argue here, Rancière believes that an activist and engaged social science must begin with an alternative set of assumptions.

18.   Here, we follow the spirit of Caroline Lee's (2013) book, *Down Market Democracy,* which tells the story of professional facilitators of participatory processes. She is critical of corporate consultants but also respectful, avoiding the cynical presuppositions that such individuals are "greedy corporate consultants" or that their work is bringing down "radical social movements" with the "conservativism of organization life" (18).

our own contributions to knowledge will do (Sedgwick 2003). We aim to produce knowledge that creates and expands possibilities, as opposed to knowledge that is dismissive, destructive, or paralyzing. Thus, we illuminate not only the pitfalls but also the potentials of various forms of civic engagement. Sedgwick calls this mode of critique "reparative" for its intention to mend, not further destroy, what is already broken (2003). It is contrasted with "paranoid critique." While both types unmask power and unveil domination, paranoid critique stops there, leaving us without possibility and limiting our ability to identify and promote agency. For example, paranoid critiques might explain how already powerful people reproduce systems of privilege, but they fail to identify how this insight might be useful for people working toward alternative futures. Reparative critique, on the other hand, is attentive to creativity and agency, and it points to renewed possibilities and avenues for change. Our analysis answers this call for a knowledge that can be used to repair that which readers find broken.

THE STAGE: PROVIDENCE, RHODE ISLAND

Today's typical American city is racially diverse, faces a challenging postindustrial economic transformation, and struggles with budgetary crises and a variety of social problems. Providence, Rhode Island, a medium-sized city with a population of 170,000, provides a specific instance of those general trends. Traditionally, Providence is known for having large Italian, Portuguese, East European, and Cape Verdean populations, but today it has an increasing Latino presence (Itzigsohn 2009; US Census Bureau 2011b). In 2010, 50 percent of the city's population was non-White (American Community Survey 2011), and voters elected their first Latino mayor. Although Providence hosted a thriving manufacturing sector in the nineteenth century, shifts in manufacturing, deindustrialization, and post–World War II suburbanization led to economic decline and a shrinking population. In the 1980s and 1990s, government community development funding and public-private development partnerships attracted investment and invigorated growth, but today, the city's economy remains tenuously dependent on five colleges and universities, an extensive hospital system, and a budding reputation as a hub for entrepreneurial innovation. After the 2008 financial decline, Rhode Island competed with Michigan for the nation's highest unemployment rates, and Providence joined many cities across the United States in being unable to balance its budget. In 2010, 26 percent of its residents lived below the poverty line (US Census Bureau 2011a). In this setting, social justice organizations proliferated, and new groups have emerged to pursue creative ways of engaging the state.[19]

---

19. The social science literature about Providence has described its civil society organizations (Perrotta 1977; Sterne 2003; Rappleye 2006), the (re)development of the city (Motte and Weil 2000; Peck 2005), and gentrification of some neighborhoods (Jerzyk 2009; Silver 2009).

Although Providence is a typical American city, it is also unusual in two respects. First, like Rhode Island as a whole, elected officials are overwhelmingly Democratic in party affiliation (Rhode Island State Board of Elections 2008). Second, Providence has an infamous history of corruption and mob activity that may continue to color how residents consider politics—perhaps making them more suspicious of political processes.[20] Although these place-specific attributes likely have some effect on the values and expectations of Providence citizens, we believe that meaning-making in this city can tell us something about political culture, more broadly, in the United States today. Our investigation has little to do with partisan politics, and distrust of politics and politicians is a nationally reported sentiment. Thus, such contextual particularities do not account for our research findings.

Like more commonly researched cities, such as Chicago, New York, or Los Angeles (e.g., Sassen 2001), Providence is large enough to host diverse approaches to civic engagement, including an Occupy Providence protest in 2011, yet small enough for a group of researchers to become intimately familiar with the civic landscape and its key players. Providence is thus an ideal "stage of action" that facilitates understanding of general processes of social action, interaction, and boundary formation (Fine 2010).

Fieldsite Selection

Our research examined civic groups and individual citizens who were engaged in civic life through those groups.[21] We consider each group to be a "fieldsite," although we often interacted with the individuals from those organizations outside their group settings. Each of our seven fieldsites met three criteria. First, each group was oriented toward making Providence a better city by influencing, reforming, or participating in politics. Some interfaced directly with the state—by attending meetings at the statehouse, protesting at city hall, lobbying elected officials, or speaking at public

---

20. For a thrilling account of these stories, see Mike Stanton's *The Prince of Providence: The True Story of Buddy Cianci, America's Most Notorious Mayor, Some Wiseguys, and the Feds* (2003). Of Mayor Buddy Cianci, a beloved but corrupt mayor of twenty-one years sent to federal prison on a racketeering conviction, Stanton writes, "He was equal parts visionary, cheerleader, rogue and lounge singer.... He was a larger-than-life political character *unique to Rhode Island and yet reflective of America....* Cianci, who boasted that he could ride around his city blindfolded and recognize each neighborhood by its sounds and smells, embodied Providence" (xiv–xv, emphasis added).

21. All of the individuals and groups have been given pseudonyms, although we realize they may still be identifiable to those familiar with civil society in Providence. Researchers distinguish between *external confidentiality*, the ability of outsiders to identify participants and the confidentiality that institutional review boards and researchers are generally most concerned with, and *internal confidentiality*, "the ability for research subjects involved in the study to identify each other in the final publication of the research" (Tolich 2004, 101). Our goal is to preserve external confidentiality, while recognizing that internal confidentiality may be impossible, because in-the-know readers will recognize stories or descriptions.

hearings. Others interacted with the state in less direct ways—by raising awareness about an issue, calling on residents to communicate with one another, or educating themselves on political topics. Despite these activities, many of our research subjects would not identify themselves or their groups as "political." Instead, they describe their activities as "neighborly," or "community-building," or simply "getting involved."

The second criterion was about groups' principal purposes. We chose not to work with partisan groups or organizations formed to campaign for particular candidates. This is not to say that our research subjects were not involved in electoral politics, but rather that the groups' primary objectives were not oriented around elections or political parties. We also eliminated religious institutions (e.g., Episcopalians for Justice), organizations based on a shared national heritage (e.g., the Portuguese Social Club), unions, and local chapters of national associations. These decisions helped us target groups that were locally organized, taking their directions from the citizens of Providence, as opposed to national or international leadership.

The final criterion for selecting fieldsites was that we were able to participate actively alongside the members and talk frequently with leaders. All of our fieldsites welcomed us to attend meetings, participate in events, interview members, volunteer our time, and build relationships. This played out differently in each group: while some invited us to attend public events, others regularly included us in "closed-door" meetings; while some invited us to lead, others preferred we mostly observe. Although we abstained from accepting positions of leadership, we found ways to contribute to each group's mission. This reciprocity took many forms: we distributed flyers, assisted with grant writing, recorded meeting minutes, compiled survey data, and accepted general gruntwork (such as picking up pumpkin guts after the Halloween pumpkin launch). Active participation helped us reciprocate, in part, the time and energy that groups gave us—in the form of interviews and introductions to projects—and gave us a more intimate understanding of the groups' work. Differences in access to groups were minor—in all cases we were able to experience life as "insiders" of the organization, and thus gather the detailed ethnographic data we sought. Of course, more than seven organizations fit all of these criteria. In choosing among eligible contenders, we aimed to study groups that seemed "different" along several dimensions, including demographic composition, mission, organizational form, tactics, history, age, and geographic location. Again, this process of selection is described in detail in Methodological Appendix A.

Although we could parse our groups into myriad categories—big groups versus small groups, old versus new, or technologically advanced versus technologically arcane—we do not find these categories particularly meaningful. Throughout the book, the seven fieldsites align and diverge in many, and often unexpected, ways. In this chapter, for the purpose of introduction, we categorize according to organizational form: we studied three neighborhood associations, two civic innovator groups, and two social justice organizations. Note that one of the neighborhood associations is also a social justice organization (as we discuss in Chapter 6). Although boundaries between groups can be blurred in many ways, our description of these groupings is intended to orient the reader around what might be familiar and to highlight how each group is often perceived by outsiders.

Neighborhood Associations

Several neighborhoods in Providence have formed collectives to improve the quality of life for people living in that area. We studied three, selected in part for the demographic differences of their neighborhoods: Oceanside Neighbors, Parkside Coalition, and Neighbors Driving Change.[22]

Oceanside Neighbors—The Oceanside neighborhood is (unsurprisingly) located on the waterfront. A historical home to immigrants from a variety of countries, about a third of today's population claims a strong Portuguese and Portuguese-speaking heritage, and delicious Portuguese baked goods are easy to find. The neighborhood's close proximity to Brown University and the Rhode Island School of Design has also made it home to many university students, faculty, and staff. The neighborhood is relatively clearly geographically divided: in one area, lower- and middle-income residents live in multifamily homes, the streets suffer from more potholes, and few trees grace the tiny yards, many of which have been paved over to accommodate the ban on street parking; in the other area, upper-income and wealthy residents live in beautifully preserved historic homes on streets lined with hundred-year-old trees. The first area includes many Portuguese, Latino, and Cape Verdean neighbors, while the second is predominantly White. The leadership of Oceanside Neighbors lives in the latter area. The group, founded nearly twenty years ago, seeks to enhance life in the neighborhood and to protect its historic resources. One of its greatest successes was closing down a controversial business in the neighborhood. Currently, land use and waterfront development are two of its top priorities. During our year of fieldwork, the group actively discussed problems with traffic noise, led opposition to controversial public art, advocated new uses for a run-down building, and hosted political candidates for community discussions.

Parkside Coalition—The Parkside neighborhood is racially and economically diverse, with a mixture of single-family homes and rental units, and real estate values on the rise. For nearly thirty years, Parkside Coalition has been organizing its neighbors and businesses to promote the area as a diverse, historic, and desirable urban community. Parkside Coalition members are predominantly White professionals with college degrees, and most own their homes. Participants express pride in their role in making the neighborhood a better place to live, reducing crime, attracting successful businesses, and gaining the attention of city officials. The association has been touted by other neighborhood associations and elected officials as a great example of community members coming together to improve their neighborhood.

---

22. According to Trulia, an online real estate guide, the 2010–2011 median sales prices for homes were roughly $300,000 in Oceanside, $110,000 in Parkside, and $75,000 around Neighbors Driving Change (www.trulia.com).

In our research year, they actively engaged in school debates, pursued historic districting, introduced an incentive program to support shopping locally, held block parties, hosted crime watch meetings, and organized a food drive.

Neighbors Driving Change—The Neighbors Driving Change office is an open, airy space with tall ceilings and huge windows. The walls are covered with large posters and banners in English and Spanish that communicate messages about civil rights, economic revolutions, progressive causes, immigration, housing, and Latino issues. While technically a neighborhood association for a neighborhood with a large Latino population, Neighbors Driving Change works to improve life for Latinos and immigrants living in any part of the city. The group's leadership and members include Blacks, Whites, and Latinos, primarily lower and middle income. The group frequently collaborates with social justice, immigrant rights, and religious organizations. In our research year, Neighbors Driving Change advocated a change to driver's license laws pertaining to immigrants, protested in several public spaces, met with police, managed a legal assistance hotline, and hosted holiday parties.

Civic Innovators

In recent years, activists have increasingly borrowed values, language, and tactics from the business world, and applied them to civic organizing. We call these people and groups "civic innovators" because of their desire to create new forms of engagement in the civic sphere (see Chapter 5). Innovators tend to be college-educated professionals whose careers often involve innovating—such as entrepreneurship, marketing, and the creative sector. In Providence, two groups stood out as examples of this type of engagement: Open Source and Engage.

Open Source—This organization was started by a group of friends who wanted to influence the 2010 mayoral election. Instead of backing a particular candidate, the friends wanted to ensure that the dialogue around the campaign—and thus the new administration—was focused on needed improvements to government transparency, efficiency, and civic accessibility. They wanted the new mayor to be someone who would enthusiastically engage community members, reach out to civic leaders, and advocate citizen participation in city decision-making processes. They built public interest in the election, facilitated dialogue by hosting morning coffee meet-and-greets where voters and candidates could mingle before work, and gave civic education presentations in local schools. After the election, the group became less active but occasionally expressed ideas or concerns about public life via blogs and social media.

Engage—In 2009, the mayor of Providence asked a friend, who was already active in Providence civil society, to form a civic organization to provide a "citizen's voice" in city politics. The goal was to counter corruption, combat Providence's "uncivil" political discourse, and go beyond the "hyper-localized, small, neighborhood association." With a small group of friends, the active citizen founded Engage. In our research year, the group worked to acquire nonprofit status, wrote grants, hosted a discussion between citizens and the mayor to discuss the budget crisis, and opened social media accounts, using these technologies to increase communication among citizens and between citizens and government. One of their accomplishments in this area was having a member attend city council and other public meetings and post updates on Facebook or Twitter in real time, allowing others to follow and comment on the proceedings.

Social Justice Organizations

Social justice organizations are groups that advocate for civil rights; race, class, and gender equality; poverty reduction; and environmental stewardship. Oftentimes, their discourse and tactics follow in the footsteps of social movements of the 1960s. Neighbors Driving Change, the neighborhood association described above, could also be considered a social justice organization. Here, we describe Youth, Action, and Knowledge (YAK) and FIGHT.

Youth, Action, and Knowledge (YAK)—YAK's founder is a middle-aged Black man whose participation in the Million Man March in 1995 inspired him to make a difference in the lives of boys and young men of color. He began by organizing a trip for inner-city boys to attend a museum exhibit. The trip's sponsors included the exhibit organizers, the Department of Recreation in Providence, and drug dealers from his neighborhood. To the latter, he implored, "Here's your chance to make it right." In our research year, YAK met with city officials, participated in a process to reform school district policy, collaborated with other organizations, and attended protest events to advocate that the Providence School System change how boys of color are educated. The members actively bring YAK's goals to their respective neighborhood associations and other activist groups. The founder believes that the Black community can and should improve their own lives and the larger community by greater understanding of the institutional racism that surrounds them, and by getting involved. Well-spoken and passionate, he makes many public appearances, hoping to "raise the consciousness of Black people."

FIGHT—Over twenty-five years ago, residents of one of Providence's economically depressed neighborhoods sat around a kitchen table to talk about how to address the pressing problems facing their community, including violence and discrimination. They founded FIGHT to organize low-income families and communities of color to work for social, economic, and political justice. Today, they are a racially diverse group of primarily lower-income citizens who continue to fight for similar issues. They strive to empower marginalized persons and groups, giving those voices a central role in their organizing and outreach. FIGHT aims to identify and address the sources of structural oppression. In doing so, they engage city councilors, administrators, and even the mayor. They have succeeded in reforming city-level criminal justice policies to improve police accountability and due process for defendants, and they are proud to provide information about their financial options to low-income residents facing eviction.

WHAT IS "POLITICS"?

One of the first things we noticed when we began joining groups and following activists is that "politics" has many meanings. As we noted in Chapter 1, the conventional definition of "politics" is the diverse array of institutions, processes, and actors affiliated with the state, though people attribute many different meanings to the word in everyday usage. In this chapter, we pointed out that although we identify all of our fieldsites as being "politically active"—that is to say, they each interface with the state in their efforts to make Providence a better place to live—often they do not identify themselves as being political. As one engaged citizen explained, "I don't know what people thought of politics fifty years ago, but today it's definitely negative. Politics evokes notions of electoral politics and parties, [but] civic engagement can be planting trees in your neighborhood, and what's so bad about that, you know?" By participating alongside, and taking seriously, organizations and activists, we can begin to understand what politics means to them, and how these meanings inform their activism. We turn to these topics now, in Chapter 3.

Chapter 3

"I Am Not Political"

MAKING SENSE OF
SKEPTICAL ENGAGEMENT

"I'm a nonpolitical guy, *big time*. I don't think it matters." The school department official threw up his hands and raised his eyebrows at the audience, pausing as if to allow the statement to sink in. His comment caught us by surprise. This was a public policy maker addressing concerned citizens at a neighborhood association meeting, and he was talking about the newly elected mayor's influence on school policy. Given the history of politically motivated school closures in this neighborhood, his claim that politics did not matter for school policy struck us as inaccurate. His statement, however, was provocative: it signaled an understanding of the "political" as something with which he did not want to be associated, despite his career in city government and his willingness to engage community members in discussing school management.

The school department official was not unique in asserting that he is not "political" in order to communicate something important to his audience. Throughout our research, we heard very different civic groups and engaged individuals make similar statements, proclaiming their distrust of and disconnection from political processes, politicians, and government, in order to say something about their own identities as citizens. "People need to get over their expectations that the government is going to fix their problems. It's not.... At its worst, government is a barrier. At its best, an enabler. That's as far as it goes." These statements from a leader of Open Source, a civic innovator group, are emblematic of the deep skepticism of government efficacy that we frequently observed in our work. "We can't complain about what schools and government are not doing.... It's up to us to do it ourselves," was another refrain we heard echoed in various ways. Mistrusting the government's ability to solve problems often went hand in hand with the notions that citizen engagement would improve government, and that people can and should "fix it themselves."

Notably, the people who made these statements were some of the most active people in Providence's civil society and local government—many of whom were explicitly engaging with the state. For example, the professional White woman who called government "at its best, an enabler" was working to improve legislative processes, meeting with officials, attending city council meetings, and writing publicly about the importance of an educated and connected citizenry. Six months after our interview, she even became a political appointee in the new mayor's administration. Similarly, an activist who advocated "do-it-yourself" citizenry works regularly and directly with the superintendent of schools and other government officials. Americans from different backgrounds, pursuing change in different ways, are nonetheless similar in asserting that they are not political. Yet this "disavowal of the political" does not necessarily signal apathy or withdrawal from political life. On the contrary, it can be a prelude to civic participation.

"I am not political" is a chorus line of political life in America. No matter what critique of politics an individual expresses—that it promotes elite interests, consists of meaningless struggles between political parties, or suggests broken processes that embody societal inequalities—"not doing politics" is a central part of how engaged citizens understand what they do. This denial is more than a quirk of language. In fact, distancing oneself from politics is *productive* for political activity. The school department official whose comment opened this chapter sought to obtain approval, as he interacted with members of the neighborhood association, by claiming a nonpolitical identity. He presented himself as one of many individuals who can be trusted because, although he is a public official, he does not *do politics*, and does not rely on politicians or political solutions.

In this chapter, we explore the meaning of being an engaged citizen in a time when declaring, "I am not political," seems central to political action. We address the questions: Why do activists, members of political parties, and government employees, among others, claim, "I am not political," while participating in politics? Why does disenchantment with the political system fail to stop citizens from engaging with vigor? What does skeptical engagement mean for politics and democracy today?

Across the broad spectrum of Providence-based civic organizations we described in Chapter 2, and across race, class, gender, social background, and political party affiliation, we found that citizens hold politics in low regard and consider being political to be unsavory. But our research also showed that, surprisingly, having a negative view of politics and government does not necessarily cultivate commitments to the public good that are only instrumental or self-serving. In contrast, rejecting politics often goes hand-in-hand with civic engagement. Residents are skeptical *and* engaged. Rather than posing a threat to democracy, disavowal of the political allows people to creatively constitute what they imagine to be appropriate and desirable forms of citizenship and civic participation.

SKEPTICAL ENGAGEMENT AND AMERICAN DEMOCRACY

Scholars, public leaders, and citizens have long been interested in how Americans' attitudes toward politics affect their involvement in civic activities and, in general, the health of American democracy. Social scientists have documented political apathy, cynicism, and distrust of government in America and analyzed empirical trends in civic and associational life. As discussed in Chapter 1, these topics came to the fore in the 1990s, as Americans' political attitudes appeared particularly sour, and scholars warned about declining associational life and civic engagement (e.g., Craig 1993; Pharr and Putnam 2000). Many social scientists argue that political disaffection leads individuals to withdraw from social and political life, and that this sort of apathy corrodes even the most vibrant of democracies and modern civil society.

Like other scholars, we use the term "skeptical" to capture this broad assortment of disapproval, disaffection, mistrust in politics and politicians, and cynicism about government. The word incorporates the positions of those who believe government *could* work (but does not), as well as those who believe the system is more fundamentally broken. Some scholars argue that skepticism engenders a form of selfish citizen engagement that is corrosive to democracy and leads to constricted and confrontational forms of participation (e.g., Putnam 1996; Macedo 2005; Bellah et al. 2008 [1985]). Others suggest that skeptical citizens withdraw from politics and turn to close, community-level concerns that do not make a difference in the big picture and cannot confront the central struggles of democratic life, such as power imbalances, inequality, and belonging (e.g., Calhoun 1998; Žižek 1999; Herbert 2005). Finally, the most pessimistic of scholars argue that skepticism, in and of itself, threatens democratic stability because if citizens conclude that government is damaged beyond repair they are unlikely to engage in the political system at all (e.g., Offe 2006; Keane 2009; Jackson, Mondak, and Huckfeldt 2009).

These views might lead us to expect an unraveling of the American democratic fabric, yet by many measures, that is far from the case. Indeed, in spite of their profound skepticism of politics, politicians, and the political system, Americans are participating in civic life at extremely high levels (CNCS 2006; ANES 2010; Pew Research Center 2010).[1] Research shows that times of distrust can spur unconventional forms of engagement (Inglehart 1990; Cain, Dalton, and Scarrow 2003). Even in times of widespread skepticism, citizens are motivated to participate in the public sphere by their hopes and dreams for democracy (Dalton 2004; Norris 2011).

We build on the work of scholars who have been drawn to this seemingly paradoxical combination of skepticism and engagement in American life. As cultural sociologists have shown, what may appear to be apathy actually takes significant work to produce. Apathy is a mechanism that people have developed in order to preserve

---

1. We recognize that measuring participation in civil and political life is complicated. On this, see Norris (2011, Chapter 4).

faith in democratic ideals even when they feel powerless in a given context (Eliasoph 1997, 1998; Norgaard 2006). Like these scholars, we turn the question of *whether* Americans are skeptical of their political system into a question of *what* that skepticism means for their engagement, their communities, and the political system. Like Nina Eliasoph (1997), we investigate the ways that Americans simultaneously navigate their sense of disappointment with their democracy and their desire to improve their communities. While Eliasoph sees a turn to "local-only" civic engagement as a retrenchment away from political problems that people believe they cannot fix, and argues that something important is lost in this negotiation, we see people's disavowal of the political as their attempt to *rescue* what they feel is good and valuable in democracy.

We are not the first to express interest in the meaning of skeptical engagement. However, scholars have paid scant attention to the role of skepticism within political cultures and to the daily customs and practices that make this skepticism compatible with civic participation. The role of disavowal of the political in contemporary American civic life helps to explain how skepticism and engagement go hand-in-hand. By paying attention to the everyday discourses and actions of a wide assortment of active members of society, we can begin to understand how Americans make sense of the political. And by examining the phenomenon across seven diverse fieldsites, we are able to expose how this disavowal is a common language of civic life—even if people mean widely varying things by "politics" and the "political."

DISAVOWAL OF THE POLITICAL

When Americans claim they are not political, they are not simply defining themselves by what they are not. They are *disavowing politics*—rejecting knowledge of, connection to, or responsibility for the processes and consequences of the political—and simultaneously self-identifying with a more positive ideal of public engagement and social change.[2] This disavowal is an active process of distancing from what is

---

2. "Disavowal" is commonly used as a psychological term. In psychology, disavowal refers to an ambivalent psychic distancing that is ego-preserving in the face of trauma or taboo (Freud 1959; Bass 2000; Gemerchak 2004). For Freud, some awkward facts were "too terrible to confront, but impossible to ignore," and were dealt with by simultaneous knowing and not-knowing, or "acceptance and disavowal" (Cohen 2001, 25). Our usage is closer to Melanie Klein's psychoanalytic usage, in which disavowal is related to the productive act of idealizing (Klein and Mitchell 1986; Sedgwick 2007). Likewise, the German philosopher Peter Sloterdijk (1987), in a framework similar to ours, develops the concept of "kynicism" (as opposed to cynicism), which he understands as subversive and simultaneous knowing and not-knowing (see Magee 2004). In sociology, Pierre Bourdieu has used the term "disavowal" (*dénégation*) to refer to the "cultivated disinterestedness" that defines a field (Bourdieu and Nice 1980; Bourdieu 1990, 1996). For Bourdieu, some spaces are defined by the apparent and constant rejection of outside influences that do, in fact, play an important role. In the case of art, for example, a strictly cultural or aesthetic "disinterested interest" is deliberately

seen as contaminated in order to identify with what is seen as desired. Disavowal is intertwined with how people understand and define politics. In what follows, we illustrate the concept of disavowal by telling the story of one individual, Joe, and his complicated relationship with the "political."

"If you want to get people engaged, throw a party and turn the music on!" Joe enthusiastically told us in an interview. As an activist and a DJ, he does just that—throws parties and plays music in public parks. Fun events give people "a reason to get involved," he explained, an impetus to visit new places in one's own city, to meet new people, and to learn about other events. In this way, Joe sees what he does as building a path toward broader civic engagement. Joe also directs an after-school program for the city's underprivileged teens, and is the co-leader of the civic group Engage. Joe says that Engage promotes better communication between citizens and city government—to "put the 'public' in public policy." Through his civic engagement, he acts upon his conviction that change comes from everyday citizens. In an interview where Joe described his values and activities, he concluded by saying, "I don't like to think of what I do as political." He then grinned, self-consciously, and added, "I'm sure you get that a lot."

Joe's comment would have been surprising had it not been so typical. We heard similar statements from across all our fieldsites—repeated skepticism of anything political or related to government. "The government won't solve our problems." "Providence politics are corrupt." "Current avenues for participation aren't going to bring about change." This is how the residents of Providence describe their city government and its political processes—discourses characterized by harsh critique of a wide array of political issues. Yet taken out of this context where such statements are commonplace, Joe's comment raises many questions. If he does not view his political activities as "political," then what are they? What is Joe's understanding of "political"? Why was it important for him to make this distinction?

According to Joe, Engage was founded as a response to the mayor's desire to "shift the power base away from the eighteen hoodlums who currently have power." This description embodies Joe's understanding of what politics is all about—a realm co-opted by the powerful, catering to special interests, and unconcerned with serving the broader public good. Other people in our fieldsites define "politics" and the "political" differently—as corruption, or as consisting of personal relationships, or as bipartisan battling. Whatever the definition, and no matter how it might change from one situation to another, "politics" is generally understood as an obstacle to how democracy ought to function if it were to truly serve the public good.

---

produced by writers and artists who depend on the economic interests of their cultural products, but who also claim autonomy from those same economic interests (Bourdieu 1994, 172; Schinkel 2007). In these spaces, symbolic interests—like the symbolic value of one's identity as an artist—are set up in opposition to economic interests—like earning a living by selling paintings. In this way, our own concept of disavowal of the political is not unlike disavowal in other realms and spaces.

Inspired by a classic anthropological argument, we suggest that the disavowal of the political establishes a taboo against the polluted elements of politics. Mary Douglas (2002 [1966]) argues that societies create taboos to deal with social disorder and ambiguities, those parts of life that are not black and white but instead complicated shades of gray. According to Douglas, taboos shape societies by generating norms and values of appropriate ways of thinking and behaving. By extension, our observation of taboos on politics and the political suggests that these taboos generate norms of appropriate ways of being good, engaged citizens. In the context of our research, people must deal with the vast ambiguities that result from their desire for a better democracy, and their concomitant disillusionment with democratic politics as they actually exist. Thus, disavowal is the enactment of a taboo against those aspects of the political considered to be polluted, providing a cultural mechanism that shelters commonly held democratic ideals from the ambiguities and contradictions of politics in practice. In the example above, Joe distances himself from a sphere he views as contaminated in order to protect his work as an activist and engaged citizen, drawing this boundary in order to deal with the ambiguities of democracy in practice and continue to work as a public activist within the political sphere.

Disavowal of politics is also identity work. In stating, "I don't like to think of what I do as political," Joe identifies himself as a good activist and civically engaged citizen. Here we draw on Erving Goffman's (1961) concept of "role distancing," the deliberate and active attempt to demonstrate a lack of attachment to an implied role. Individuals engage in role distancing when they enact roles, associate with others, or utilize institutions that imply social identities inconsistent with their actual or desired self-conceptions. For example, homeless people engage in role distancing by distinguishing their behaviors and identities from common stereotypes attributed to the homeless (Snow and Anderson 1987). Likewise, a worker who feels overqualified and constrained by his menial job might distinguish himself from satisfied employees—those who feel content in accepting this sort of employment—by grumbling and making sarcastic jokes about the nature of the position (Riemer 2001). In our case, activists disavow politics to separate themselves from the negative stigma associated with the perceived nature of politicians or other political actors. In this way, members of civil society draw boundaries between themselves and the political in order to establish a positive identity for themselves and gain trust and legitimacy in the eyes of others.

The process of forging one's identity is never complete. It is not sufficient for Joe to disavow politics once in an interview—it must happen over and over again. Disavowal is enacted repeatedly, to different audiences, and across contexts, as people continually establish themselves as appropriately engaged citizens. Every interpersonal interaction provides the opportunity to negotiate this identity for themselves and for others. In particular, when Joe takes on political roles, associates with political people, or uses political institutions, he creates a disjuncture with his identification as "nonpolitical." This ambiguity inspires subsequent disavowals of the political.

Joe's story and the scores of stories of people we met who are like Joe in their disavowal highlight how disavowal functions, and to what end. It is not only instrumental but also symbolic. In drawing a boundary between "good" civic engagement and "bad" politics, they express shared understandings of what democracy should be. When people like Joe describe their work as nonpolitical, they reinforce the idea that good, engaged citizens working to make Providence a better place should do so outside of politics. Even elected officials—like a bureaucrat discussing school policy at a neighborhood association meeting—use this idiom. With this understanding in mind, we explore how and why disavowal of politics emerges.

THE AMBIGUITIES OF POLITICS

Why is "the political" so polluted? When and where do we see disavowal emerge? We argue that disavowal is a cultural idiom that attempts to resolve the ambiguity that people experience when their expectations about how politics *ought* to function are contradicted by how they believe political decisions *actually* take place. Disavowal takes many forms, but we saw it emerge most commonly in response to three areas of ambiguity: (1) when people suspect that special interests are at stake, even though the conversation is about the broader public interest; (2) when people want polite, rational public discourse, but instead see angry, conflict-ridden politics; and (3) when people are mistrustful of government capacity, yet remain engaged in influencing government activity. This is not an exhaustive list of all possible forms of disavowal of the political; instead, these categories reflect the most salient manifestations of ambiguities that we observed in our fieldsites. Individuals may disavow one aspect of politics or many, and the object of disavowal may change between contexts.

These ambiguities are connected to people's definitions of politics and the political. As discussed in Chapter 1, this book emphasizes popular definitions of politics. When people talk about "politics," they mean many different things, ranging from normal democratic practices, such as voting, to abstract judgments about corruption, power, and influence. Here, we show how these definitions of politics are interwoven with people's imaginations of a better future democracy.

Skeptical of Special Interests, but Engaged in Promoting Community Interests

One evening in the spring of 2010, a neighborhood association hosted the spouse of a candidate for local public office as a special guest at their monthly meeting. Sitting at the head of the room, the guest explained that she was there to "say hi" on her husband's behalf. In her efforts to promote her spouse as a candidate, the guest said two things about herself: first, that she did not have a history of being "very political"; and second, that she was the principal of a public school. These two statements were intended to bolster her credibility and to help those attending the meeting believe that her husband was a good person and a good candidate. For this guest, "I am not political" communicated, "I am trustworthy." Likewise, "I am a public servant" communicated, "I am not self-interested." The guest's pronouncement had the intended effect, as evidenced by a transformation of the facial expressions of several board members—from mildly hostile to cautiously welcoming. By disavowing self-interested politics, the guest gained credibility as an advocate for the common good.

There is a disjuncture between the common perception that politics is about the promotion of self-interest or special interests, and the belief that politics *should be* about the promotion of universal interests or public goods. It is this ambiguity that leads engaged citizens to disavow politics, defined as activities or practices that benefit few people, narrow interests, and personal gain. Thus, a "political" agent is someone who uses the state to pursue selfish interests, lacks a commitment to the public good, or allows elite interests to crowd out benefits to the masses. These types of political activities include both illicit behavior, such as bribery, and legal profiteering, such as benefiting from one's access to influential decision-makers. This disavowal rests on the assumption that when one promotes *self-interest* or interests connected to a defined, identifiable group in the political arena, one necessarily becomes *self-interested*. Being political means being selfish or greedy.

People disavow a political system that benefits a small group at the expense of the broader community. Participation and engagement are put forward as the antidote to this type of political action. We saw this clearly with Joe, whose organization Engage aimed to shift power from "eighteen hoodlums" to the people of Providence. We also heard this expressed during heated debates over whether to close public schools to balance the city budget. At a well-attended public forum, in which school board members were to listen to members of the community, a parent asserted that the mayor's decision to close several schools was political because it was based on the recommendations of "two for-profit companies" who "stand to benefit financially" from decisions to close or repurpose public schools. For this parent, politics meant allowing a few companies to gain profits at the expense of the education of hundreds of schoolchildren.

This sentiment was common throughout our fieldwork. Political activity was disavowed for being closed, corrupt, serving narrow interests, and ignoring the general good, but accepted and encouraged when it was the opposite. To be nonpolitical was not just to be free of these narrow interests, but also to be community minded, to work for the general good, and to embody public-spiritedness. In this way, disavowal is not only a rejection of politics, but also an active redefinition and an aspirational rendering of the political.

Skeptical of Conflict, but Engaged in Polite Problem Solving

The civic group Engage identifies the acrimony that characterizes Providence politics as one of the city's primary problems, and thus Engage aims to promote "harmonious" relations among citizens and city government officials. According to one of the organization's leaders, "Mutual respect for each other as neighbors and friends should determine the tone of any and all conversations." One of Engage's main tactics is to publicize city council meetings, organize residents to attend these meetings, and use social media to report what was discussed and decided. Leaders told us repeatedly that merely having Providence residents attend city council meetings would improve city government, because it would encourage councilors to be more civil and "well-behaved."

In these discourses, Engage exemplifies an aversion to political conflict commonly held by Americans of all backgrounds (Hibbing and Theiss-Morse 2002). Ambiguity results when people take political action or participate in political activities, which often involve conflict. During our fieldwork, we often saw people and groups distancing themselves from contention and confrontation. This type of distancing was clear in an interview with a leader of Oceanside Neighbors. Describing her group's goals and strategies, she said, "I have learned that you can't start out by attacking. You have to first talk about what they have done that is good, and then go into [your goals]." She spent much of the interview describing a multiyear campaign to shut down a neighborhood business, whose noisy activities and clientele were perceived as dangerous and harmful to residents' quality of life, by talking to local officials and fund-raising to hire a lawyer. The leader did not mention any direct actions, such as protests or picketing, nor did she talk about contentious meetings between residents and city leaders or the business owners. Even surrounding these highly charged political issues of public space in the neighborhood, she said, "We try really hard to get along with people—we don't want to be naysayers."

In another case, a volunteer who teaches civic skills to students in public schools said his organization's lesson plans "avoid politically charged issues," which he defined as issues that are too contentious for the classroom and cannot be solved by student discussion. Here, politics takes on the connotation of inciting unproductive conflict, the sort of thing that is inappropriate for young people to discuss in school.

These are examples of disavowing politics as conflict. This form of disavowal sets up the expectation of a different form of politics—one defined by civility, communication, and participation. In particular, we saw this type of disavowal surface around issues that are by nature contentious, and in moments when no single solution could be agreed on by everyone. To disavow politics, in this sense, is to deny the potential productivity of conflictive behaviors or processes, and to simultaneously promote norms of good civic engagement as polite and harmonious.

Some civic groups and individuals seem to defy this more general trend of distaste for conflict in political life. They imagine that society will be improved by leveling out inequalities, and in order to work toward this goal, direct and confrontational action is sometimes a necessary tactic. For example, as part of their campaign against the criminalization of immigration, Neighbors Driving Change held polite and rational meetings with the police commissioner, and also organized confrontational protests in front of elected officials' homes. In their own meetings, however, the group went to great lengths to avoid and smooth over conflict, and their discussions were marked by respect, order, and equal opportunities to be heard. Thus, some groups have an orientation toward conflict that is more fluid across contexts. Often these are the very same groups who, in many situations, openly claim to be engaging in politics and whose disavowal of the political is thus worth examining more closely. We discuss this in more depth at the end of the chapter.

Skeptical of Broken Political Processes, but Engaged in Influencing the Government

In one of the anecdotes that opened this chapter, a civic leader described government as "at its best, an enabler" of citizens' actions, and emphasized that because government is not going to "fix people's problems," citizens need to take matters into their own hands. In a similar call for self-sufficiency from government, a leader of a Black advocacy group expressed nostalgia for a communal past when people took care of other people, rather than relying on government services. He believes that "it's on us": people must hold themselves accountable for making the changes necessary to improve their community. He works with Black families and non-Black allies to address the structural racism that continues to create an unequal society. As is characteristic of disavowal, his advocacy for communitarianism and self-reliance is complemented by directly engaging the state through actions such as testifying on a bill or partnering with school officials.

This third type of disavowal emerges in response to the ambiguities that arise when people work within political systems while believing that those systems cannot or do not solve community problems. While the people in our study may disagree on what, exactly, is broken, they nearly always agree that the government apparatus alone cannot solve the city's problems. In grappling with this tension between lack of faith in government and the need to work within the political system, people disavow politics in favor of self-sufficiency and community engagement, as described above. Correspondingly, people speak about trying to change the political process to incorporate greater citizen involvement. "We have to stand up and take our city back," explained a neighborhood resident at an Oceanside Neighbors meeting. He described his efforts to improve communication between civic organizations and political bodies, and talked about making some noise on an issue of concern to the neighborhood, explaining that residents did not want a council that does not talk to each other or a mayor that does not talk to the council.

Sometimes people disavow everyday politics because they believe that significant structural changes are required to transform the political system. For example, members of FIGHT often make veiled references to the possibilities of revolution and socialism, implying that only massive overhauls to the political system can address entrenched race, class, and gender inequalities. Likewise, an activist with YAK said that institutionalized racism was visible in political decisions made by the city council, state legislature, and mayor. For him, the policy proposals on the table today are insufficient for addressing what he understands to be the root of society's problems.

These sentiments were common among many engaged citizens of Providence. At a public hearing on proposed school closures in Providence, a young Latino student asked why the city was not closing schools in the more affluent, White neighborhoods. Another student echoed this critique: "Why do they pick on the poor kids all the time?" The implication was that school closures were *not* just about solving budget problems for the common good but also about unequal distributions of power. Joe, the activist DJ who works with Engage, explained that schools inspire a lot of people to get involved but are equally good at shutting people out. In his case, feeling the system is fundamentally broken is part of why he works to supplement public schools with an after-school program, instead of working for small changes within the public schools themselves. In these examples, the political process is rejected on the basis that it unfairly excludes vulnerable segments of the population.

Activists who disavow political processes often attribute their political victories to the ingenuity of their tactics, as opposed to the responsiveness of politicians or political systems that work. For example, when Governor Lincoln Chafee was running for office in 2010, Neighbors Driving Change requested that, if elected, he rescind an executive order from the previous governor. The order was related to the use of "E-Verify," a federal program to check the immigration eligibility of potential employees. He promised to do so, and in his first days of office held a press conference to talk about E-Verify and announce his decision on that executive order. Members of Neighbors Driving Change were skeptical that he would stick to his promise. As they gathered to walk together to the press conference, one leader shouted to the group, "Who's ready to get angry?" The response was enthusiastic. At the press conference, the governor did, in fact, rescind the executive order, stating that the policy was divisive, that it had failed to reduce costs for the state, and that immigration policy was best addressed at the federal level (Tucker 2011). One of the activists credited this "success" to his group's direct action tactics, arguing that the only reason Chafee agreed to rescind the whole executive order was that he saw activists in the crowd. For him, the victory was attributable to the threat of activists making a scene—not to an elected official's own policy positions or commitment to respond to his constituents, or to a democratic process that worked. In this type of disavowal, individuals at once claim that the political system is broken, push for structural change, and attribute victories to contentious tactics, not institutionalized processes.

EMBRACING POLITICS AS CONFLICT

At times, we did hear people say that what they do is political. Anecdotes in this chapter have hinted at who these people generally are: those who believe politics is broken because it embodies social inequalities. Often, their civic groups are oriented around advocating for social justice and improving the well-being of marginalized communities in Providence. These are the same people who are likely to view conflict as a necessary tactic, even if they avoid contentiousness at their own groups' meetings. In an emblematic comment, Dave, a member of FIGHT, told us about his activities, "If it ain't political, then it's no justice, because there has to be a reason why we are doing these things. We need political and social change, and that doesn't happen unless you get into the political arena." From this perspective, explicitly political activism is both worthwhile and necessary.

Others in our fieldsites expressed similar sentiments, even as they simultaneously professed their dislike of or disbelief in politics. In an interview with Darnell, the leader of YAK, we asked, "Do you view your activities as political?" At first, he responded that no, his work was not about politics, but then he clarified, "I mean, yes, it is political. You know, I go to the State House." But, he continued, "politricks" is not something he *likes* to do, it is something he *has* to do. In this instance, Darnell contradicts himself, both disavowing politics and admitting that he engages with the political. He understands the political as polluted but has the sense that he needs to engage with it in order to create the social change that he desires. While these types of comments were relatively rare during our fieldwork, they are worth investigating. How can we understand the sentiments expressed by Dave and Darnell, in the context of widespread disavowal of the political? Far from being exceptions to our argument, we suggest these are part of the same trends in contemporary civic life that prompt disavowal.

Dave and Darnell, like others across our fieldsites, view the current political system as hopeless, polluted, and broken. FIGHT, for example, is organized around the premise that the current political system in America is unjust and full of racial and class prejudices. Social justice organizers at FIGHT and elsewhere are particularly attuned to several of the definitions of politics we described above: they are extremely skeptical of special and elite interests taking over politics, disillusioned with a broken democratic system, and mistrustful of government capacity. Their disavowal of politics is interwoven with these understandings, as they engage in direct actions to convince Providence city government to improve policies to protect the rights of, for example, ex-prisoners, the jobless, or those in danger of losing their homes to foreclosure. Like anyone else who disavows politics, they are grappling with the ambiguities presented by the disparity between their ideal politics—how politics should be—and how politics actually plays out on the ground. In general, they view the state as a self-serving political system that lacks the capacity to make real social change that improves the well-being of the most marginalized populations.

However, there is a key difference for activists who openly and regularly claim that their work is political. Whereas many Americans disavow conflict and want a democracy without confrontational politics, these individuals and groups view conflict as a necessary strategy. Fighting for one's beliefs is seen as a necessary avenue toward change. They see themselves as the only people willing to directly confront the political system that everyone agrees is broken. This finding was clarified toward the end of our fieldwork, when we explained our preliminary results to leaders in each fieldsite. At FIGHT, as we were explaining our concept of disavowal of politics, saying that people disavow but still engage, a leader interjected, "*Some* people do [engage]." This person may have misunderstood our point, but his interjection was revealing. In emphasizing that *some* people engage, the implication was that *others* do not. Essentially, he was suggesting that he and his colleagues were the ones willing to roll up their sleeves and do the dirty but necessary work of engaging with politics. Thus, when these individuals say they are political, it is in part a defiant stance against the predominant cultural discourse that appropriately engaged citizens are polite, rational, and avoid confrontation.

In sum, even when people seem not to disavow politics, they are often partaking in the contemporary idiom of political disavowal. These people disavow politics by asserting that the political system is almost irreparably broken, even as they engage directly with government partners and processes. When they say, "Yes, I *am* political," it is an indication of their view of the necessary role of conflict in democracy, that it is interwoven with the need to fight structural inequalities, and that in this belief, they are different from other citizens. As we show later in the book, this is a key difference for conceptions of how these people and groups envision and carry out attempts to make positive social change.

IMAGINING A FUTURE THAT DOES NOT YET EXIST

This chapter has illustrated how engaged citizens disavow politics as a prelude to, or justification for, getting involved. Disavowal thus creates links between people and facilitates participation by those who are otherwise critical of politics. The ways that people respond to the ambiguities of actually existing politics generate avenues for good forms of civic engagement that stand in opposition to politics that is corrupt, focused on narrow interests, and full of broken processes. Rather than reproduce a kind of political life that is contaminated, they see their engagement as a departure from politics as it actually is.

Disavowal makes it possible to work for a political campaign, be a public official, or interact with government—in other words, to do political things—by signaling that one is not entangled with the contaminated sphere of politics. At the beginning of the chapter, we described how the leader of Open Source professed her disbelief in government. It should now be clear that she was signaling that her path diverges from traditional politics, which has not effected the kinds of change she wishes to see. When she worked on political campaigns, and eventually in the mayor's office, it was in the spirit of imagining that a different and better path is possible. Similarly, activist DJ Joe's vision of himself as nonpolitical allows him to work for a better city government and support struggling teens, without being associated with the negative features of the political sphere. His disavowal is intertwined with the belief that bringing people together in public spaces and building community will create positive changes for his city. Disavowal, then, is about imagining and pursuing a future democracy that does not yet exist.

Through people's disavowal, we begin to see the contours of the democracy that people wish to have. What do Americans understand to be good and desirable forms of action? What are the characteristics of the democracy they envision? We start to see some commonalities and patterns—if politics is focused on narrow interests, involves conflict, and entails broken processes, then a better democratic system is inclusive and representative, respectful of everyone, and efficient at serving and responding to citizens. As we see in the next chapter, disavowal is intimately connected to "civic imaginations," which are people's theories of how to bring about a better society and democracy.

Of course, people imagine problems and possible solutions in different ways. The leader of YAK promotes a Black community that self-organizes and takes care of itself, without relying on government. The leader of Engage, however, believes in making change by shifting the culture within government and improving communication with and responsibility to an active citizenry. Yet because these individuals engage in disavowal, this creates a space for them as people of different political beliefs to connect and work together. Even when people have widely diverging understandings of politics—as corruption or discrimination or broken systems—or different ideas about an ideal future, disavowal of the current system signals a desire to do things differently, and that is common ground. Even public officials, people that others might identify as clearly political, disavow to express that they are on the same page as their audience. "I am not political" and "I am a public servant" communicate a more friendly feeling and facilitate trust.

CONCLUSION: THE PRODUCTIVE CONSEQUENCES OF DISAVOWAL

This chapter has illustrated the ways in which individuals and groups maintain their skeptical attitudes toward politics while at the same time actively engaging in civic and political life. We found that skepticism does not preclude involvement with political activities, participating in governmental committees or working groups, engaging public officials, or other civic mobilizations. That is to say, skepticism and disengagement need not—and do not automatically—go hand in hand.

On the contrary, "political disavowal" provides citizens with the symbolic capital and notions of good citizenship needed to engage in politics. By asserting that one is "not political," an individual may engage politics without feeling or being perceived as self-interested, participate in civic life while rejecting political conflicts deemed unproductive, and become an activist despite feeling that government and political processes are ineffective in solving society's problems. Disavowal not only allows individuals to deepen their sense of community, it also allows them to harness that community for political activity and engagement and step into the public arena in leadership roles. By avoiding the contaminated sphere of politics, activists can collectively engage with the political structure without polluting their identities or feeling compromised.

Skeptical engagement and disavowal were displayed across *all* of our diverse fieldsites. Tech-savvy civic innovators, radical social justice activists, and nonconfrontational neighborhood leaders all identified shortcomings in contemporary politics, struggled with common ambiguities, and disavowed the political. Indeed, the use of disavowal to justify political engagement is not limited to demographic groups or constrained by political ideology. Disavowal is a widespread cultural mechanism for protecting widely held democratic ideals from the ambiguities and contradictions of politics in practice.

By exclaiming, enacting, and promising that an activity "is not political," citizens simultaneously generate new personal and group identities, alter cultural notions of appropriate and desirable forms of civic engagement, and create multiple avenues to engagement. In this way, disavowal serves as an attempt to rescue democracy from the contamination of politics as is. It is a productive way for people and groups to distance themselves from actually existing politics in order to imagine and politically reorient the world around them. While disavowal raises questions about the consequences of constantly affirming that politics is a dirty, corrupt, and polluted sphere—a topic we return to in Chapter 7 and an important issue for future research—it offers relief from the notion that skepticism begets democratic demise. Citizens are actively creating new notions of what it means to be a good citizen and city resident, thus developing and enacting ways to rescue engagement in an era of skepticism. In Chapter 4, we turn our attention to these acts of imagination.

Chapter 4

The Civic Imagination

Shortly after taking office, Mayor Angel Taveras, a young lawyer-turned-politician, recommended that the Providence school board close several schools in order to address a severe budget crisis. This announcement surprised residents and disappointed many of the mayor's supporters. A series of public hearings was held to allow Providence residents to voice their opinions directly to the school board. During these meetings, a number of unlikely allies—including the majority of our fieldsites, parents, teachers' organizations, and public officials—found themselves working together toward a common goal. Speaking one by one into a microphone— or shouting out of turn from the audience—community members tried earnestly to reason with the school board, pleading that they vote no on the closures, that they save the schools.

At one of these meetings, we greeted activists from FIGHT and Parkside Coalition, and took our seats next to members of YAK. Emotions were running high, and already citizens seemed disenchanted with the process. "They are doing these meetings so they can check things off their list. They need to legally have these meetings, tell us the information they want, and pretend it's been a real community meeting," someone at our table remarked. "They call this a community meeting but don't want to really hear from the community," smirked Darnell, the leader of YAK.

A school board official started the meeting with a presentation of facts and figures about the city's financial woes and the school district's plan, and then opened the floor to public comment. Dozens of people shared stories and opinions, all adding pressure to vote no. Some asserted that the proposed closures disproportionately affected students of color. Others argued that the closures disrupted each school's sense of community. At the end of the meeting, the mayor himself took the microphone. Facing a hostile audience, he asked if the people of Providence thought he actually *wanted* to close the schools, and he explained that there are no easy solutions to fiscal crisis. He defended the closure decision-making process as transparent and open, insisting he wanted to hear people's ideas.

Mayor Taveras reinforced this sentiment at another public meeting later that month: "These aren't political decisions. If I was trying to be political, do you think this is what I would be doing? Don't think for one second that I don't care. This is the hardest thing I've ever had to do." Citizens' cynical comments continued, but their overall tone began to change as a cautious sense of hope emerged. After all, the fact that the school board, the mayor, and city officials were listening to public comments had to mean something, right? Even Darnell, whose skepticism during the first hearings could not have been more pronounced, said he felt the school board was listening to the large number of people who testified at each hearing against the proposed closures. Perhaps the school board would be persuaded, by their participation, to vote against the mayor's suggested course of action.

For some concerned Providence residents, this was an opportunity to fight for their beliefs and put their ideals into practice. From her seat at the back of the room, a member of FIGHT addressed the school board members, who sat above the crowd on an elementary school stage. "You've heard the change, people expressing their opinions ... this is democracy! I don't know how you can vote to close these schools when you see democracy in action!" she yelled at top volume. Another man gestured toward the packed auditorium and shouted, "*This* is what democracy looks like ... *right here.*" FIGHT members in the room struck up a chant: "Show me what democracy looks like!" some called out. "*This* is what democracy looks like!" responded others. In these moments, for these activists, there was a sense that the people would be heard. Of course, the yelling out of turn and occasionally hostile language was not appreciated by everyone.

For other activists, whether the schools stayed open or closed was less important than the fact that the school closure debate opened a space for dialogue between citizens and the state. Engage, for example, hosted a related event dubbed "Budget and Beer." It was one stop on the mayor's "Fiscal Honesty Tour," a series of meetings to explain to the public why Providence was experiencing such a severe budget crisis. During the event, one attendee commented publicly that the budget presentation indicated the schools would close, yet in his understanding, this was a decision yet to be made by the school board. The mayor confirmed this was correct, but explained that he had called the school board and urged them to vote for the closures, despite heavy public pressure to vote no. Some attendees followed up by pressing the mayor for specific information, while others changed the subject. As facilitators, Engage members were not interested in turning the event into yet another advocacy meeting for schools. At the end of the night, members of Engage gave Mayor Taveras a standing ovation. Shortly after, they published in the local newspaper that the meeting was an excellent example of convening "different" and "more attractive" types of public discussion. For Engage, the process of holding debates, inviting dialogue, and sharing ideas was a notable success—no matter the outcome.

On April 28, 2011, the school board gathered on the stage of a high school auditorium to see one last presentation from a school official, hear a final round of public comments, and vote on the fate of six schools. The auditorium was packed. One news reporter called it "one of the most heated meetings" he had ever attended.

After a full month of meetings, citizens still had a lot to say. "That's bullshit!" someone shouted as a school official once again offered figures of projected savings from school closures. Some audience members testified about the decision-making process. "This is true democracy—all of us coming out and listening to each other," said one attendee. Others invoked a sense of the community's responsibility: "The only way Providence schools will get better is if we do it—it's not if these guys [*motioning to the board*] do it. We have to do it!" Various protesters disrupted the proceedings with bursts of "Hey hey, ho ho, Mayor Taveras has got to go!"

Finally, it came time for the board to vote. Roll-call style, as each school's name was announced, each board member was to say "aye" (to close) or "nay" (to keep open) into their microphone. They went down the row for each school, a single "Nay" and a chorus of "Ayes." "Aye." "Aye." "Aye." "Aye." "Aye." Members of Neighbors Driving Change moved from the back of the auditorium to the middle of the audience. They remained standing but turned their backs to the stage. Nearly everyone in the auditorium stood up and followed suit. After the last vote, a devastated audience, many of them children, many of them crying, turned around to face the school board. "Shame! Shame! Shame!" they screamed. Fists pumped into the air and fingers pointed at the stage. "You wasted our time! *You wasted our time.*"

THE CULTURE OF AMERICAN CIVIC LIFE

These scenes took place in Providence over the course of a few months in 2011, but they are by no means unique. Across the United States, and throughout history, issues about which people care deeply have brought diverse groups together to work for a common cause. This simple observation speaks to the culture of American civic life and confirms a line of scholarly thought stretching back to Alexis de Tocqueville (2003 [1840]): Americans value involvement, volunteerism, and associative democracy and are inspired by these "habits of the heart" (Bellah et al. 2008 [1985]). Most people at the school-related meetings in Providence valued an *active* version of citizenship: the idea that it is worthwhile and important for citizens to be involved in their communities and in the issues that affect them. Indeed, esteem for participation was nearly universal in the seven civic groups we studied, as a good in itself and as crucial to the health of our democracy. Yet Providence residents remained divided in their interpretations and ideas of what should be done, and how to do it. This raises the question: What does participation mean, and how is it understood in relation to the political system and to civic change?

In Chapter 3, we discussed the centrality of disavowal of politics to Americans' civic engagement. The world of politics—whether seen as a top-down corrupt enterprise that serves elite interests, an electoral strategy of pandering to would-be constituencies, or a spectacle that simulates actual democracy—is understood as polluted and contradictory to democracy and community. Civic life, on the other hand, is constantly redefined as distinct from the political. Critics have dismissed this turning away from politics as a narrow cynicism or as a gateway to apathy. We disagreed with this pessimistic interpretation, and instead showed that disavowal is a common language that makes certain alliances and engagements possible, but that also expresses a kind of yearning for more autonomous and democratic civic engagement. In this chapter, we explore those yearnings in more detail, expose their contours and contradictions, and illustrate the ways in which they shape and limit the possibilities of civic life.

Civic Imagination

Following the seven civic groups in our study, we heard and saw how a wide range of people articulated what good engagement looks like and what it means to be a citizen engaged in creating positive social change. We were struck by the observation that people are continuously, actively engaged in prospective thinking about a better society and political system. Our concept of "civic imagination" captures this constant simmering. As we define it, the civic imagination consists of the ways in which people individually and collectively envision better political, social, and civic environments. Civic imaginations are people's *theories of civic life*. They are the cognitive roadmaps, moral compasses, and guides that shape participation and motivate action. These underlying frameworks help people make sense of their place in the world and help generate notions of what it means to work for change. Civic imaginations underpin the processes of identifying problems and solutions, envisioning better societies and environments, and developing a plan to make those visions of a better future into reality. We use the concept of civic imagination to examine Americans' diverse motivations for and styles of engaging the political sphere.

In the context of the Providence school closure debates, the diversity of civic imaginations was overwhelming. Early on, we noticed that there were different conceptions about which tactics might work. There was widespread agreement among the people who testified at the public hearings that saving schools from being shut down was the right solution, and that citizen involvement was the answer, but there were fundamental disagreements about how to make the school board agree. If one person pushed for street protest, another called the idea needless disruption. If one group proposed an alternative policy, another group would argue to leave policy making to the city. As we listened to debates, followed activists, and participated in events, it became apparent that these disagreements were not only about strategies, tactics, or even styles of engagement; they were also fundamentally different assumptions about what engagement *is*, what it is *for*, and how it *works* (or does not). As philosopher Ludwig Wittgenstein writes, these were not so much disagreements in opinion, but in "forms of life" (1966, 241).[1] We were experiencing a clash between different ways of understanding the social world.

---

1. Wittgenstein argued for careful description of ways of knowing as they were actually lived by people. Similarly, we attend to the differences between the multiple bodies of knowledge held by, and lived realities inhabited by, each citizen. As we take up this notion that "traditional categories of knowledge, objectivity, and truth are socially constituted and determined by the norms, needs, and interests of particular socio-cultural groups" (Friedman 1998, 241), we also call into question the limits of those groups, highlighting the potentials of agency in a way that Wittgenstein did not.

One Language, Many Grammars

There are many different grammars of civic life—in other words, sets of rules about the *meaning* of language, not the *form* of language, that are loosely drawn on but not always followed—for seeing the world and speaking about it. As we followed individuals and groups throughout our research, we found that their civic imaginations tended toward three common emphases: "power," "solidarity," and "problem solving." Each of these emphases, or points of orientation, represents a different understanding of what civil society *is* and *does*.

In brief, for imaginations that emphasize "power," the role of civil society is to reduce current inequalities and redistribute who has influence in the political sphere. To solve social problems, people should challenge structures and systems. In this way of thinking, justice, equity, and social change are paramount. For imaginations centered on "solidarity," civil society influences the political by fostering a sense of community. Civic life requires feeling connected to others. This is the world of fellowship, neighborliness, and camaraderie. Finally, for imaginations emphasizing "problem solving," civil society creates the conditions for deliberation and dialogue about common problems. It is this kind of communicative action that will improve political processes and outcomes. This is the world of thinking together, being pragmatic, and finding technical solutions. If commitment to democracy and distance from politics make up the common language of American civil society, civic imaginations are its principal dialects.

Explaining the concept of civic imaginations and identifying these three variants help us understand that while people may use the same words to describe what they want—for example, increased public participation or government transparency—the civic imaginations behind those words can give them radically different meanings. Such was the case in discussing school closures. As people voiced opinions, protested, and came into conflict with one another, we noticed that arguments were clustered around the three dialects of civic life we described. Some people (emphasizing power) were primarily concerned with the fact that the school closings primarily affected students from poor, racial minority neighborhoods. For other people (oriented around solidarity), the important thing was that people came together to voice their opinions to city officials. For yet others (focused on problem solving), what was needed was space for community members to come up with a plan and for ordinary citizens to feel responsible for helping the city solve its budget problem.

Common Language

Civic culture is at once widely shared and hugely varied. That is, within a common cultural idiom that values citizen involvement and eschews politics, words like citizenship and participation come to assume a variety of different meanings within our three groups of imaginations. Describing civic culture as a language is an appropriate analogy, in which civic imaginations might be thought of as dialects or as variations on a theme.

At this point, it is important for us to be clear about what civic imaginations are *not*. First, they are not synonymous with political views—that is to say, imaginations and political beliefs do not line up neatly. Tempting as it may be to equate imaginations focused on power with the political Left, or problem solving with the Right, for example, the reality is more complicated. Tea Party activists who mobilize to decry the conspiracy of professional politicians in Washington, DC, and the injustices of the tax system express an imagination centered around power. And when President Obama calls for health care reform in the name of pragmatic solutions, he is expressing the problem solving imagination. Second, it is important to underscore that these imaginations, or moral grammars, are not rules that people must follow, but instead are cognitive tools or "shorthand" for different understandings of civic and political life. They make sense of complicated facts, organize overwhelming amounts of information, and link together ideas and realities that seem dissonant. Unlike a formal set of rules, civic imaginations are loose frameworks, supportive of thinking, not commanding of thought. In contrast to philosophical ideas that suggest humans act within a given set of parameters or possibilities, civic imaginations do not derive from a fixed or predetermined set of rules of how people think about and act toward the future, nor are their expressions merely improvisations on such fixed rules. In this way, we find room for agency, despite the influence of structure.

Why do people have different civic imaginations? Where do they come from? How do they change from context to context, and what are their limitations? In what follows, we examine how each family of civic imaginations underpins, informs, and shapes civic engagement in a different way.[2] We also look at how imaginations guide the tradeoffs activists make and how the logic of different imaginations can create blind spots, or issues that are easily ignored. First, however, we describe how our idea of "civic imaginations" follows on the pragmatist theoretical tradition and from sociologist C. Wright Mills's (1959) concept of the "sociological imagination."

Inspirations

In developing the concept of civic imagination, we use "civic" because we are interested in imagination that is concerned with society, as opposed to, for example, individual aspirations for a better life. We adopt the word "imagination" because of its creative dimension, since imagination implies thinking of things that do not (yet) exist. To imagine is an act of prospective thinking that brings forth a possible future. In this way, it is similar to what philosophers have sometimes referred to as *poiesis*, meaning "to make." As an act of bringing-forth, the civic imagination informs and

---

2. Here, we urge readers to recall the limits of our study. We studied only those individuals who are active and engaged in civil society and in voluntary associations. We suspect that some of these imaginations may have traction among uninvolved citizens, but we observed these civic imaginations come to life clearly in the context of intentional group life. Strictly speaking, our study does not capture the range of imaginations of people who do not participate and who are totally removed from the political sphere.

guides action, directly bearing on how individuals think about diagnosing social problems and creating social change. Imaginations are fluid and in motion, and are constantly created and re-created as people confront reality and seek out their visions of the "good" amid changing circumstances.

Our methodology, as we described in Chapter 2, is inspired by the pragmatist approach developed by Luc Boltanski, Laurent Thévenot, and colleagues at the Center for Moral and Political Sociology at the Ecole des Hautes Etudes en Sciences Sociales in Paris.[3] Like them, we are less concerned with norms and values, as might be asked in a large-scale survey, than we are with people's moral *evaluations*.[4] The pragmatists urge social scientists to take people seriously as moral beings who are seeking to understand and enact a version of the good, and who are forced to adjust their imaginations in this process. To make judgments about the present—the kind of judgments that civic organizations and activists are often called to do—requires imagination about others but also about the future. As we have argued, imagination and judgment are intimately related, for judgment reveals both the frame through which someone understands the world and the future they imagine.

We also find commonality with sociologist C. Wright Mills's (1959) concept of the "sociological imagination." Mills argues that people's lives are shaped by historical and societal changes, but it is overwhelming for people to think about the structural forces that impact their lives. In order to make sense of the relationship between individual lives and historical structures, people develop sociological imaginations that allow them to see their position in historical context and relative to other individuals. For Mills, this ability to make sense of the connections between one's personal troubles and public issues is empowering, in that it relieves some of the discomfort of not knowing how one relates to history.

If the sociological imagination helps people answer questions about their place in a larger *historical* context, then the civic imagination helps people answer questions about their place in a larger *political* context. These civic imaginations, though, serve as more than just diagnostic tools. As civic imaginations make sense of relationships between personal actions and political contexts, they provide insight into how to work for change, thus driving civic, social, and political action.

---

3. We see this kind of pragmatism as quite compatible with the US cultural sociology that provides so much of the anchor for our approach. We concur with Silber (2003) that pragmatism outlines the "structural and structuring features" of cultural repertoires (such as our three imaginations), rather than seeing those cultural repertoires as only loosely assembled without any dependence on structures.

4. Norms and values were the mainstay of political culture research for many years, but we agree with contemporary scholars who now see this as a somewhat static approach (e.g., Lichterman and Cefaï 2006). The focus on *evaluation* implies an active role for people, as well as reflexivity. That is to say, people critically evaluate using their own frameworks, though these frameworks are not always coherent, and not necessarily the same from situation to situation.

THE DIALECTS OF CIVIC LIFE

Where do people converge and diverge in their quest for good citizenship and improved futures? What are the limitations of imaginations? In this section, we turn our attention to such questions. We also connect the contemporary imaginations resonant in our fieldsites with those of activists, philosophers, social scientists, public intellectuals, and political officials throughout history. These connections provide familiar reference points and illustrate how imaginations have guided actions and shaped politics in other moments, helping us understand their potential in politics today.

Redistributing Power and Privilege

Each of the school closure hearings opened with a PowerPoint presentation in which a school official would explain why budget cuts were needed, review the proposal to close schools, and describe the plan to relocate students. At one such presentation, in a high school auditorium, we sat with Darnell from YAK. Together, we watched as the official displayed a map of the city. Dots appeared where schools might be closed. Darnell whispered to us, "There are dots from all other parts of the city except the East Side." The East Side of Providence, we all knew, was the wealthier and Whiter side of town.

Later, during public comments, Darnell said this to the school board:

> You have already chosen the schools to close, but you don't know where the kids will go. On the maps it looks like the East Side isn't part of Providence. It's as if our students in the rest of the city are running amok. Do we have to revisit *Plessy vs. Ferguson*? As people of color, we have to pay attention. The people of color will take the brunt of the changes. We should send our children over to the East Side. If you want to show good faith to the Black and Latino communities, then send our kids over to those schools.

Many people at the meeting shared Darnell's anger at the unequal distribution of burden between White and non-White students. They felt that the school closings were, at their root, linked to factors such as race and neighborhood income. As one activist declared to the school board, "I am here fighting for equity!"

These statements express civic imaginations that focus on issues of power and inequality. In these understandings, nationwide or societal patterns are important, and things seen and experienced at the local level are understood to reflect broader structural forces. A leader of Neighbors Driving Change, a neighborhood association that advocates for immigrants, explained that "local" problems are never just that: "Because of our members, we see problems outside of our neighborhood, and how our neighborhood fits in our city." Though Neighbors Driving Change offers direct services to Latino immigrant members, including translation and legal assistance, the group also organizes extensively around city, state, and national policies, even traveling across the country to protest restrictive immigration policies in other states. FIGHT's director echoed this emphasis on connecting the local with broader scales: "It's important to connect local, individual experiences to global processes. These local things aren't isolated events." People act at the local level even as they perceive their actions as contributing to a much broader struggle against structural inequalities.

For civic imaginations that are oriented in this way, redistribution of power and privilege is at the heart of working for social change. Often, to address the problem at hand, a privileged group is asked to share some of its privileges. For example, Neighbors Driving Change sees the privilege of holding a driver's license as one that should be shared with immigrants, legal or undocumented. Likewise, FIGHT argues that wealthier individuals should pay more taxes than the poor.

Partly because redistribution is highly contentious and necessitates a shift of the status quo, conflict is often considered a necessary element of working for social change. As a sign at a "Unity Day" rally at the statehouse read, "A Better World Is Possible ... But We Have to Fight for It."[5] This imagination commonly involves naming an opponent or adversary and using confrontational and militaristic language. As one activist told us, "We certainly have some formidable opponents who are working against just about every principle we believe in." Others talked of "storming" the statehouse and "shutting the state down."

People who emphasize power and privilege thus tend to adopt more confrontational tactics, including nonviolent direct action, which historically has included sit-ins, freedom rides, freedom walks, prayer pilgrimages, wade-ins, pray-ins, human chains, and makeshift blockades. As public intellectual Howard Zinn notes,

> Whatever the specific form, this technique has certain qualities: it disturbs the status quo, it intrudes on the complacency of the majority, it expresses the anger and the hurt of the aggrieved, it publicizes an injustice, it demonstrates the inadequacy of whatever reforms have been instituted up to that point, it creates tension and trouble and thus forces the holders of power to move faster than they otherwise would have to redress grievances. (2011, 39)

People motivated by a power-centered imagination argue that direct actions are often necessary because they are the only way for marginalized people to transform existing power structures and thereby gain some measure of equality. During our year of fieldwork, we participated in about a dozen direct actions with FIGHT and Neighbors Driving Change, including street protests and small confrontational rallies

---

5. Unity Day was celebrated in Providence on April 4, 2011, to commemorate the anniversary of the assassination of Martin Luther King Jr. and to open up space for discussion about equality and domestic politics. It was organized by a coalition of progressive organizations in the state, including FIGHT. Other signs read, "NOBODY should have too much until EVERYBODY has enough!" "The Banks Got Bailed-Out; We Got Sold Out," and "Feed the People, Not the Pentagon."

directed at specific elected officials, and the groups organized many other direct actions that we did not attend. As a longtime Providence activist who participated in many of these events explained, "This is how change takes place. We can't expect to elect people and stop there."

The organizations developed by people who are motivated to address structural inequalities often prioritize the opinions, voices, and actions of those most affected by injustice. For FIGHT, the best people to speak on issues of oppression are those directly affected by oppression. As a leader told us, "When we're working for criminal justice reform, we're working with former inmates. When we're talking about foreclosures, we look for someone who has been recently foreclosed upon.... That is different from many groups, which see themselves as *advocating for* the oppressed." From this perspective, official "experts" who acquire their pedigree by thinking about or studying a subject—as opposed to *experiencing it*—can be unnecessary, and sometimes even to blame. At a small meeting with school district officials, one YAK member pointed out that bringing in experts from another city, as the officials proposed, would be a mistake, because local knowledge matters. "*Experts*," added another member, "have put us where we are." In this way of thinking, formal expertise—as measured by academic degrees or professional status—has not led to better outcomes in the past. Instead, these experts are considered a source of the problems faced by the city and its residents.

In sum, a civic imagination that sees fighting power and advocating for greater equality as central to the role of civil society is marked by the following traits: connecting local problems to larger systems, accepting conflict as part of working for social change, believing direct action is necessary to address structural problems, privileging the voices of marginalized populations, and questioning elite and expert sources of knowledge. We saw FIGHT, Neighbors Driving Change, and YAK express this civic imagination by organizing for social justice causes.

In doing so, these groups often venerated the activism of important historical figures who have emphasized the role of power and advocated for equality in their accounts of the world. Martin Luther King Jr., Malcolm X, and Emma Goldman are just a few of the notable activists in US history who expressed a civic imagination based on power. They confronted structural inequalities through direct action, empowered marginalized populations to engage with others to fight for equality, and did not back down from conflict. Classic and contemporary scholars, as well, have been guided by civic imaginations based on power. Karl Marx paid close attention to structural inequality and the class conflict he saw as a fundamental feature of society (Marx, Engels, and Hobsbawm 1998 [1848]), Antonio Gramsci (1971) developed the concept of hegemony to explain how the ruling class ensured the consent of the rest of society, and W. E. B. Du Bois described the color line as the defining feature of the twentieth century (Du Bois 1999 [1903]). More contemporary thinkers like Pierre Bourdieu (1990) and Michel Foucault (Foucault, Rabinow, and Faubion 1997) have similarly emphasized power and inequality in their accounts of social life. These scholars draw on historical evidence to explain the unequal societies in which they live, and provide ideas for what may be needed to make alternative futures a reality.

Building Community Solidarity

We saw a different grammar of civic life emerge when a teacher pleaded with the school board to give the community a year to develop a new plan. "We need to get organized *together*," she explained. "Give us a voice on this!" By simply working together, the logic followed, the community could identify solutions that were better than the school board's proposal. Later in the meeting, when some attendees began to show their anger toward the school board by booing, yelling, and even throwing the microphone, we saw another example of this dialect of civic life at play. In this particularly heated moment, James, a city councilor, gently intervened and brought the meeting toward a close. He calmly thanked everyone for their participation—the mayor, the superintendent, the kids, the teachers, and even the belligerent activist in the back who yelled, "What about me?" Then James said, "Let's not end it on this note. We've been so *constructive* today."

The family of civic imaginations that underpins these expressions is oriented around a belief in the importance and efficacy of community solidarity. These sentiments are expressed in calls for people to come together, in organizations that support community identity and collective culture, and in efforts to strengthen shared spaces. We saw this focus on solidarity expressed by a wide variety of people, including social justice organizers, civic innovators, and neighborhood leaders from across racial, class, and ethnic backgrounds.

According to the logic of this grammar of civic life, when people participate in public decision-making processes, they build solidarity. As a member of Engage explained, "If people have more civic awareness, they are more likely to be better neighbors." People holding these civic imaginations value such feelings of togetherness. A FIGHT leader told us about a rally she had recently attended in Washington, DC, and described it as a "success" because hundreds of activists gathered together to "motivate each other and connect." They had not accomplished a specific policy objective or reached new benchmarks in their quest for social change, yet this feeling of solidarity was celebrated as an achievement. Likewise, a leader of a civic innovator group said her goal was to connect "pockets of people that should be connected but who are not." Her colleague described one of the organization's meetings as highly successful simply because "new relationships were formed."

In this way of thinking, solidarity is not only good on its own, but it is also a means to achieving other desirable outcomes. Under conditions of solidarity, people are more likely to work together, to solve problems together, and to create positive change in their communities. In other words, solidarity leads to civic engagement, and civic engagement begets solidarity.[6] The idea that public participation fosters solidarity helps us to make sense of James's closing comment in the school board meeting. In the midst of public displays of anger and outrage, James was able to

---

6. This perspective very closely reflects Robert Putnam's argument in *Making Democracy Work: Civic Traditions in Modern Italy* (1993).

call the meeting "constructive" because community members were coming together around a common cause, building solidarity, and thus creating the type of community where people can make social change.

For James and others focused on building community solidarity, the most important ways to be a good citizen are to get to know your neighbors, organize together, attend community gatherings, patronize local businesses, and care for the local environment (for example, by planting trees along your street). One should act locally to make change at the local level. Whereas civic imaginations attentive to power and privilege often make connections between local issues and national and even global problems, here the emphasis is on connections between the local problems at hand. James, for example, is concerned about schools and jobs in his community. He talks about how they are related to one another at the *local* level, not in terms of broader trends or larger systems. As he told us, many areas of Providence are poor, but "if you have good schools, you can attract people to the neighborhoods. And if you have a good job base, in the neighborhood and across the city, you can attract resources. Then employers thinking about where to locate new businesses will look at where the good schools are, because they know those things matter for their workers." Thus, change is both achieved and experienced at the local level.

Two of the values that characterize this imagination are neighborly relations and minimizing conflict. *Building a neighborhood* is different from just *being neighbors*, a civic leader explained, in that neighborhoods generate and nurture connections between people. Parkside Coalition was an organization where the solidarity civic imagination was highly visible. The organization promoted block parties, tree plantings, neighborhood clean-ups, book collections, Christmas caroling, Halloween parades, and crime-watch activities. At Parkside meetings and events, being "neighborly" was highly valued. Also important was being polite, avoiding conflict, minimizing disagreement, and preventing ruptures in community. As a past president of Oceanside Neighbors, another neighborhood association, explained to us, it is important to approach city officials on a positive note, instead of attacking right away.

In sum, these civic imaginations emphasize the centrality of solidarity, fellowship, and feelings of togetherness in underpinning efforts to solve social problems. Though we saw solidarity and community building in each of our fieldsites at one time or another, Parkside Coalition and Oceanside Neighbors expressed this civic imagination most clearly, and we suspect that neighborhood groups throughout the country draw on similar logics of civic life to guide their activities. Neighborhood crime watch programs, for example, have become commonplace in many parts of the United States.

Questions of solidarity and community-mindedness have long been part of the conversations and advocacy that comprise American civic life. Over a century ago, Alexis de Tocqueville (2003 [1840]) recognized that associational spaces created a vibrant and active civil society and thus a better functioning democracy. Dorothy Day, a social activist and devout Catholic, helped establish the Catholic Worker Movement in the 1930s that advocated for and created communal living environments in both urban and rural areas as a way to support the poor. More recently, Amitai Etzione and the communitarian movement have called for communities to "respect and uphold society's moral order as you would have society respect and uphold your autonomy to live a full life" (Etzione 1996, xviii). Social scientists also recognize solidarity as a central dynamic of civic life. Émile Durkheim (1964), a founder of sociological thought, worried about how the modern division of labor might impact community solidarity. Jeffrey Alexander (2006), a more contemporary scholar, theorizes the way that solidarity may extend from the civil sphere to other domains. Robert Putnam (2000) maintains that the fabric of American democracy depends on the quality of social capital, or networks and ties between people. The solidarity imagination, as these examples show, has broad resonance in the United States, among scholars and citizens alike.

Solving Problems

In yet another public schools hearing, collective anger accumulated as citizens accused the mayor of betraying the community. An audience member tried to introduce a voice of reason: "We are dealing with reality here. People are coming down too hard on the mayor. He came into this problem. The reality is that some teachers need to go. We need to stop putting so much pressure on the school district. We need to find ways to help, need to take responsibility. *It's on us.* We need to look at ourselves."

This comment, and the rational way in which it was spoken, exemplifies a third type of civic imagination: one focused on collective problem solving. People with this imagination believe that by bringing people together—and giving them the right tools, information, and means of communication—they can create solutions to even the most complicated social problems. In this perspective, Americans are problem solvers, pragmatists, "can-do" people who are not afraid to experiment with novel ideas—and whose ideas improve their society. According to this logic, differing perspectives can be resolved by discussing issues in a civil manner.

Like the focus on building solidarity, this way of thinking highlights the power of coming together with others. However, the objective is not only to build solidarity but also to spur creativity and generate new ideas. Months before closing schools became a topic of debate, the school issue that captured citizens' attention was students' uniforms. A member of Engage moderated a public meeting on the subject. "I don't want speeches," he admonished the crowd. "I want ideas!" After the meeting, the moderator commented, "That went well. That was a good conversation. Boy, people raised lots of issues." This comment was particularly striking because many others in the room felt differently about the meeting: instead of thinking it "went well" or was "a good conversation," they complained about its premise, tactics, and lack of results. For the moderator, however, the goal was simply to create a space for an assortment of people to come together to voice their ideas and generate possible solutions.

The discourses that construct this type of civic imagination are centered on the need for rational debate and conversation. A leader of Open Source told us that change comes from small, incremental wins, not revolutionary campaigns led by "angry activists." Another member of Open Source explained,

> I'd much rather have a reasoned dialogue, and I think most politicians would, too, to have a normal tone of voice, without people shouting at them.... No one likes getting shouted at.... As much as we criticize politics for enjoying fight for the sake of fight, a lot of people are protesting just to make waves. There's, like, no accountability. There's no pressure to be rational, I guess. You can be as outlandish as you want. You don't have to sit down and explain in a calm tone of voice why you believe what you do.

Conflict in civic life is considered not only unsavory but also counterproductive, and should be avoided because it limits the amount of progress that can be made. Instead of conflict, groups that express this logic host "friendly" meetings with public officials, write nonconfrontational letters to the mayor, and organize committees to generate ideas about a topic or problem. Sarah, a Parkside Coalition leader, explained that being persistent but congenial helps you get what you want. This idea is common among Parkside's members. In a planning meeting, when Sarah announced that she had submitted the group's ideas to the city planner, an attendee commented in approval, "We've got to be the squeaky wheel."

For these problem solvers, experts and people with special skills or training are welcome additions to civic dialogue and public debates. At times, ordinary citizens struggle to contribute informed ideas—perhaps because "citizens aren't used to being asked" for their ideas about policy, or "many folks struggle when put on the spot," or people lack necessary information to contribute. As one such activist put it, "Democracy is great when people are educated," but in Rhode Island, "we have a relatively uneducated voting base, and that's the problem." Problem solvers place great value in expertise that has been acquired through education and professional experience.

According to this problem-solving civic imagination, then, the good citizen is one who communicates rationally in collective decision-making processes, who generates good and informed ideas, and who thinks and acts creatively with others to solve city problems. Civil society is, principally, a space of dialogue and problem solving. We found that Engage and Open Source, groups we describe in the next chapter as "civic innovators," expressed this imagination most often in Providence, but other individuals and groups shared some of the same perspectives.

Similar ideas have also been expressed throughout history and are of particular appeal in the contemporary moment. John Dewey (1954) and other pragmatist scholars, as we described in Chapter 2, advocate a democracy based on effective communication that fully incorporates citizens, experts, and politicians in the decision-making process. Contemporary thinkers animated by this vision include Roberto Unger (1975) and Jürgen Habermas (1989 [1962]), who emphasize the capacity of civil society to experiment and find new, discussion-driven solutions to common problems.

IMAGINATIONS IN MOTION

Why do individuals have the particular civic imaginations that they do? Imaginations about civic life are not formed in a vacuum or isolated from society. We agree with political theorists who argue that "aspirations are never simply individual (as the language of *wants* and *choices* inclines us to think). They are always formed *in interaction* and *in the thick* of social life" (Appadurai 2004, 67, emphasis added). Indeed, individuals' imaginations are formed in intimate interactions with their social interactions, their positions in society, and their material interests. However, social location, demographics, and local culture cannot fully explain why certain people adopt particular values and beliefs. People also think independently of the structures and systems of the social world. Their reflective agency—their ability to see themselves within a broader context—and creative ingenuity inform their civic imaginations. That is to say, civic imaginations are shaped by both "structure" and "agency." The relationship between structure and agency is a foundational debate in social science research: to what extent are people's actions in the present constrained and directed by their social location, their race or class, their collective experiences, or their own self-directed desires and perceptions? Put another way, how can we understand the ability of individuals and collectives to shape their own worlds, if these worlds are also governed by external structural forces? To shed light on these relationships between structure, agency, and civic imaginations, we return to two individuals, James and Darnell, both introduced earlier in this chapter, and each with distinct civic imaginations.

James, a newly elected city councilor, is a White, college-educated man and an active member of his local neighborhood association. He first became involved in city politics several years ago, when his children's neighborhood elementary school was shut down due to fire code violations. He was a member of the Parent Teacher Organization at the school, and in response to the school closing, he joined other parents in protesting, attending school board meetings, meeting with the superintendent, and getting city council members involved. James was encouraged when the school department announced they would renovate and reopen the school, and while this did not come to fruition during our year of fieldwork, he saw great success in the community's ability to work together and keep this issue on the agenda of both the school board and the city for more than three years, in part due to his leadership.

Empowered by his success in political organizing, James ran for a city council seat in his ward. His campaign platform was based on generating local jobs and supporting neighborhood schools, and rather than relying on the well-established Democratic political machine, his campaign strategy was to walk through the neighborhood, engaging small groups of people in conversation. The approach was time consuming but satisfying, and his win strengthened his commitment to building community solidarity. James believes that the best way to build a better future for his city is to build connections between residents. This imagination is reinforced every time he participates in a neighborhood cleanup, tree planting event, holiday party, or street music event sponsored by his local neighborhood association. At a lively neighborhood Halloween party in the local park, James told us, "This is what community is all about—coming together with your neighbors and friends to have fun on a Saturday afternoon."

We can see how James's theory of civic life was fostered by a personal experience of organizing with neighbors, his relatively privileged socioeconomic status, his participation in his neighborhood association, and his success in winning the community's support by building solidarity. James has the financial resources and the social networks to see his civic imagination come to fruition. As cultural anthropologist Arjun Appadurai would say, "The better off you are (in terms of power, dignity, and material resources)," the more developed your "capacity to aspire," as you are better able to link justifications, narratives, and abstract norms and beliefs to concrete, immediate needs (2004, 68).

In the time we knew James, this cognitive scaffolding was shaken only by the community's failure to stop the proposed school closures we described above, which was a disappointment for him, as it was for many Providence residents. After all the community mobilization, participation, solidarity, and debate, the school board still decided to support the mayor's recommendation to close the schools. For many of the citizens who had hoped their active engagement would save their schools, this was a transformative moment. At a parent-teacher meeting after the vote, a teacher said, "I felt like such a chump at the end" for being hopeful and saying that "I was cautiously optimistic" in front of the cameras. Someone else responded, "It was theater! We were duped, everyone was." Another woman agreed, saying, "I am so angry. I feel like we've been played for fools. I want direct action! We've played by their rules, but now enough with the *talk*. Let's *do*!" The support for a community-based solution was replaced with frustration and resentment when a good process—full of participation and problem solving by residents—did not lead to a good outcome.

Here we see civic imaginations and tactics evolving with changing circumstances. When the school board voted to close the schools even though the vast majority of testimony at public hearings urged them to vote no, many parents and teachers felt they had been "duped" into thinking their voices mattered and came to the realization that they were unequal players in a more powerful system. As a result, some turned to confrontational language and tactics, a characteristic style that results from civic imaginations concerned with power and inequality. Thus, individuals' civic imaginations can gravitate toward this concern when people's experiences make them realize that power is at stake.

Engaged citizens often start at this same point when their lower levels of economic, social, and cultural capital incline them to better understand the role of inequality and power in society, and hamper their capability to easily make their visions a reality.[7] Darnell's experience as a Black activist and the leader of YAK provides an exemplar of this experience. As a poor Black teenager in Providence,

---

7. This is not to say there are not privileged people whose civic imaginations gravitate to issues of power and inequality—indeed, a number of social justice activists we worked with in Providence came from privileged backgrounds, as do many progressive academics.

Darnell was enmeshed in "street life" and spent over a decade in prison. While there, Darnell began to educate himself, starting with the dictionary. Eventually, he read Malcolm X's autobiography, and it "changed his life." He joined the Nation of Islam and read deeply on subjects of race and inequality. Two years after leaving prison, he participated in the Million Man March, a civil rights event in 1995 that gathered hundreds of thousands of activists in Washington, DC, to unite against the challenges facing Black Americans.

When he returned to Providence after that event, Darnell learned that a Smithsonian exhibit was coming to the city, and he secured a donation of forty-five free tickets for local children and their adult chaperones. Darnell then called the city's department of recreation, which agreed to donate boxed lunches for the field trip. He was even able to garner financial donations for other expenses associated with the trip from neighborhood drug dealers by telling them, "Here's your chance to make it right." This was an empowering moment for Darnell. He learned he could "get stuff done." Shortly afterward, he founded Youth, Action, and Knowledge (YAK), to address the "young Black men problem." Today Darnell is a frequent, if polemical, figure in city debates on school-related issues. He is known and recognized by many in Providence, from his neighbors to city officials. Because of his active, vocal lobbying to prevent a neighborhood school from being shut down several years ago, he has won awards from a neighborhood association and the school system for "parent leadership training" and was asked by the school district superintendent of schools to make recommendations on how to close the gap in quality of education for Black and White youth.

Darnell's trajectory shows us how and why people might form an imagination based on power. Frequent and persistent encounters with political, economic, and social inequalities; early "successes" in making a difference to counter this inequality; and finding like-minded peers engaged in the fight for more equality can lead an individual to express this kind of imagination. In Darnell's case, this path has led to his enthusiasm for discussions about enduring racial inequalities and has paved the way for the projects he organizes with YAK and other allied organizations. Although he is a provocative figure who does not shy away from confrontation, Darnell's drive and charisma have allowed him to forge social networks with many parts of Providence society, including city officials. He has therefore had some, albeit limited, success in seeing his imagination become a reality.

Darnell is strongly focused on the need to address inequality between Whites and Blacks, but he also expresses discourses of problem solving and solidarity that lead him to collaborate with city bureaucrats, technological entrepreneurs, and neighborhood associations in different contexts. Darnell is a key member of another civic group that works to provide opportunities for members of the Black community to take responsibility for improving their own situations, independent of government welfare programs. He also regularly participates in and supports the activities of Parkside Coalition, and he frequently talks about the need for communities to come together to solve problems. Thus, Darnell often expresses elements of both a power-centered and a problem-solving imagination. His story shows how individuals' civic imaginations incorporate different and sometimes contradictory principles, not only in changing circumstances but sometimes even in the same speech or conversation.

James's and Darnell's civic imaginations are clearly different, but these two descriptions show that civic imaginations are shaped by a similar combination of social location, personal trajectory and experience of the political sphere, and group culture. Both James and Darnell experienced an early success that showed them that they could accomplish social change. They also found like-minded individuals with whom they could share and construct their civic imaginations—either geographical communities of actual neighbors, or intellectual and spiritual communities of peers. Undeniably, however, James, a city councilor, and Darnell, a vocal Black activist, have very different opportunities to make their "vision of the future become a reality" (Holland et al. 2007, 132). Without a doubt, race, social capital, money, and networks play a role in determining the extent to which individuals can influence political life. Yet focusing only on social positions or material interests obscures the creative agency that these people exercise when they imagine what is good for their communities, and when they act on those imaginations.

Importantly, civic imaginations are often formed collectively, and this collective imagining is an important aspect of associational life. Individuals with similar imaginations tend to organize together, which, in turn, leads to groups that consist of people with similar imaginations. The group reinforces and solidifies these imaginations through their discourses and practices, such as storytelling, group nostalgia, and founding principles, which serve as tools to orient the group. Darnell's and James's participation with others reinforced their particular imaginations, even as their individual imaginations went toward strengthening the culture of their groups. For these reasons, we argue that civic imaginations are formed at the intersection of collective life and personal history, or at the crossroads of social positioning and individual reflection. As people evaluate their world and seek to create a better future for themselves and their communities, their imaginations are constantly changing.

TRADEOFFS AND BLIND SPOTS

Being five ethnographers working at seven fieldsites, we had a unique opportunity: because we could see many imaginations, and their convergences, divisions, and collisions, we could also see the tradeoffs and blind spots that accompanied the expressions of each imagination. What tradeoffs do individuals and groups make when acting out their civic imaginations? What do these diverse visions fail to see or choose to ignore? We do not suggest that these tradeoffs and blind spots are *necessarily* associated with each imagination, but rather that, based on what we saw, these are the *tendencies* associated with each imagination. As researchers whose fieldwork crossed very different groups, we offer engaged citizens glimpses of other realities, and the opportunity for greater reflexivity regarding the pitfalls inherent in only understanding one point of view or primarily interacting within only one organization.

Fighting Power with Confrontation

As school closures unfolded in Providence, many civic groups continued to pursue other objectives on their advocacy agendas. Neighbors Driving Change wanted to draw negative attention to a public official who supported an anti-immigration policy harmful to Latinos in their community. In a members' meeting, they discussed a plan. "He goes to church and says he is a Christian. . . . We can highlight his hypocrisy by going there!" suggested one member. The group agreed. They would go to the official's place of worship and position themselves inside and outside of the building. As parishioners and church leaders gathered for a service, Neighbors Driving Change would spread the word that the public official supported an anti-immigration policy that is inhumane. To appeal to the faith-oriented audience, they would highlight how the official, as a member of their faith community, was a hypocrite. Another member added that they could stage a protest outside of the church, and if some members of the faith community were already inside when the public official arrived, they could make faces or draw attention to his arrival. "Agitating in church? *Yeah ...*" giggled one young man, in approval.

The meeting facilitator asked if anyone had further thoughts or suggestions. One man raised the concern that the public official may not attend church services every weekend, adding that he thought the chances were quite slim. Other members nodded in agreement. Aside from this caveat, however, the unanimous consensus was that the plan was well laid out, and, with solid organization, could be executed successfully. Tasks for planning the event were assigned, and the meeting moved on.

In their advocacy for pro-immigration legislation, the members of Neighbors Driving Change identified an opponent and aimed to divest some of his power and influence by shaming him in front of his community. We were surprised that the group's only concern was about the plan's feasibility. We, on the other hand, felt uncomfortable with the idea of heckling someone at their place of worship. Perhaps others in attendance had similar reactions, but nobody commented. Would this approach open the eyes of parishioners, as the activists hoped? Or, would crossing what we saw as a line between appropriate and inappropriate forms of protest alienate them, as we feared it might?[8] In choosing contentious tactics over an institutionalized

---

8. The members of Neighbors Driving Change are not alone in employing this logic. In the words of Martin Luther King Jr., written from a jail cell in Birmingham, Alabama, "Nonviolent direct action seeks to create such a crisis and foster such a tension that a community which has constantly refused to negotiate is forced to confront the issue. It seeks so to dramatize the issue that it can no longer be ignored" (April 16, 1963). In this way of thinking, the tension and discomfort created by contentious tactics are not a negative externality, but instead a useful tool in working for political change.

approach (e.g., petitioning), these activists are making a tradeoff: they draw greater attention to their issues and ideas, at the risk of alienating more moderate audiences.[9] We found this to be characteristic of imaginations centered on fighting power and inequality.

When people understand their work to be just, see themselves as righting societal ills, and seek inspiration from historical figures who have used nonviolent direct action to bring about social change,[10] they may overlook or choose to ignore the potentially negative consequences of contentious styles of protest. For example, one person in our study called them "angry activists," and another told us that those groups were not being taken seriously by political leaders. As political scientist Sidney Tarrow (1994) points out, disagreements about whether to rely on disruptive action or adopt conventional, less extreme approaches can also create disruptions and factions *within* an organization. In our fieldwork, we saw that by fighting power with confrontational tactics, organizations forfeited opportunities to collaborate with more conventional groups, found it more difficult to attract members, and were sometimes dismissed for going "too far."

Solidarity That Excludes

> *Public Schools Planning Series:* We are being given an incredible and unprecedented opportunity as a community to help redesign our neighborhood schools. Please attend a planning meeting tomorrow at Parkside Coalition to give input on what YOU want and need our public schools to be. *The School Department will be present to give feedback on what neighbors discussed at our last meeting.*

Down the page, the announcement explained, "Tomorrow night's meeting will continue our discussion on ideal configurations and programming for public elementary schools. Please attend—your input is key to creating the best school options for our neighborhood! *Kids Welcome.*"

Parkside Coalition's announcement was telling in what it said. It promoted participation, voice, and input, and it gave the sense that community, working together with local government, can achieve the best results. The announcement was also telling in *how* it communicated this message: it was only in English and was circulated online—via Facebook and email—to a preexisting network of the coalition's members, regular meeting attendees, and friends. This surprised us because

---

9. Political scientist Marco Giugni points out that there is no consensus among scholars who study social movements about if, when, and how using "disruptive and violent protest" is causally related to achieving institutional goals (1998, 376–379).

10. Here, we think of Mahatma Gandhi's work for India's independence from Great Britain in the first half of the twentieth century, and Martin Luther King Jr.'s advocacy for American civil rights several decades later. A more current example is the School of the Americas Watch, which aims to close a US training facility for Latin American military personnel.

the organization's office sits across the street from a busy Dominican bodega that specializes in travel arrangements and remittances, and half a block from a Central American restaurant that is a hangout for migrant workers in the neighborhood. The neighborhood itself is predominantly Latino (US Census Bureau 2013), and many families live in rented multifamily homes and struggle to make ends meet.[11] The members of Parkside Coalition, however, stand out against this backdrop: most are White, speak English as their first language, and own their own homes. Oceanside Neighbors follows this same pattern: the neighborhood is economically, racially, and ethnically diverse, yet the organization's board is made up of White homeowners.

The meeting advertised by Parkside Coalition was conducted in English, and without translation, which was typical of the organization's events. But in this case, the fact was especially poignant because the meeting was about the neighborhood's public schools, where the vast majority of students speak Spanish (US Census Bureau 2013), and many parents speak little English. The issue of translation was frequently raised in such settings. In another meeting, a participant brought language barriers to the fore by making a statement in Spanish—which she could safely assume not everyone would understand—followed by an argument, in English, that many parents are excluded from important discussions because of the lack of translation. Heads bobbed in agreement around the room, but no immediate actions were taken, and the conversation moved to other topics. A Parkside Coalition member told us that when community groups provide translation at meetings, Latino families are usually active in the discussion.

At another meeting, Darnell noticed that the discussion focused on what would be best for "all kids," rather than specific racial groups of kids who were more likely to be struggling. He interrupted the facilitator and demanded to know what was being done for *Black* children, who represent such a high proportion of the dropouts in the city, and noted that people of color were poorly represented in the room that night. Indeed, of the over twenty participants, Darnell, an older man, and the school official were the only Black people in attendance. The school official responded that the district is aware of the problem and that they are working to ensure that Providence education is good for *all kids*. Darnell responded that he is tired of the focus on "all children," because issues related to Black youth are always moved to the back burner. The conversation moved on, and nobody returned to Darnell's point.

The problems of translation, participation, and avoiding talk about inequality are all part of a bigger struggle: being inclusive. In principle, diversity was valued (in fact, "valuing diversity and the environment" was painted on one of the inside walls at Parkside Coalition's office as one of the organization's principles). And we suspect that most members of the Parkside Coalition and Oceanside Neighbors would say they support multiculturalism in their neighborhoods. One Parkside

---

11. For interactive data and analysis on the demographics of neighborhoods in Providence, see the Prov-Plan website: http://provplan.org/data-and-information/people-and-housing.

Coalition member told us that it would be nice to "bring in more renters and other diverse people," and several comments in meetings indicated that people are trying to build a more inclusive environment. Yet, at the same time, several moments in our fieldwork highlighted Parkside Coalition's exclusivity: a Halloween trick or treat map directed children to the homes of families that had sent their RSVPs to the association, immigrant families lingered at a festival perimeter instead of joining in the fun, and crime watch discussions included updates on where the "young Spanish guys" were hanging out. Despite constant talk of "finding good neighbors," the group's practices attracted only one type of good neighbor. The contradictions between a stated commitment to "multiculturalism" and practices that promote exclusivity are partially the result of an imagination that centers on solidarity. Seeing the world in this way can magnify the commonalities between *some* neighbors and downplay the discrepancies in privilege that divide them from the rest of the community. There is an assumption that everyone can be part of the "we," without much attention to who is absent and why. Individuals and groups focused on solidarity may imagine their community in a way that does not correspond with demographic reality, and their actions may reinforce existing divides by being exclusive of less visible groups.

The Limits of Problem Solving

As the fiscal crisis deepened in Providence, threatening to extend beyond school closures and engulf the whole city, the founders of Engage published a letter in the local newspaper titled "A Call to Action." The authors of the letter open by inviting readers to think about what *really* goes on when city officials negotiate with unions behind closed doors, asserting that without voters in the room, "tax dollars are given away." Next, they lay out an alternative approach to government decision making:

> Imagine if our city government solicited solutions to community problems and challenges from the citizens who are most affected. What if elected officials convened regular round-table meetings with leaders of neighborhood associations and community groups for collaborative creative problem-solving? ... Our vision is of a city with broad civic engagement, where Providence residents have shifted their view of themselves from customers of government to active participants in, and partners with, government.

The letter highlighted the mayor's "fiscal honesty tour" as a good example of this approach, and suggested that citizens blog from city council meetings and that the city work to develop more interesting forms of public debate.

The civic imagination expressed in the public letter asserts that transparent, nonconfrontational conversations are the most productive ways to work for change, and that technology can facilitate such interactions. But this imagination tends to overlook deeply entrenched structure and privilege, and the limited reach of new technologies. Like solidarity builders, problem solvers often acknowledge the problem of inequality and express concerns about exclusion, but they differ in what they identify as the solution. Whereas the solidarity builders believe in the power of coming together, the problem solvers look for answers in new ideas, processes, and technologies.

For example, a founder of one civic innovation group told us that she recognized that lack of diversity was "a problem, but nothing that could not be fixed with a good app." When we questioned whether an app—however great—would be able to engage a large and representative portion of the population, Ernie, the other founder, replied, "When you go to the poorer parts of town, how many people are on their cell phone?... Everyone has a cell phone, and even if they don't have digital cable, they pay their cell phone bill and they pay for unlimited texting." He noted that in the poor countries of Kenya and Haiti "cell phone minutes serve as currency," and said, "It's pernicious that we think that poor people and brown people can't use technology or can't engage with technology.... This isn't the case." When we pushed him to acknowledge the "digital divide," he was dismissive, saying that it is tempting to think about "rich pink people" and "poor brown people" using technology in different ways, but that we need to break out of that way of thinking: "People use what's useful to them." Ernie felt technology was broadly accessible and could solve difficult problems. His comments display the problem-solving imagination's tendency to overlook or underplay the notion that endemic and intractable problems may be at stake, and that these issues require more than a quick technological fix.

As individuals and groups express the problem-solving imagination, they often strive to develop new processes rather than work toward a particular outcome. In this focus on process over outcome, they are concerned with rational communication, polite dialogue, and greater transparency. This reflects the belief that better processes will inevitably lead to solving problems, even problems as intractable as inequality. However, this idea comes with an inherent tradeoff, for a better process does not necessarily ensure a better outcome for all. Processes can exclude groups and reinforce existing inequalities if egalitarian goals are not established from the start.

Additionally, activists focused on problem solving can overlook the narrow scope of their proposed solutions. For example, an Engage document states that "the organization is not seeking to issue policy—our goal is to take the pulse of the city and see what are the issues that are rising to the top, to help convene positive and productive dialogue." Yet because Engage relies on social media and the social networks of the group's leaders to gauge citizen perspectives, the problems that it identifies as "rising to the top" often reflect the passions and projects of the leaders themselves—such as reducing red tape, cutting taxes for landlords, and limiting the salaries of union members. These are the city's concerns as defined by the professional and social circles of the organization's leadership. Other groups and activists may point to problems such as police violence, hunger rates, food deserts, and failing schools, but for Engage those issues do not rise to the surface. This omission is a blind spot in the problem-solving imagination: new processes and innovative approaches can be severely limited in their reach, resulting in a democracy that is by—and for—only a small number of its people.

LISTENING TO THE IMAGINATION

What guides the actions of people who choose to engage with the political system? How do people come to understand and work toward achieving change? How do civically engaged individuals and groups define and understand what it means to be a good citizen? Answering these questions helps us understand the different forms of civic engagement and how each has the potential to create social and political change.

In this chapter, a controversial public debate around the closing of several Providence schools provided a window into Americans' radically different imaginations of what a better social and political future might entail. Engaged citizens share a common desire to improve their cities and their democracies. Yet often their unity ends there, as their visions diverge around defining a better future and figuring out a way to make it happen. In Providence, everyone supported "public participation," but what they meant by "participation" varied dramatically. Their activities around this common goal include events as different as marching on the statehouse, hosting a neighborhood Halloween party, and planning a roundtable for businesspeople to discuss city planning with the mayor, to name a few.

Civic imaginations are the ideas and understandings, cognitive roadmaps, and guiding beliefs that citizens use to diagnose problems with the social world and identify ways to solve them. We witnessed imaginations oriented around the common themes of fighting inequality, bolstering citizen solidarity, and generating community-driven solutions. Imaginations are fluid, changing over time and across contexts, and are expressed in both words and deeds. They are formed at once by social locations and by the constant, agentive processes of learning, reflection, and evaluation in people's personal experiences. Imaginations are nurtured by collective life—people imagine *together*, and they create organizations that reflect this process of collective imagining. In turn, collective imaginations shape the beliefs of the individuals who help generate them.

All of the imaginations we witnessed have the potential to guide people in working for positive social change, deepening democracy, and combating inequality. Yet people's actions are at once *enabled* and *constrained* by civic imaginations. How they express their imaginations—the tactics, habits, and styles of activism in practice—has tradeoffs and blind spots that may limit their appeal or effectiveness, or pervert their intentions. No one we studied aimed to reify inequalities, entrench social divisions, or marginalize important issues, but we show how some of their actions may do so.

It is difficult, as Arendt (1978) put it, "to train your imagination to go visiting"—to put oneself in another's shoes. It is challenging to see one's own activism through the lens of another's imagination. However, by spending time with alternative perspectives, by comparing ideas, by analyzing the ways in which our imaginations diverge, people can begin to be more reflexive about their own imaginations and the words and deeds that express them. Through this act of visiting, citizens can begin to see tradeoffs for what they are, weighing the benefits and the challenges of how we approach working for change. In the next chapter, we look more closely at "civic innovation," which has become a popular way to work for political change and often expresses imaginations focused on problem solving.

Chapter 5

Participation 2.0

THE POLITICS OF CIVIC INNOVATION

In 2009, Mayor David Cicilline asked a friend in Providence to start an independent civic organization that would act as the citizens' voice in city politics. Cicilline believed it was necessary to counter corruption, combat the "uncivil" discourses that plagued city politics, and create collaborative relationships beyond the "hyper-localized, small, neighborhood association." His friend invited a neighbor—someone engaged in community affairs—and together they started circulating the idea of getting more citizens to weigh in on community issues. After meeting with individuals all over the city, hosting a planning meeting at a local business, and talking late into the night with friends around kitchen tables, they formed the group Engage. Engage continues to operate around its founding goals, publicizing government meetings, organizing forums about high-profile public issues, and contributing to citywide dialogues about the future of Providence.

One of the first events that drew our attention was Engage's "un-protest." It was 2009, and Vice President Biden and other high-ranking members of Obama's administration had canceled their planned appearance at the annual Conference of Mayors, to be held in Providence. This decision was a response to a threat by the Fire Fighter's Union, which had been working without a contract since 2000, to picket in front of the conference venue in protest (WPRI 2009). The members of Engage were disappointed that the administration would not be visiting their city and disapproved of the firefighters' plan to use the conference as an opportunity to air their grievances. A few weeks before the event, Engage had hosted a planning meeting in a local independent cinema. How could they stop the firefighters from derailing the conference? Attendees repeated what seemed to be collective sentiments: we need to "move beyond politics"; we must "neutralize special interests"; we can come up with "creative win-win solutions." Much of the meeting was reminiscent of a corporate brainstorming session, with two skilled facilitators working hard to keep the energy going, writing especially creative ideas on the board, and moving the group past a handful of non sequiturs on garbage collection and bureaucratic red tape. If the firefighters stopped their picket, they reasoned, it would save the Conference of Mayors, promote the city nationally, contribute to the struggling local economy, and generate goodwill for the union. They decided to appeal to the firefighters' sense of community by holding an "un-protest"—a protest in protest of a protest! On the designated morning, about thirty Engage members and "concerned citizens" picketed in a downtown park. Their signs read, "I ♥ Providence" and "Firefighters, Please Call Off Your Picket" (NBC 2009). As one leader explained, calling their plan an "un-protest" signaled *collaboration*, as opposed to *conflict*. And this, for the members of Engage, was a good thing.

Not long after this event, another civic group was created after an informal gathering of friends, similar to the meetings that launched Engage. When Mayor Cicilline announced that he would not seek reelection, seven Providence residents—many part of the city's technology and design communities—gathered in a living room to discuss how they could seize the opportunity to "change the conversation in politics" and start a movement for increased civic engagement in the city. One of these founding members recalls,

> We got together ... to ask, "Do we need to do anything about this?" We decided we did. Our PR stunt was a job ad for mayor on Craigslist, then a website in English and Spanish with a text and voice "idea line." The goal was not to pick the candidate. It was a neutral organization politically. It was to make sure the dialogue and issues were the ones we cared about—transparency, efficiency, and civic accessibility—so if people wanted to contribute to what is going on, they can.

In this "PR stunt," the group named themselves "hiring managers" and set out to recruit candidates for the executive position of mayor. The group posted a job description on Craigslist in Providence and other "like-minded" cities—cities reputed to be progressive, with hip urban centers and strong tech, entrepreneurial, and artistic communities—including Austin, Texas; Portland, Oregon; and San Francisco, California.[1] This bold move caught national press attention and kick-started their organization, which we call Open Source.

CIVIC INNOVATION

The members of Engage and Open Source are "civic innovators," a name we give to a new generation of politically engaged people who apply business values, language, and tactics to the civic sphere. Civic innovation generates new ideas for solving social

---

1. Craigslist is an online classifieds website that coordinates activities such as used car sales, apartments rentals, and employment postings in hundreds of locations throughout the country and abroad. The Providence, RI, page can be found at http://providence.craigslist .org.

problems, creates ways for citizens to address problems independently of government, advocates for increased government transparency, and provides opportunities for citizens and public officials to collaborate through polite conversation and reasoned debate. Like the civic innovators that make up the "civic renewal movement" described by Carmen Sirianni and Lewis Friedland (2001), these activists find innovative solutions to new and enduring public problems without working directly though political parties, often highlighting the shortcomings of electoral politics and the state.[2]

This approach to working for social change has broad resonance in America today. It follows an ideological turn of the late twentieth century, when "market rule" began to shape culture and politics. "Market rule" is the term that anthropologist Dorothy Holland and her coauthors (2007) use to describe the predominance of the ethos and discourse of neoliberalism in American political life. Neoliberalism is the idea that the state should shrink, reining in its regulation of social and economic spaces. Given the supremacy of market rule in contemporary US society, it is not surprising that civic innovation has become a popular pattern of civil society engagement.

Innovation as an Expression of Civic Imagination

In Chapter 4, we described our concept of civic imaginations, the working theories that people use to understand how civic life is organized, to envision a better future, and to think about how everyday citizens can work for political change. Civic imaginations guide civic participation, and in this way we can see individuals' discourses and actions as *expressions* of these cognitive roadmaps. While civic innovation can be part of the expression of any civic imagination—whether oriented around power, problem solving, or solidarity—we found that it was most often taken up by individuals and groups focused on solving problems. As we described in Chapter 4, imaginations centered on problem solving reason that by bringing people together—and giving them the right tools, information, and means of communication—they can generate solutions to social problems. In this way of thinking, differing perspectives can be resolved by discussing issues in a civil manner in order to arrive at good solutions.

The synergies between imaginations focused on solving problems and the expression of civic innovation are obvious: both believe in bringing more voices to

---

2. The people we call civic innovators fit into this pattern of civic renewal in their use of technological solutions, their support of self-sufficiency from the state, and their ability to harness personal and communal social capital to achieve their goals. But while Sirianni and Friedland (2001) describe a shared language of civic renewal that cuts across issues and social spheres, we focus on the characteristics of civic innovators that set them apart from other activists. Goals like participation or increased governmental transparency are compelling to a variety of groups, but in this chapter we identify the distinct traits that differentiate the civic innovator groups from other forms of activism in Providence.

the table, both highlight a need for rational debate, both value polite communication, and both feel that even the most complex political and social problems can be solved by creating new processes for making decisions. However, a problem-solving imagination and civic innovation are not necessarily synonymous. A clear example of this distinction is the case of Darnell, the leader of YAK, mentioned in prior chapters. When Darnell professes a strong belief in self-reliance—that members of the Black community must work together to solve their own problems, independently of government—he is expressing a problem-solving imagination. This does not, however, mean that he is a civic innovator, as will become clear in what follows.

Civic Innovation Groups

Engage and Open Source are both emblematic civic innovator groups, but they are not similar in every way. Civic innovation takes different organizational forms. For example, while Engage worked hard to become a 501(c)(3) registered nonprofit, the leader of Open Source said the day the group gains 501(c)(3) status is the day she wipes her hands of it, because her group "doesn't conform to conventional patterns."

Moreover, these groups perceive their relations with government in different ways. Engage, following its original mandate to be the "people's voice" in city-level decision making, works hard to connect everyday citizens with public officials. Members use Facebook, Twitter, and the group's website to publicize city news and tell residents when and where city council meetings will be held, and they facilitate dialogue between citizens and elected officials at public meetings. One of the Engage founders explained that they want the group to be a forum where voices and ideas can come together. He hopes that Engage can serve as an incubator that supports people to use their imaginations, to pilot projects, and to put new ideas together. Ultimately, he said, the group wants to shine light on issues and bring transparency to government decision-making processes. Another organizer for the group highlighted that they try to get residents to hearings and city council meetings in order to show that the public is not a *consumer* of government. Instead, she explained, they want to connect the government with the people in more meaningful ways.

Open Source takes a different approach: "We are not a location for information about government, but a discussion of what government should be," a leader explained during an event at a local high school. To this end, the group hosted a "listening party" in which the typical town hall practice of the audience asking questions of political candidates was reversed. Instead, Open Source members facilitated a dialogue in which mayoral candidates asked questions of the audience about how to improve the city, and then remained silent as the community discussed possible solutions. The idea was to highlight the capacity of citizens to generate new ideas, offer creative solutions, and bring fresh thinking to a tired political system. Open Source also sponsored a phone line and website where citizens could pass along suggestions for what the new mayor should do to improve the city.

In sum, if Engage wants to bring people to politics, Open Source aims to bring "good ideas to government." Both ultimately hope to make Providence better by bringing people and technology together to solve problems and to generate new ideas about democracy, elections, and government. And both regard their strategies as successful: "I think we played a small part in opening the door to new players and new ideas," said a member of Engage. Likewise, Open Source claimed, "I think that a lot of the ideas are actually finding a way into [the mayor's] policies and positions.... He actually really [takes] advantage of the opportunity to feel out what people are thinking." Here, it is clear that despite their emphasis on new solutions, civic innovators still mobilize around some of the most traditional aspects of politics—in these cases, city council meetings and political elections. We turn our attention to connections between civic innovation and democratic values later in the chapter.

Though most emblematic, Engage and Open Source were not the *only* ones among our fieldsites to draw on modes of civic innovation. Some people can be considered innovators in some aspects of their work, but not others. Groups that would not be considered "civic innovators" on the whole occasionally express their imaginations in this way. The social justice group FIGHT, for example, coordinated a flashmob protest, a tactic often used in corporate advertising and marketing campaigns in which seemingly random members of a crowd join a dance or other coordinated action. Using this type of business language and strategy for social protest is a feature of civic innovators' tactics, as we describe in greater detail below. Civic innovation is deployed by diverse groups, across the political spectrum. However, some organizations and individuals have stronger leanings in this direction.

Who Are Innovators?

Civic innovators are typically professionals in the entrepreneurial and creative sectors. In Providence, most people closely involved with Engage and Open Source work in the arts, design, or information technology industries or are business entrepreneurs. Civic innovators in Providence are predominantly White, often from middle-class or affluent backgrounds, and highly educated—privileged in many ways, though not necessarily high-profile icons of power, business, or wealth. Most have lived, studied, or worked outside of Rhode Island. The leaders of Engage and Open Source have strong social networks that include leaders of local and state government, the business community, nonprofits, philanthropic organizations, and influential residents of the city. They often refer to politicians by their first names and have personal relationships with the city's young "movers and shakers." As one noted, "Everybody can be best friends with the mayor if they want to." During our research period, several innovators were appointed by the mayor to serve on influential city governance committees.

Civic innovators believe in developing and using networks and technology to open the gateway for citizens' ideas to affect city government. Often, they rely on their personal networks. As one innovator described,

> I hosted a reception for [then mayoral candidate] Angel Taveras ... about a week before the election ... but that reception was more about getting people access

to the candidate. It was not a fundraiser. It was a discussion forum; there was no contribution required.... It reinforced my belief in equal access. I find it very frustrating that we have a system where you pay two hundred or five hundred or more dollars to even talk to a candidate, and you're basically buying access.

In their individual activism and with their groups, civic innovators network, employ technology, open lines of communication, and work hard to solve the city's problems—both in collaboration with and on behalf of the city government.

Innovation and the Creative Class

Civic innovators, because of their focus on creativity and the entrepreneurial spirit, and their overlap with people working in arts and design, can be seen as part of an emerging "creative class." According to urban studies theorist Richard Florida, the creative class—scientists, professors, artists, designers, high-technology specialists, and others whose work it is to "create meaningful new forms"—is the driving force in regional economic growth (2003, 8). Florida argues that urban development and fortune depend on cities' capacity to attract and retain this class of young, educated, and enthusiastic professionals. In this way, creativity can be billed as a strategy for economic development in urban areas. This has become a seductive idea for civic leaders around the world, perhaps based on a belief that it is easy and inexpensive to invest in arts and culture, and that the impact is primarily a positive one. Yet, as scholar Jamie Peck (2005) has shown, a focus on creative capital may provide benefits to elites and successful entrepreneurs while paying little heed to the need for broader distribution of these benefits.

In many ways, Providence embodies this call to create a hub for the creative class. Providence has long been the home of several creativity-oriented institutions, including the Rhode Island School of Design, with the nation's top ranked fine arts programs; Brown University, with respected theater and music programs; and Johnson and Wales University, with a renowned culinary arts institute. In 2009, Providence city officials launched a campaign for the city to become the "Creative Capital" of New England, ranking among the nation's and world's creative centers. The plan, titled "Creative Providence: A Cultural Plan for the Creative Sector," outlines how Providence can "realize its full potential as a creative center and deliver on its promise of innovation and change" (City of Providence 2009). Today, Providence is often recognized for a thriving arts, music, performance, and food scene. It also has a burgeoning entrepreneurial community, offering several opportunities for training and networking ("incubation" and "ecosystem building" in the language of social enterprise).[3] The banner on the city's official website reads, "Providence: The Creative Capital," and city events such as WaterFire, a summer public art event, invoke the

---

3. On this, see the Social Enterprise Ecosystem Economic Development website at http://seeed.org.

city's identity as a place where innovation thrives. In a moment when cities such as Providence work to attract the "creative class" as a pathway to economic development, perhaps it is not surprising that other manifestations of creativity—such as civic innovation—have risen to the fore.

Innovation and Elite Social Movements

Given the demographic characteristics of innovators, some may assume that civic innovation is an example of an "elite social movement." Elite social movements, unlike traditional populist movements, benefit elites and their institutions instead of the general public or disadvantaged populations (Boyle and Silver 2005; Lee 2007, 2013). Such movements include "empowerment projects" (Eliasoph 2009; 2011), "new public participation" (Lee, McQuarrie, and Walker forthcoming), industry-funded grassroots lobbying and corporate activism (Walker 2009), and "civic partnerships" with specific economic and civic goals (Pacewicz 2010). Elite social movements employ and redefine many of the terms commonly used to contest authority—terms such as "empowerment" and "public participation"—in order to reinforce their own power. For example, Michael McQuarrie shows how an elite-sponsored public deliberation project in Cleveland that engaged tens of thousands of neighborhood residents redefined "participation" as something that "reinforce[d] hierarchies, discipline[d] public behavior into non-controversial dialogue, and undermine[d] social solidarity" (2013, 169). Participation can reinforce elite or institutional interests, even as participants themselves experience their participation as natural, voluntary, productive, and not dictated by particular economic interests (Eliasoph 2009; 2011; Walker 2009; Pacewicz 2010).[4]

This scholarship on elite social movements provides an important background for our discussion of civic innovation, yet our analysis differs in that we focus on the *meanings* that animate innovators. While foregrounding a class-based analysis might have led us to speculate on, for example, the influence of corporate interests or the closed nature of social networks, our approach—of listening to what people say about their intentions and observing how these intentions play out, of taking people seriously—leads to a different kind of analysis. That is to say, we do not assume that people's speech and practices merely reflect their privileges and social positions, though we observe and account for evidence of this when it surfaces. As a result, we see civic innovators having more in common with the governance reformers of late nineteenth- or early twentieth-century America than they do with elite social movements. Like the "goo-goos" who supported reformist political candidates in the late nineteenth century, the "mugwumps" who switched political parties in the 1884 election in search of less political corruption, or the "Progressives" who pushed

---

4. Caroline Lee (2013) examines the emergence of a new profession, in which public engagement consultants design and implement participatory projects. She points out the investments made by everyday participants and questions whether the outcomes deliver a worthwhile return to those groups.

for better working and living conditions in response to industrialization throughout the early twentieth century, civic innovators believe in the strength of civil society and in the potential for better governance (Barry 2009). Much of civic innovators' work expresses a genuine desire to strengthen democracy via the direct contribution of citizens to government, as opposed to delegating this necessary work to government employees or elected officials.

BUSINESS AS CULTURAL IDIOM

The job ad that Open Source posted for mayor drew on language and tactics normally used by the business sector: "Job Summary: The Citizens of the City of Providence seek applications for the position of Mayor...." It posed a striking contrast to how elected positions are normally filled—through a process of campaigning and voting. With this tactic, Open Source aimed to repair a broken political system by introducing business-style efficient thinking and tactics.

In Providence, as in other places across the United States, business models and social goals are increasingly merged. This is by no means a new trend: as far back as Victorian Britain, so-called enlightened entrepreneurs pursued both commercial success and social responsibility, motivated to invest in philanthropy by political and religious values (Mair and Marti 2004; Bradley 2007). Today, however, under market rule, the transfer of business ideals to other parts of social life is flourishing. Many institutions of higher education, including Brown University and the Rhode Island School of Design, have recently developed programs in social enterprise (socially responsible business practices) or social entrepreneurship (the use of business-style thinking and tactics to solve social problems), catering to a generation of young people for whom business ideals are appealing, but who are also interested in creating positive social change. Businesses touting "triple bottom lines" (people, planet, and profit) and developing corporate social responsibility strategies are also merging market-based and social ideals.

In this context, it makes sense that business idioms are increasingly being leveraged to improve political processes and deepen democracy. There is a distinction here between the increasingly popular concepts of social enterprise and social entrepreneurship and our related notion of civic innovation. While social enterprise and entrepreneurship likewise refer to the merging of business values with social goals, our concept of civic innovation refers specifically to the use of business logics *in civic life*—toward improved civic engagement, public processes, and community organizing.[5] Civic innovators believe that where other types of civic engagement have fallen short, the central tenets of business, such as efficiency and innovation,

---

5. Although the origin of this civic innovation is not our subject of inquiry, we note that some scholars attribute the introduction of business language into civil society to the influence of foundations' increasing insistence on impact measurements and business-like efficiency in their financing of grants to civil society organizations (Bishop and Green 2008).

hold the potential to solve political problems. If innovation can increase profits for businesses, then similar types of innovation should lead to better democracy and a better city. Civic innovators participate in training programs for entrepreneurs and attend events like CityCamp, "an international unconference series and online community focused on innovation for municipal governments and community organizations" (CityCamp 2012).

Civic innovators adopt the language of business, embracing the concepts of "efficiency," "supply and demand," and "marketing." As an Open Source leader said, "We wanted to give people the info they needed to vote appropriately.... We wanted transparency, coffee meet-ups, real transparency for consumers of information, for voters." At a workshop led by another Open Source leader, students were instructed to think of the mayor as the CEO of the city and to design an appropriate job description. Here, residents and voters are "consumers" of information and politics; elected officials are "CEOs." Innovators regularly use these types of idioms drawn from the business world.

INNOVATORS AND THEIR IMAGINATIONS

In what follows, we examine some of the logics common to civic innovators: generating new ideas, advocating citizens' self-sufficiency, promoting government transparency, using new technologies, and favoring polite conversation over conflict. We note, however, that not everyone we identified as a civic innovator subscribes to all of these ideas.

New Ideas

Whether spearheading an urban agriculture project, developing a vacant downtown property, or building an online tool, what matters to innovators is that citizens generate and implement new and good ideas. As a leader of Open Source explains, Providence needs "problem solvers" who "support and engage each other," and initiatives that are "citizen led, free of government." There is an implicit critique that people outside of government can generate better ideas more effectively than people within it.

So what counts as a "good" idea for innovators? During Open Source's listening party, as community members answered questions posed by mayoral candidates, one participant suggested that the city begin a composting project. Despite criticism from some people in the community that this project would paint Open Source as just a bunch of hippies, a founder of Open Source later told us they supported and were working on making this project a reality because it "just makes sense" considering that every trash bag in the city costs money, and the city buys a lot of soil and fertilizer. In Open Source's eyes, this type of project tackles a social problem (unnecessary waste), while saving money. Our interviewee followed this example by saying she has "modest expectations" for Open Source, but she hopes they have "busted enough balls" that the government "pays attention." For this group, innovative ways of engaging the community can lead to financially sensible projects that cause government officials to take note of what the community wants and needs.

Self-Sufficiency

For civic innovators, the onus for improving the city rests squarely on citizens' shoulders. Local residents should identify problems, generate solutions, and find the best ways to implement those solutions, either independently of government, in conjunction with government, or by telling the government how to fix problems. As one innovator put it, "Government can't do it all by itself. People can't do it all by themselves." Another elaborated, saying that people are wrong if they expect the government to fix their problems, because at best, the government is an *enabler* of change, and at worst, *a barrier* to making the city a better place.

While solutions may involve the government, they certainly do not come from the government. A founder of Open Source said that it was easier to get people engaged by challenging them to take on city issues than by asking them to get involved with government. So he tells people that Open Source "isn't about getting people to engage with their government: it's about getting people engaged with their city and learning about how people engage with their city." We found this idea to have broad appeal. A leader of YAK, for example, noted that the slogan "it's on us" resonated with the Black and low-income communities in which he worked.

Of relevance here, many scholars have noted that the state's retreat from public service provision (as mandated by market rule) has devolved responsibility for welfare to community organizations and voluntary groups. This shift in responsibility from the state to citizens is often considered, or disguised (depending on one's perspective), as community "empowerment." Some studies have found that grassroots activists have internalized these structural changes and ideas about the role of the state, leading them to embrace the notion of self-responsibility or to distrust the state, or both (Marinetto 2003; Ilcan and Basok 2004; Herbert 2005; Fuller and McCorry 2011).

Transparency

Innovators often describe the government as a dark hole where information and ideas are hidden from the light of public scrutiny by the corrupt or closed nature of politics. An Engage leader said the organization exists to take public matters "out of the dark" and into the public light. Closed-door negotiations were considered bad governance. Another innovator used the same metaphor in discussing electoral politics. "By us shining a light on the candidates, we can shine a light on what their ulterior motives are, their answers and solutions," she stated.

For civic innovators, sharing previously hidden government information with the public is a means of promoting citizens' participation and therefore democracy. Many are believers in "Government 2.0," the Internet technology–based movement for open, accessible data on public matters. With full access to data, mass citizen collaboration can bring transformative change to "the business of delivering public services" and "the nature of democracy" (Eggers 2007; Tapscott, Williams, and Herman 2008, 1). A member of Open Source told us that transparency and participation are the two "vectors" of "Government 2.0." The state, he says, should release data to the public in a raw, unbiased format—as opposed to analyses, which he argues are biased—so everyone can use it and "so then they own the bias." For Engage, this similar goal has been translated into a "transparency initiative" that aims to "get as much info as possible on how government works, how do you reach them and interface with them, when are city council meetings, when does the finance committee meet. It's basic info about how decisions are made, how budgets are allocated, etc., and getting that out to the public, through our website, Facebook, [and] Twitter."

By knowing what is really going on, city residents become "consumers of information" and have the data they need to make informed decisions about whom to vote for and how to engage. Increased transparency puts the onus on citizens to *do something* with the data and information they obtain about government and city processes.

New Technology

"Technology allowed us to get to places where we hadn't already gone," one civic innovator explained. Innovators use new technologies, including smartphone apps and social media websites, to provide access to information, promote ideas and events, and facilitate communication between citizens. For example, one of Engage's primary tactics is to increase awareness of what happens at city council meetings by providing real-time updates through social media. The group devised a system whereby a member of the community would attend the meeting with a smartphone, upload messages to Facebook and Twitter during the meeting, and ask for comments from their community of Facebook friends. As the director explained, "We'll have a place to tell us who is going to what meeting and [who is] willing to post [on Facebook].... You don't have to be Engage sanctioned. It's actually you as a person, speaking through the lens or the forums of Engage."

Discourses of new technology have a double meaning for groups like Engage and Open Source. In addition to utilizing technology in their work, these groups also describe what they do as a form of "social technology" for promoting democracy. That is, they understand their work as a new tool for citizens to directly engage with and contribute to government. During a public presentation, an Engage founder explained, "We want to be a disruptive technology. Just like the iPhone changed the way people used phones, we want to change the way our city government engages with its citizens and the way that we engage with our government and our city." For example, Engage was working to find a way for citizens attending city council meetings to be able to text seven hundred people at once and quickly receive replies from those people. This way, "the person at the meeting can raise their hand and say that, for whatever it's worth, they have had fifty people who say one thing and fifty people who say another thing." Although Engage did not implement this during our year of fieldwork, it is an example of how the organization thinks about combining new technology with direct democratic engagement to lead to a technological shift in how citizens interact with their government.

Polite Engagement, Not Conflict

As we noted in Chapter 3, when Americans talk about political engagement, they frequently disavow conflict in favor of polite conversation or consensus building. Likewise, the innovators of Providence argue that the heated public conflict that often characterizes politics is "uncivil and not rational" and does not help to resolve issues. Thus, one of Engage's primary missions is to create "harmonious partnerships between elected officials and individuals." Innovators believe that citizens are able to civilize the discourse of political life: "Especially when there are controversial issues, when people are polarized, when there is antagonism, where there's difficulty in reaching a common agreement, we want to come forward as a convener and facilitate dialogue."

This goal comes from the founders' observation that Providence city council members are frequently "ill-behaved" toward one another in their sessions, and that if members of the public would attend the city council meetings, their mere presence could "bring down acrimony." That is why one of Engage's main lines of action is to publish the dates, times, and locations of the city council meetings online—information that, in Providence, is notoriously inaccessible—and get more people to attend these meetings. Public attendance is seen as a worthwhile and productive goal, even in the absence of any other interaction. Civic innovators believe that engaging residents to go to public meetings and thereby getting the city council members to be nice to each other is a way to create better municipal policies.

TRADEOFFS AND BLIND SPOTS

In Providence and across America, civic innovators are working to make a difference by eliciting new ideas, increasing government transparency, employing new technologies, and challenging the acrimonious aspects of politics. The numbers at their events and online forums show that their logics are broadly appealing. In Providence, the Open Source "listening party" drew nearly two hundred people, and Engage has over 3,000 Facebook "friends."[6] Thus, civic innovators have generated new avenues for citizen engagement.

Like all expressions of political values and civic imaginations, however, civic innovators prioritize competing goals, make tradeoffs, and have blind spots. In this section, we highlight two notable blind spots of civic innovation: prioritizing process

---

6. These are higher numbers of constituents than at most events sponsored by other civic groups in our study.

over outcome and downplaying the productive nature of conflict. As we discussed in Chapter 4, "blind spots" are aspects of civic innovators' imaginations and activities that people either do not see or choose to ignore.

Process or Outcome

A feature of the civic imaginations expressed by innovators is a focus on process rather than outcome. Neither Engage nor Open Source regularly organizes around specific policy goals or takes sides on contentious issues. Instead, they organize events and outreach efforts to bolster government transparency and citizen participation, which they feel are worthwhile goals on their own. As one Open Source founder said, the organization stands "more for the process than specific positions."

During our fieldwork, we were struck that civic innovators often did not seem to have a particular vision of what would constitute a better city, beyond an engaged and educated citizenry. From our fieldnotes after an interview with Richard, a civic innovator: "Richard did not seem to have an idea of what a better Providence would look like, or what he would like to see changed, or what goals he would work toward. What he *does* seem to know is that by talking nicely, building relationships, spending time together, and connecting people, desirable outcomes will be achieved. But I don't know what those are for Richard."

Thus, such things as transparency and participation are often seen as ultimate goals. No one can deny the value of greater government transparency. But instead of talking about what data and information from the government can be used for, civic innovators often promote transparency as an end goal in itself, rather than as a means to an end. Innovators rarely ask questions that are central to other types of activism, such as, "Transparency to what purpose?"

A comparison with other civic groups in our research sheds light on such an alternative. We found that social justice organizations—like FIGHT and YAK in our fieldwork—typically take a different stance. For example, FIGHT often seeks to increase and broaden public participation in order to make demands on city government for workers' or ex-prisoners' rights. Participation is used as a campaign strategy to further tangible political goals, and at FIGHT planning meetings, substantive campaign topics and goals are decided on first and then campaign tactics are chosen and planned. This means that a campaign at FIGHT might be devoted to a new piece of legislation, and one tactic to support that legislation is to get people in the community to write letters to elected officials or to attend public hearings. Participation is seen as a useful tool that can help the organization achieve its substantive goals. In contrast, innovators tend to view participation, in and of itself, as a good outcome.

Believing that a smoother and more participatory process is a worthy goal on its own comes with an inherent blind spot: a good process does not necessarily lead to good outcomes for everyone. In any decision-making process, the "good" ideas are those that appeal to the participants, so if marginalized communities do not participate, decisions are likely to reflect elite interests. In this way, *who* is included is very much related to *what* issues are included.[7] For example, a "collective" decision-making process about projects worthy of municipal funding, in the hands of people from different social classes, can lead to projects of varying degrees of transformative potential. Wealthy community members might decide they need funds to create a new dog park, whereas the same process led by more marginalized residents might lead to needed municipal infrastructure in poor neighborhoods. We found that the problems identified as significant by innovators, whether abstract problems like an unengaged population or concrete problems like potholes, generally differ significantly from those problems prioritized by social justice organizations. Moreover, civic innovators, preoccupied with scaling up and spreading their innovations, sometimes fail to pay attention to the importance of local context and forget to listen to those for whom they are supposedly targeting their programs. Thus, a focus on greater participation for its own sake might emphasize engagement and the development of new ideas at the expense of the full inclusion and benefit of disadvantaged communities. This is an issue we address in greater detail in the next chapter.

Smoothing Over Conflict

Civic innovators privilege rational debate and polite dialogue over conflict and emotion-driven activism. They critique city councilors as "ill-behaved," especially when the public is not watching, and express disdain for the type of engagement that is based on shouting out loud in street protests or using political theater to make public officials feel uncomfortable—frequent tactics used by many social justice groups. One leader of Open Source dismissed members of these types of groups as "angry activists" and criticized them for "not proposing anything useful," in other words, for not understanding the type of engagement and problem solving needed to create meaningful, pragmatic change.

As theorists of democracy have shown, a focus on consensus over conflict may undermine true democratic engagement. Political theorist Chantal Mouffe argues that the contemporary celebration of consensus and partisan-free democracy does not represent progress in democracy. Instead, an emphasis on consensus is actually

---

7. Political theorist Slavoj Žižek warns against the unthinking promotion of good ideas, defined as "ideas that work" (1999), without any inquiry into the ideological context or history of where these ideas come from. To say that an idea works without such an inquiry is to accept a socially predominant, often elite-driven explanation for what works and what does not. Žižek claims that a truly political act does exactly the opposite: it calls into question the predominant frameworks in society. Žižek raises a relevant point for our consideration of civic innovation. Applauding a new idea for the sake of its novelty, rather than for its disruption of existing patterns of injustice and inequality, could reinforce the inequalities and injustices of market rule instead of promoting positive social change. Thus, the new ideas of civic innovation can be exciting and appealing, but it is important to think critically about their origins and effects when evaluating whether they should be put into action.

demobilizing, for "mobilization requires politicization, but politicization cannot exist without the production of a conflictual representation of the world, with opposed camps with which people can identify" (2005, 25). Marginalized people, in particular, use political conflict, or at least disruption of accepted norms, to make claims for increased recognition (Rancière 1995; Žižek 1999).

Thus, when civic innovators call for politeness, they may decrease the possibility that people with alternative voices to the mainstream (or to their own) can voice other opinions. Their ability to engage in society without anger may come from their relatively elite social positions, and this socioeconomic or racial privilege might make them less supportive and understanding of those who express frustration and anger in their activism. Indeed, the critique by an Open Source founder that "angry activists" feel "entitled to jobs or whatever" reveals a lack of empathy for the unemployed. By advocating for consensus and moving beyond conflict, civic innovators act out theoretical arguments that the lack of confrontation in a "post-political" era actually restricts mobilization, therefore harming democracy (Rancière 1995; Mouffe 2005). Thus, despite their best intentions, civic innovators may actually be dampening democratic practices of full and equal participation by restricting avenues for political contestation in favor of a supposedly more pluralistic, consensus-based, problem-solving model.

GRAPPLING WITH LIMITED REACH

In their preference for technological innovations, business logics, and polite engagement, civic innovators thus can sometimes pursue projects that are less inclusive of nonelites. Though most civic innovator events are open to the public, they are most often frequented by individuals from their own social networks, who are attentive to their own social and geographical communities but may have a narrow perspective on the city's problems.[8] Civic innovator events attract these attendees because they are typically advertised through social media or social networks and are held at such venues as downtown restaurants, far from most residential neighborhoods. An organizer described such an event: "We're having it at [a trendy bar in downtown] and having drinks.... Hopefully it will be well attended. You have to buy your

---

8. For example, we heard civic innovators describe their communities as having only amicable relationships with the local police force. This perspective is in sharp contrast with those of other activists in our study, who believe that Providence residents of color often experience injustice at the hands of police officers. As another example, one Open Source leader asserted that potholes were one of the most significant and widely discussed problems in Providence. As a testament to the popularity of this idea, another member described potholes as a "gateway drug to civic engagement"—a surefire way to attract the attention and resources of individuals in their social circles. Attention to potholes contrasts dramatically with the priorities identified by social justice organizations in Providence.

own beer. We'll have some cheese and crackers." However, even when there is no admission cost or when hors d'oeuvres are provided, not all residents feel welcome at expensive restaurants or can attend on a weeknight. And in their organizing activities, civic innovators often fail to reach beyond their comfort zone. On occasions when we tried to make connections between civic innovators and other organizations and leaders from our fieldsites, we rarely saw civic innovators interact with or acknowledge social justice or low-income organizers. This was true even when they were interested in the same issues or attending the same public events. These kinds of limitations on civic innovators' social networks may serve to narrow the horizons of possibilities for change.

Many of the civic innovators with whom we worked are reflexive about whether or not their projects are inclusive. They often focused on the issue of language, which seemed to represent their limitations in reaching out to broader populations. For example, though we met no innovators who were native Spanish speakers, they attempted to reach out to the many Spanish-speaking residents of Providence in various ways. A member of Engage described efforts to reach out to Latinos through popular Spanish-language radio shows, and Open Source's website includes a Spanish-language translation of the homepage.

Likewise, innovators have "mixed feelings" about new technologies, recognizing they can have limited reach to diverse segments of the population. For example, a leader of Open Source noted that retirees often fall behind the latest technological trends. She said the organization realizes that "not everyone has a laptop," and the group hopes to overcome these technological barriers and "reach the widest number of people possible" by also using text and voice messaging. Another member of Open Source spoke favorably about a smartphone app, "SeeClickFix," which allows people to take pictures of such municipal infrastructure problems as potholes, and post photos and descriptions on the Internet in order to call for them to be "fixed" by local government (SeeClickFix 2013). He noted that this type of engagement is growing; however, it is still limited: "Only a certain number of people engage with the mechanisms of government." He concluded by saying that within this movement for greater access to government information, tools to increase transparency were more developed than tools to increase engagement. Although a new smartphone app might inspire some disengaged citizens to participate in civic life, its appeal and accessibility are limited. He continued that technology-focused activities are not, in themselves, elitist, saying that people use technology if it is made "useful to them," and therefore technology can be inclusive if it is targeted to certain populations (who might use text messaging more than the Internet, for example).

Despite doubts that their projects might not be reaching everyone they could, civic innovators justify these choices. We heard civic innovators defend their work with mostly White and educated communities, arguing that more privileged people, just like anyone else, need to deepen their civic and political engagement. An Engage leader explained, "We can't address all the places at once. When we talked about this issue we decided to start with where we have the most affinities. If we only worked on the South Side, that would be phony. We would be out of our depth. You have to start where your strength is."[9] This is a well-reasoned justification for the group's focus, but it does not include a plan for broadening this narrow focus in the future. An Open Source founder put it more bluntly: "I'm not too concerned with being representative. If it's just fifteen people who put the manifesto [on changes to government] together, then fine. They are the ones who took the initiative to do it. It's usually the same kinds of people who do that, anyways." This statement speaks to this person's imagination that the most essential factor in creating social change is that people take the initiative to make it. Other considerations, such as representativeness in political decision-making processes, are secondary. This is a tradeoff that civic innovators sometimes recognize and are willing to make in their quest for serving the public good.

These omissions, doubts, and questions of civic innovators in regard to their reach and representation indicate that, as we discuss at length in the next chapter, social inequality is difficult to talk about and harder to address. We would pose the following questions to those grappling with these issues: Can democratic practice and local communities truly be improved without engaging all individuals? How transformative is it, for democracy and society, to target and reach only relatively well-off segments of the population?

CONCLUSION

The civic innovation we observed in Providence is a contemporary expression of a problem-solving civic imagination. Civic innovators are motivated by a cluster of goals, including generating new ideas for social and political problems, calling for citizens to work for civic and political change, advocating for government transparency, employing new media and cutting-edge technologies for outreach and campaign work, and finding alternatives to conflict-based politics. A quick Internet search is enough to reveal that Providence civic innovators are not unique: similar organizations are active throughout the United States and there are innumerable in-person events or virtual networking platforms for people who work for civic change in this way.

In light of the emerging popularity of civic innovation, what can we make of business ideals being brought into the world of civic engagement? Many social scientists take a cynical view of these developments, interpreting them as an invasion of capitalist and neoliberal values into more and more arenas of civic and political life. Some scholars express concern that the focus on creativity may overshadow the importance of equally distributing benefits across society and that technological solutions are not evenly available to all. As Peck (2005) writes, discourses that

---

9. In Providence, the South Side is a predominantly minority and poor area of town, so this innovator was suggesting that it would be ineffective for them to focus on this type of neighborhood.

equate creativity with "good" development may empower elites at the expense of distributive outcomes that benefit other segments of society. Other scholars have raised concerns about importing business idioms into civic life. Dorothy Holland and her colleagues (2007) warn that market rule is imperiling US democracy. They note that while democracy rests on three principles—freedom, equality, and community—the ideology of market rule compromises equality and community in order to promote freedom of the market.

While some scholars have a cynical view of the merging of business ideals with civic engagement, other scholars pay attention to how people act within neoliberal and capitalist systems in ways that can actually serve democratic ends. Sociologists Luc Boltanski and Eve Chiapello (2005) argue that today's form of capitalism has incorporated a "new spirit" that includes a *moral* dimension. This new spirit enables capitalist values and ideals to travel out of the marketplace, engaging and mobilizing people in many different ways. Scholar Nigel Thrift (2005) argues that the relations and practices on which capitalism rests are not "all bad": for example, many people find creativity and innovation enjoyable. By appealing to people's gut feelings, the everyday practices of capitalism are sometimes the very same ones needed to overcome some of capitalism's harmful elements. Other scholars have pointed to people's creativity in appropriating neoliberal ideologies in order to serve emancipatory ends (e.g., Postero 2007). Here, scholars do not see people as blind followers of market rule but instead as individuals who reason, think carefully, and act out their theories of the world.

This stance resonates with our own analysis of civic innovation. In our ethnography, we found that in civic innovators' everyday practices, they creatively appropriate the values and ideals of market rule in order to further their goals of improving their cities and their democracy. Their tactics have the potential to deepen democratic engagement for many Americans. Many people believe in civic innovators' goals and are attracted to innovators' efficient business-style practices. In a time of deep political skepticism, these kinds of trends provide a rallying cry for more people to get civically engaged. Civic innovators' creation of new spaces for civic engagement reflects the value they place on the purest forms of democratic decision making, where more people have a voice, decisions are made together and by the public, and transparency is paramount.

Yet we offer a word of caution: if there is no reflexivity about how strategies of civic innovation relate to questions of equal access and poverty reduction, civic innovation could perpetuate inequality and injustice. Civic innovators in Providence often focus on process rather than outcome by pursuing civic participation for its own sake and emphasizing cutting-edge technologies for outreach and participation while overlooking the important role of conflict in democracy. These tendencies serve to obscure important questions of inclusivity and representativeness. Languages and tactics of civic innovation that seem attractive and efficient, and draw in participation by certain populations, may also constrain participation in some ways, because not all residents will attend flashy events, take advantage of new technological solutions, or respond to an ad for mayor. Moreover, civic innovators' emphasis on new ideas, problem solving, and building consensus portrays their viewpoints as "just making sense," or as natural and neutral, even when these views are based on privilege or particular social locations. These blind spots, even when they are consciously chosen tradeoffs in favor of other priorities, may prevent civic innovators' policies and tactics from achieving the good outcomes they intend.

Chapter 6

Inequality

A DIFFICULT CONVERSATION

In this chapter, we turn to the question of inequality and how it is understood, framed, and discussed (or not) within activist settings. The fieldwork for this book took place at a time when the national economic recession was impacting the lives of nearly all Americans. The working class saw wages cut and positions downsized or eliminated, and the middle class, after dwindling in numbers for decades, was suddenly and harshly squeezed by the real estate collapse and financial crisis. Students graduated to find there were no jobs, homeowners faced the heartbreak of foreclosure, and baby boomers saw their retirement savings disappear. Providence, Rhode Island, was among the cities hardest hit. The numbers of unemployed, homeless, and poor swelled; reliance on food banks climbed 45 percent; and Depression-era scenes, such as hundreds of people lining up for a few dozen jobs at a new hotel, were noticeable throughout the city (*Providence Journal* 2010; Rhode Island Community Food Bank 2010). As the global economic crisis cascaded into a city-level fiscal disaster, the thin safety net standing between the working poor and the growing population living in poverty began to dissolve. Public transportation, social services, and public assistance were reduced; cuts to public education led to teacher layoffs, larger classes, and closed schools.

In this context, we looked to activists and civic organizations with the goal of understanding how they made sense of this inequality. After all, it is often in civil society that solutions are explored, solidarity is extended, and justice is pursued. Unlike our optimism about American participation, our diagnosis about inequality is less clear. Inequality is ubiquitous in contemporary American society and presents seemingly intractable challenges—it is difficult to speak of, hard to understand, and overwhelming to address. In this chapter, we offer an explanation for why this is so. It is not that citizens are self-interested. In fact, as we described in Chapter 3, people

96

go to great lengths to avoid being seen (even by themselves) as the type of person who would pursue narrow, selfish interests. Nor is the difficulty with addressing inequality a consequence of widespread cynicism. In Chapter 3, we detailed the verbal and intellectual acrobatics that activists employ to preserve hope that it *is* possible to reform what they see as an utterly broken political system. Rather, it is that inequality often falls out of focus. We discuss the reasons for this throughout the chapter.

To examine activists' relationship with inequality, we tell the story of participatory budgeting in Providence. The idea of allowing people to directly participate in budgeting decisions intrigued citizens of all stripes, but their motivations and strategies for pursuing it were unarguably distinct. In following how and why diverse groups were drawn to this common project, we saw how inequality can be placed at the fore of activism or, alternatively, relegated to the margins. There are also marked differences in how people speak of inequality: while some people use euphemisms to talk about race, gender, class, privilege, and injustice, others speak of these issues directly. As groups evaluate one another as possible allies, or potential foes, their decisions on with whom to collaborate are, in part, informed by the degree to which their perspectives on inequality align. For example, social justice groups sought out partners such as immigrants' rights groups, but avoided working with civic groups that were against unions. Despite these differences, all civic groups find ways to gloss over issues of inequality and privilege *within* their own organizations. In short, we show in this chapter that it is simply too easy for inequality to fade from view, especially for those who do not experience its discomforts. And for those who *are* focused on inequality, the problem becomes identifying tactics and employing discourses to reposition inequality within everyone's line of sight.

THE BROAD APPEAL OF PARTICIPATION

The notion of giving citizens more voice in government decision making is nearly universally appealing. This became very clear one evening toward the end of our year of fieldwork when, instead of disbursing to attend events throughout the city, our fieldsites came to us. Activists from Parkside Coalition, Neighbors Driving Change, FIGHT, and Engage gathered in an auditorium at Brown University to learn about participatory budgeting, a process that grants citizens the authority to collectively decide how a pool of municipal funds will be spent. Participatory budgeting originated in Brazil but has since been replicated in various cities in the United States. At this event, over fifty activists, students, faculty, and members of the community gathered to explore the potential of participatory budgeting in Providence. Speakers included Joe Moore, the alderman who facilitated the process in Chicago; an interested Providence city councilor; and our co-author Gianpaolo Baiocchi.

Gianpaolo had participated in, and written about, participatory budgeting in Chicago and Brazil (Baiocchi 2005; Baiocchi, Heller, and Silva 2011), and his experiences had piqued the interest of neighbors and friends in Providence. During the course of our research, interest in participatory budgeting grew at several of our fieldsites. As organizing efforts materialized, we thus found ourselves in the position of experts, providing suggestions and support to efforts to initiate participatory budgeting at the city level. Although we did not assume leadership roles, we observed people from several different civic groups talking about and planning their advocacy strategies and imagining what a city budget allocated "by the people" might entail.

Two groups were particularly interested in bringing participatory budgeting to Providence: FIGHT and Engage. FIGHT, a social justice organization, invested time and resources in the idea as part of their broader campaign to make city governance more accountable to the city's poor. FIGHT leaders met with the mayor and city councilors to identify eligible funds and eventually won the support of several city councilors who agreed to champion for each councilor's discretionary funds to be allocated to the participatory budgeting process. Engage, a civic innovator group, took a different approach. Leaders focused on spreading the word to key players around the city and advertised meetings using social media. For this group, the draw was a more direct form of democracy, which resonated with their mission to use innovation to increase participation in city government.

While these two groups were the most engaged of our fieldsites, most of the actors in our research expressed some interest and participated in discussions about participatory budgeting. This is how we found ourselves in a Brown University auditorium, greeting activists from our different fieldsites. One of us sat with FIGHT organizers; another joined Neighbors Driving Change activists in the middle of the room; and the others lingered in the back, chatting with Engage and Parkside Coalition members as they arrived. At this event, civic imaginations were articulated and acted upon in telling ways. Notions of how a better city *could* and *should* be organized were at the heart of the conversation. A FIGHT member explained, "For me it's like a breath of fresh air.... There is some stale bread in that city hall." Another FIGHT member thought that the funds in question were quite small, but said that participatory budgeting was still worth the fight. And a member of Engage considered the potential for enhanced transparency, quoting Alderman Moore on the group's Facebook page: "Participatory budgeting is more than just having people participate more. It goes to accountability—people ask questions that should be asked. Sunlight is a powerful disinfectant and this process allows sunlight to shine on your government.... When people aren't engaged it gives more power to corporations and other special interests."

In particular, talk and action around participatory budgeting highlighted the different ways that civic imaginations are oriented around the issue of inequality. Participatory budgeting is about policy outcomes (*how* money is spent) as well as political processes (*who decides* how money is spent), and we witnessed different perspectives of how policies and processes should address inequality. FIGHT, the social justice group, wanted the process to help the urban poor by allowing them to allocate money to necessary projects, especially those focused on job creation. However, they knew that not all groups would share this objective. They were aware that in Chicago, when middle-class residents dominated the participatory budgeting process, some of the results—dog parks and beach showers—reflected middle-class interests. FIGHT worried about this type of co-optation of the process, and expressed concern that if they took the lead in organizing, the mayor's office might just discard it as another one of FIGHT's many projects to address socioeconomic and racial inequalities in Providence—and thus, not extend needed support.

WHY PROMOTE PARTICIPATORY BUDGETING?

Beneath common goals and similar language, activists can have different interpretations, objectives, motivations, and tactics for civic engagement. Their ideas about what needs to be changed, and how, are guided by their civic imaginations. As we described in Chapter 4, civic imaginations are the ways in which people individually and collectively envision better political, social, and civic worlds. Individuals and groups express their imaginations through words and actions, as they engage with their communities and with each other. Because participatory budgeting can be—but is not necessarily—used to promote equitable outcomes or equality in decision making, activists' words and deeds in their promotion of participatory budgeting were especially revealing of how their imaginations relate to contemporary patterns of inequality.

In our fieldwork, activists' imaginations cluster around fighting power, promoting solidarity, or solving problems. The next three sections examine how people drew on participatory budgeting as a way to fight against inequality, to promote community solidarity, and to solve a social or political problem. Here, we ask *whether* and *how* each of the three dialects of civic imagination grapples with issues of inequality, and how expressions of these imaginations put concerns about inequality front and center or, alternatively, relegate those concerns to the wings.

Participatory Budgeting as a Way to Fight Inequality

Individuals and organizations with civic imaginations centered on fighting power see confronting injustice and inequality as central to their mission and activities. During our research, this imagination was strongly expressed at FIGHT. The group's interest in participatory budgeting dated back to the fall of 2010, when concern grew about a federal jobs bill. As originally introduced, the bill supported job creation for marginalized groups. However, in the face of constrained local budgets, this mission had eroded, and the money was instead to be used to maintain city and state employee salaries. FIGHT was skeptical that local political leaders would prioritize the "real" needs of "the people." Participatory budgeting came to the fore as the group brainstormed ways to advocate for budgets that would better serve the interests of Rhode Island's poor and unemployed. FIGHT members attended participatory budgeting workshops at the US Social Forum in 2010 and reached out to Gianpaolo for advice and help.

FIGHT pursued participatory budgeting by recruiting a coalition of like-minded groups and incorporating information about municipal budgeting into their existing programs. Neighbors Driving Change joined FIGHT in hosting and advertising organizational meetings and educational forums. For members of both organizations, participatory budgeting was a way to address the historical misuse of public money and the community's continued frustrations at how money is allocated in Providence. These groups found promise in a message from Chicago activists and politicians: participatory budgeting provides a level of transparency that counters government corruption. The groups planned an awareness campaign to raise excitement about the idea among low-income people and asked mayoral candidates to publicly pledge to implement participatory budgeting if elected.

These initial organizing efforts and their justifications make clear why FIGHT and Neighbors Driving Change were interested in participatory budgeting: it potentially provides mechanisms for meaningful participation in governance by poor, jobless, and otherwise marginalized people, and for promoting equality via policies and budgets. These groups imagined participatory budgeting to be a tool to reinstate the original mission of the federal jobs bill, to curb government corruption, to promote widespread and consequential public participation, and to serve the less powerful.

Participatory Budgeting as a Way to Promote Community Solidarity

A second family of civic imaginations focuses on promoting community solidarity by bringing people together, developing a sense of collective culture, and strengthening neighborhoods and local spaces. Expressions of the solidarity imagination were common across all of our fieldsites, but were most fully expressed by two neighborhood associations: Parkside Coalition and Oceanside Neighbors. People in these groups were excited about participatory budgeting because they saw it as providing an impetus and a forum for bringing people together to make shared decisions and promoting the hands-on engagement of neighborhood residents. In an early meeting with Sarah, the director of the Parkside Coalition, we mentioned Gianpaolo's research and experience with participatory budgeting. The concept was new to her, but she was immediately interested, and said she had learned from a recent community forum about the importance of establishing a clear, nonconfrontational process for discussion and decision making—a way for people to participate in making decisions as a collective.

James, a city councilor active in the Parkside Coalition, had a similar reaction. After an initial conversation with us about participatory budgeting, he made a point to follow up on the idea. James was drawn to the concept because he believed good ideas come from everyday people, and the process would involve getting out and talking to people to figure out solutions to community problems. As organizing efforts progressed, James became an active supporter of bringing participatory budgeting to Providence. He collaborated with members of FIGHT and Engage, met with Chicago alderman Joe Moore, and spoke publicly about his support at the Brown University event. People with imaginations based on community solidarity were interested in participatory budgeting because it could bring like-minded neighbors together, not necessarily because it could empower marginalized groups.

Participatory Budgeting as a Way to Solve Problems

The third cluster of imaginations is motivated by the idea that civic groups can generate creative solutions to political problems by bringing people together and facilitating communication. Leaders of Engage clearly express this imagination. For them, participatory budgeting represented an innovative social technology that could help achieve their goal of engaging more citizens of Providence in interactions with their government. In fact, participatory budgeting was a perfect example of what Engage wanted to do more generally—"help push the envelope" by facilitating "innovative communication models," without explicitly promoting specific policies or political parties. As the director wrote in a letter to a local newspaper, "We want Providence to become a standout model of participatory democracy in action."

Engage solicited public support and identified potential public funds via Facebook posts and word of mouth at professional and social networking events. They saw participatory budgeting as a neutral governance tool that provided the opportunity for all citizens to directly contribute to political decision-making processes.

The groups in our study were excited about participatory budgeting for different reasons, and they imagined the process taking different paths and reaching different ends. Many of these distinctions are related to their perspectives on inequality: how pressing is it, who has the responsibility to address it, and to what extent does it take priority over other issues? We found it meaningful that people spoke about inequality in extremely different ways, and that they allied with groups whose discourse was similar to their own. We also noticed that all groups—regardless of their orientation around inequality—were challenged to identify and acknowledge the discrepancies in privilege between members of their own organization, though, not surprisingly, this took different forms. The following three sections examine each of these topics: differences in discourse, the process of identifying collaborators, and the barriers to accurately assessing within-group demographics.

SPEAKING OF INEQUALITY

Ideas about inequality are central to how people and groups decide what it means to be a good citizen or to work effectively for social change. Speaking about this undercurrent, however, is more difficult. Sometimes what people do *not* say is just as revealing as what they do. Instead of addressing privilege, poverty, or race head-on, individuals often talk around issues of inequality, using colorful phrases, stereotypes, and indirect references. In some groups, this is a common way of talking—or not talking—about inequality. These *euphemisms*—innocuous phrases or descriptions used in place of offensive ones—allow people to refer to others' race, class, or gender, without having to identify those markers or think about others' status in relation to their own. In this section, we describe the pervasive use of euphemisms. As with most trends, we also find the exception—direct talk—to be revealing.

Euphemisms

Like many cities in the United States, Providence is multicultural, racially diverse, and with residents ranging from very rich to extremely poor. Some activists, however, hesitate to name racial or ethnic groups or to explicitly talk about income stratification. In some organizations, this is part of the norms of group culture. For example, Kim is a member of the civic innovator group Open Source. In describing a meet-and-greet coffee event for mayoral candidates and the public, she avoided saying "working class" or "the working poor" or "low income." Instead, she said she talked to some "really salt of the earth" kind of people, who were very different from her "peer group." She said that while these salt of the earth people were concerned about solving simple problems, her peer group—who we knew to be highly educated professionals with creative jobs and access to decision-makers—was actually developing innovative solutions. She said the conversation was "refreshing" despite a total disconnect between the interests and agendas of her peers and the people she met. In describing a cross-class experience about civic life, Kim avoided talking about privilege, income, or opportunity.

People also obscure inequalities by employing what is, on the surface, "neutral" discourse about topics like participation or neighborliness. At a Halloween event, the Parkside Coalition distributed a map of the neighborhood with addresses of houses where kids could trick-or-treat. Since it is often obvious which houses welcome children on Halloween because they turn on porch lights and decorate, we asked Sarah why this was necessary. She explained that not everyone celebrates Halloween in the neighborhood, and in general, you would not want to walk up to just any house. "It's all about finding the *right* neighbors," Sarah said. "Right neighbors," in this conversation, was a placeholder for "members" or "potential members" of the neighborhood association. After all, Parkside Coalition's objective was to build solidarity among residents to achieve common goals, and here was a way to bring together neighbors through trick-or-treating with children. However, because the neighborhood association members are largely White, English-speaking, middle-class professionals, not Black or Latino, Spanish-speaking, blue-collar workers, the map primarily directed families to homogenous and privileged parts of the neighborhood. The phrase "right neighbors" was not *intentionally* used in place of "White home-owners," but allowed the conversation to proceed without acknowledging that the map directed parents and children to parts of Parkside that were not representative of the neighborhood's overall demographics.

In other moments, people deploy a creative array of humorous euphemisms to acknowledge—and make light of—an inequality elephant in the room. This happened when Alderman Moore, from Chicago, met with Providence activists at FIGHT before his talk at Brown. Moore said his ward was diverse, but there were a few "yuppies." A resident of the West Side of Providence laughed and said, we call those people "misplaced East-Siders." Both men were referring to White people living in non-White areas of racially segregated cities. In both Chicago and Providence, the mostly White neighborhoods are more affluent than the mostly non-White neighborhoods, and White neighborhoods enjoy disproportionately large allocations of public funding. One activist illustrated this point by asserting that the East Side of Providence, which is predominantly White, has fifteen snowplows, while the larger South Side of the city, which is predominately Black and Latino, has only six. In snowy New England, this makes a big difference in residents' quality of life and the safety of local streets.

A similar conversation took place during an Oceanside Neighbors meeting. Members were discussing a rezoning proposal from the Historical Commission that would be costly to residents but had the potential to raise real estate values. Implementing this plan would require widespread agreement from the residents, and nobody wanted to raise the issue of low-income neighbors, many of whom were bilingual immigrants and would likely oppose increasing their costs of living. These residents were clustered in one corner of the Oceanside neighborhood, slightly downhill from the more affluent families, and no one at that meeting (beside us) lived in this part of Oceanside. Instead of talking about income disparity head-on, someone started, "The problem with people *down there ...*" She paused and looked around to see if everyone around the table "got" the reference. To her relief, someone laughed and repeated "*dowwwwwn therrrrre*" in a funny, slow, low-pitched voice, acknowledging a shared understanding. Everyone laughed. Problem solved! No need to mention race or class—they could simply note that some people were "down there." Relieved of this tension, the conversation continued. How would the group "pitch" historical zoning to the "people down there" who "don't want anyone to tell them what to do"? How far "down there" was too far? The euphemism became so normalized that when the visitor from the Historical Commission wanted to identify the area on a map, she asked, "Where is your 'down there'?" We jotted in our fieldnotes, "Is everyone just afraid to talk about race?" Euphemisms are used to mask differences, avoid naming implicitly excluded groups, and humorously relieve tension when avoidance is not possible.

Direct Talk

In contrast to masking, ignoring, or skirting around inequality, speaking directly about race, class, and gender was often the norm at FIGHT, Neighbors Driving Change, and YAK, groups motivated by imaginations of fighting power. The value of direct talk was clearly asserted in a FIGHT meeting, when a visiting activist broke this informal code. The visitor boldly claimed that unemployment is not a Black or White issue, but instead a worker issue. The visitor then turned to Bernice, a Black organizer with FIGHT, and explained that she did not see a Black woman, simply a person. Bernice, defending the group's norm of direct talk, responded that the visitor *had better see her as a Black woman*, because we still live in a world where we need to look at race, class, and gender. There were many instances like this in which issues of race, class, and gender were visible at FIGHT meetings.

People also moved beyond simple acknowledgment of difference and privilege, to openly describing and discussing their prejudices. A FIGHT leader once told one of us, who is White, "*You're* not the type of White person I hate." Explaining that she did not mean to offend, she qualified her comment, holding out her arms for a hug: "I only hate *rich* White people." This comment stands in stark contrast with the previous examples of skirting around the mere mention of racial divides. Similarly, another Black member of FIGHT shared at a meeting, "I got in fights with Black kids, so I have racist thoughts against Blacks. I'm walking down the street and a Black guy comes at me and I think, 'Is he going to rob me?' And I know he's thinking the same thing about me. Racism comes from our own personal experiences. We think racism is a White vs. Black or Black vs. White, but it's not always like that." By naming their biases, these individuals brought the issues of inequality to the fore. These comments created space for conversation—and potentially action—around inequality.

Openly acknowledging inequality also includes naming one's own privileges. A FIGHT meeting one evening kept going off track, with several leaders frequently talking loudly over each other, and one suggested designating a facilitator to keep things moving along. A man who had been dominating the conversation agreed with this suggestion, saying he was one of the "loud ones ... and a man, too," showing awareness of how his gender was influencing the meeting style. On several occasions, we heard White members of social justice groups wrestling openly with their own privilege. For example, a White member of Neighbors Driving Change, a primarily Latino organization, admitted in a membership meeting that the emissions inspection sticker on her car had been expired for four years, but she had never been pulled over. She said that if she were the "wrong color" and drove a car made earlier than the year 2000, this would not have been the case. Stuart, a former director of Neighbors Driving Change, reflected, "When I go to meetings of other immigrant groups, sometimes I'm the only White person in the room.... I'm grateful to bring my privilege into the space and put it to good use [by writing fund-raising proposals, for example], but I'm conscious that the more space I take up and the more leadership that I take on, the harder it is to create a grassroots social movement." Similarly, Heather, who was active at both FIGHT and Neighbors Driving Change, talked about coming from a relatively privileged background. She said she had to work hard to figure out her role in social justice work, and sometimes wondered whether her efforts would be more productive if she organized her "own people."[1]

In sum, certain groups have a culture of direct talk, in which members acknowledge difference, admit bias, and sometimes even name their own privileges. Although individuals of all imaginations avoid and euphemize inequality in some contexts, direct talk occurs more often in expressing imaginations focused on fighting power.

---

1. For readers interested in thinking more about privilege, see *Readings for Diversity and Social Justice: An Anthology on Racism, Antisemitism, Sexism, Heterosexism, Ableism, and Classism*, edited by Maurianne Adams, Warren J. Blumenfeld, Carmelita Castañeda, Heather W. Hackman, Madeline L. Peters, and Ximena Zúñiga (2000).

GROUP BOUNDARIES: WHO IS IN, WHO IS OUT

For most people, it is difficult to talk about inequality, though people who work to address structural injustice more often find ways to speak openly about it. Here, we expand on this observation, arguing that perspectives on inequality are central to the maintenance of group boundaries, or how groups define who and what is "in" and "out" (Lamont and Molnar 2002). No group in our study established official racial, ethnic, class, income, or other requirements for membership, and many groups attracted diverse participants. However, shared understandings about inequality and privilege were at the heart of each group. Thus, different perspectives on why participatory budgeting could be good for Providence, and how these perspectives relate to the issue of social inequality, were not simply varied approaches to an exciting new civic project. These perspectives reveal important differences in how people and groups draw boundaries between themselves and others.

Everybody's Welcome

Groups that express the community-building or problem-solving imaginations focus on bringing people together and creating solutions, and these groups emphasize the importance of diversity, community, and participation, but rarely place inequality at the center of their campaign goals or tactics. If asked directly, they would likely respond that equality and inclusiveness are certainly values they believe in. These activists do not see their individual actions or the structures of their organizations as directly perpetuating inequality. Yet their outreach strategies, campaign goals, meeting objectives, and programmatic decisions involve tradeoffs that often have exclusionary effects. Entire demographic groups are often absent from many of their events and meetings and omitted from their outreach tactics. For example, Parkside Coalition hosted a daytime Halloween party in a large park that is the symbolic and physical center of their neighborhood. On ordinary days, the park overflows with local life—Latino men talking on the benches, athletes organizing pick-up soccer, Asians spilling out from the church across the street, youth playing sand volleyball, and foodies at the Farmers' Market. But on this day, at an event intended to "bring neighbors together," the park was full of young, White families. In a neighborhood that is over 50 percent Latino, most of the non-White people in sight were sitting on benches on the opposite side of the park, observing—but not participating in—the festivities.[2]

We are not the only ones to notice these representative discrepancies. At the semiannual Oceanside Neighbors meeting, one of our researchers sat next to a local resident. Toward the end of the meeting, the woman, whom our team had never met,

---

2. This figure is estimated based on the 2010 census data, taking into consideration the multiple census tracts that make up the neighborhood and range from 21 percent to over 60 percent Hispanic (US Census Bureau 2013).

leaned over and said, "It's all White people here! There was one Black guy, but he left a while ago." She noted that a lot of Black people live in the neighborhood. When we questioned Oceanside Neighbors' president about the organization's orientation to racial diversity, he admitted that the group was "gentrified." When asked if there were any efforts to address this, he responded that it was an ongoing question for the organization, but that the status quo was accepted and there was no real effort to be more inclusive.

Some organizations have identified ways to attract a more representative group of participants. Sarah, the director of Parkside Coalition, knows that being inclusive in her gentrifying but mixed neighborhood is a challenge. She told us that she would like the association's newsletters, which are currently only in English, to be distributed in Spanish as well. She also mentioned that her programs that were most successful in terms of promoting diversity were those that "offered things" to residents. For example, a few years ago the city had a serious rat problem, and the association distributed trashcans with lids. Because people needed to come to Parkside Coalition to pick up these trashcans, she reasoned, it was an opportunity to teach potential new constituencies about the organization. Sarah also mentioned past success in bringing diverse community residents to their headquarters by providing English and Spanish classes, but the organization no longer offers these programs.

The examples that Sarah shared with us are striking in the implicit recognition that the group was *not* currently prioritizing what had, in the past, been successful at broadening outreach beyond Parkside's core constituency. Although the group and its leaders wanted to be more inclusive and identified in that way, they did not pursue these already identified strategies to foster inclusivity.

When organizations' leaders are homogeneous in terms of race and class, their norms and customs come to reflect this identity. For example, at an Oceanside Neighbors meeting, a board member joked that they would treat the group to Subway sandwiches. The group laughed. *Everybody* knows that fast food is not a treat! The conversation turned to favorite homemade recipes and the possibility of hosting a meeting at a family member's seldom utilized seaside home. (In contrast, Subway sandwiches were regularly served at meetings at FIGHT, often next to a tin for donations to reimburse the person who had purchased them.) This conversation revealed that Oceanside leaders took for granted that others in the room shared their disregard for certain consumption patterns, preferences strongly connected to the fact that the organization's leadership and membership was populated by affluent homeowners.

In sum, community builders and problem solvers often exclude certain populations, limit their outreach tactics, and forget to question the boundaries they create between themselves and others. Just as the omission of inequality in a conversation suggests that the speaker might not be tuned in to issues of inequality, a group's failure to consider how activities or projects potentially alleviate or exacerbate inequality has significant consequences. In the previous chapter, we showed how initiatives of civic innovators sometimes have limited reach among certain demographic constituents. For example, Engage regularly asserted that the group's target audience was *everyone* in the city, yet by sending messages to the group's Facebook friends and informally gathering input through their natural social and professional circles, their tactics likely reached only certain populations. Here we expand this point to note that all groups, not just civic innovators, can be either unaware of their limited reach, or aware of it but see it as a necessary tradeoff. Even when people want to be inclusive and promote diversity, and even when groups maintain that they are actively working to achieve these goals, sometimes they reproduce inequality by not prioritizing it as a direct concern.

We Are All Immigrants

For groups focused on fighting power, inequality is an explicitly articulated dimension of group identity in two ways. As we showed in the case of participatory budgeting, members of these groups choose to work on issues related to inequality and are committed to mobilizing marginalized populations. As an activist commented during a door-to-door canvassing campaign, "*These* are exactly the people who need to organize." He had just finished talking with a poor immigrant facing threats of foreclosure. For groups like FIGHT, YAK, and Neighbors Driving Change, the people who matter for social justice work are oppressed populations: the poor, immigrants, and minorities.

In addition to actively working on issues related to inequality, these groups form identities based on shared experiences of oppression. They view themselves, and most Americans, as victimized by and not responsible for structural inequalities. We heard a variety of claims in this regard. Rebecca, a Neighbors Driving Change organizer, articulated this identity clearly: "We have all done things that we don't like to talk about ... but *we* don't commit the worst crimes. The people in this room do not keep whole populations oppressed. *The people in this room* are not responsible for starvation and racism." At the time, the people in the room were all members of Neighbors Driving Change. Her statement reinforced a strong sense of group identity and expressed her belief that those responsible for injustice were outside the group's boundaries.

At times, this shared experience of oppression was more imagined than real. Clearly, not all members of social justice groups are from marginalized populations or regularly experience overt, overwhelming oppression. Some group members are more privileged than group customs easily admitted. For example, leaders of Neighbors Driving Change regularly expressed, "We're all immigrants," a statement that forged solidarity with immigrant communities even among US-born members of the organization. At a meeting of progressive activists hosted by FIGHT, a woman working on unemployment issues declared passionately that the group was all working poor, and that there is no middle class in America anymore. Another activist concurred, citing frustrations with tax cuts for the wealthy: "We're *all* the working poor!" However, the participants at that meeting were simply not all working poor. In addition to the members of our team, who are part of an Ivy League academic community, there were several other professionals and professors at the table. Yet no one contested her statement.

Claims of shared experiences of oppression contribute to a shared identity in these organizations. Yet these statements also have the effect of obscuring differing levels of privilege among members. The fact that these activists can be unwilling to identify and mark differing levels of privilege is yet another indication that inequality is difficult to talk about when it hits close to home, and especially when it is evident in one's own group or activities. In this regard, *all* groups struggle in some ways, and in some moments, to discuss inequality, especially with regard to their members.

ALLY OR OPPONENT? EVALUATING OTHERS

The ways in which groups are oriented to the issue of inequality help them judge who might be good allies or, alternatively, unappreciated competition. As organizational efforts around participatory budgeting unfolded, civic groups in Providence allied or competed to launch the initiative. In justifying their strategies, activists described, praised, and critiqued other groups. People's actions are in part shaped by the way they view and interact with people guided by other imaginations. Groups recognize that others engage with the civic and political world in different ways and can have opposing ideas about what needs to be done to make a better future possible. We occasionally saw these judgments surface in our research, through comments such as, "Oh, yeah, that antiunion East Side yuppie group." This evaluation of others helps people clarify and understand their own positions, though often the tendency is to dismiss others and reinforce one's own imagination.

Frequently, issues of inequality are at the heart of evaluations of others. This section highlights the tensions over goals and tactics that developed between two groups, FIGHT and Engage, in their efforts to bring participatory budgeting to Providence. We describe these conflicts in order to show how people expressing various civic imaginations perceive one another, and how inequality is at the heart of these judgments.

Fearing Co-Optation

FIGHT organizers told us they worried that groups like Engage would "hijack" the organizational efforts to bring participatory budgeting to Providence. They thought that if Engage planned the process, participatory budgeting would be used by middle- and upper-class Whites to allocate funds toward "projects we hate, like condos and mixed-use development." They called this the "dog park phenomenon," in reference to how the participatory budgeting process played out in Chicago, where projects like dog parks won out over projects aiming to serve the poor. In FIGHT's view, such a co-optation would undermine participatory budgeting's potential to create economic opportunities and improve quality of life for the poor.

FIGHT thus worked to build a coalition of like-minded allies. They began by identifying groups that spoke their "language"—people who shared their perspective that race, class, oppression, and inequality are top priorities. They worked quickly, hoping to organize before other groups could form counter-alliances. "We'll need the extra time to compete for project ideas," a FIGHT organizer explained. She added sarcastically, "Parkside Coalition could hire a $15,000 contractor to come up with a great idea for a $10,000 project." They planned to combat the superior material resources of other organizations with extra time spent mobilizing their constituencies.

FIGHT felt they had good reason to fear elite capture and public exclusion, because this had happened before in Providence, to them and to groups considered allies. For example, FIGHT talked about negative experiences with public charrettes,[3] which they sometimes jokingly referred to as "charades," asserting that their ideas, critiques, and suggestions were ignored in the final outcome. In reminiscing about a city planning process in which officials claimed to have consulted the community, a FIGHT activist held up his arms in the form of an X: "That process was all about excluding the public," he said. The fear of processes and outcomes being co-opted by those with more privilege and power seemed to be a commonsense aspect of these activists' civic organizing. Others had similar experiences: Darnell from YAK said that he had been working with Parkside Coalition on an educational advocacy campaign. Together, they developed an idea to pitch to the mayor's office, but in the end, the group excluded him from the actual meeting with the mayor. The activist believed this exclusion to be racially motivated: "They wanted to present their White face.... They thought their chances [to win over the mayor] were better without the Black face." As Bernice commented on the co-optation of public participation exercises such as the dog park phenomenon, "That happens with everything! But at least we can say *we got it started*." The "we" in this statement referred to inequality-oriented social justice groups that made up the coalition of allies that FIGHT had assembled.

Avoiding Contentious Tactics

When Engage first mentioned their interest in participatory budgeting to our team, we suggested they contact other groups mobilizing around the project. We provided contact information for James, an interested city council member, and two FIGHT organizers. Months later, Dina, a leader of Engage, commented, "Thanks so much for telling me about James.... We had a really good conversation about it and he'll be a good partner for us." She never mentioned FIGHT. At a later meeting about participatory budgeting, we directly asked Dina if she knew of a group called FIGHT. She responded without answering the question, saying that many groups were interested in participatory budgeting: "I think that there are a bunch of groups that would come on [board] ... establishment type groups like the New England Foundation ... radical grassroots groups ... others across the spectrum." She said that this diversity was good, so people could see that this was not the work

---

3. Charrettes are collaborative processes where several people work together to draft solutions to identified social problems. In city planning, charrettes have become a popular way to have diverse stakeholders come together to share and discuss their ideas.

of a "narrow" interest group. Here we catch a glimpse of why Engage never reached out to FIGHT: it was a "radical grassroots group," and one that others would see as promoting "narrow" interests. If James was an acceptable partner because of his political office and shared civic imagination, FIGHT, because of its emphasis on inequality, was not. Rather than signaling neutrality, Dina's comments illustrated the dissonance between her problem-solving civic imagination and FIGHT's imagination of the need to fight power.

Dina was not the only civic leader we heard describe FIGHT as "radical." (Indeed, FIGHT leaders themselves would likely identify in this way, citing their work as part of an overhaul of the status quo.) A civic innovator elaborated on this assessment: "FIGHT is always angry about something, because of their entitlement model. They think they are entitled to jobs or whatever." Civil society leaders critique social justice activists for relying on tactics that are seen as unproductive, irrational, and even amoral. Another interviewee similarly critiqued contentious activism: "There's no accountability, there's no pressure to be rational.... You can be as outlandish as you want. You don't have to sit down and explain in a calm tone of voice why you believe what you do.... I've never understood [shouting during meetings] as a means for social change. A lot of people are protesting just to ..." her voice trailed off, and she shrugged, suggesting that the groups' protests are not effective.

As we have described in earlier chapters, we frequently observed that social justice groups did not shy away from confrontational tactics. In imaginations that emphasize power, conflict is often considered necessary in combating identifiable "bad guys" or opponents, making such tactics both noble and exciting. We regularly heard and saw these activists exalt radical leaders and heroes. For example, at one FIGHT meeting, attendees were asked to role-play social justice leaders like Dr. Martin Luther King Jr., Audre Lorde, or Tupak Shakur. Bernice drew on the character of Harriet Tubman, praising the historical figure as a strong Freedom Fighter who she said carried a gun and was a tough lady.

We say that some civic imaginations center on *fighting* power because, more than other groups, their approach is closer to an actual *fight*. For them, disruptive or combative approaches, including nonviolent direct action, are oftentimes necessary to point out inequalities and bring about change. While the goal is to raise consciousness among the public, their tactics can rub some members of society the wrong way. The assertion that some activists are "always angry" attempts to dismiss the claims, causes, and actions of an activist, insisting that the cause of anger is within the activist, not embedded in society (Myers 1997).

THE CONSEQUENCES OF NARROWED IMAGINATIONS

What happened to participatory budgeting? The ball was in the court of the city councilors, who would have to earmark funds for the process to move forward, when energy for participatory budgeting dwindled. Some speculated that the supportive city councilors lacked the political capital required to reform budgeting procedures because they were newly elected. We never found out definitively what ended the conversation, if the activists were notified, or if the idea was simply hung out to dry. We *do* know that in our fieldsites, talk of participatory budgeting slowly lost steam, and eventually died out, without reforming the budgeting process of city government.

Despite never becoming a reality, the initiative to bring participatory budgeting to Providence offers a window into how various expressions of civic imagination relate to widespread inequality in America. Since participatory budgeting could be used to allocate funds for equality-oriented programs, or provide more equal influence in government decision making, the groups' orientations to inequality frequently rose to the fore. For some, addressing inequality was core to their mission; for others, it was an unfortunate circumstance of their neighborhood; and for others, it was neglected. For those with imaginations focused on fighting power, participatory budgeting was a way to foster broad participation—especially of minorities and the poor—in city politics. For those with imaginations centered on solidarity, participatory budgeting had the potential to bring residents together to share ideas and develop new strategies that would help them bond as neighbors and build a sense of community. And for those with imaginations focused on problem solving, participatory budgeting was an innovative way for citizens to address problems at the city level, finding better solutions through more accountability and transparency in city politics.

Inequality is a difficult topic of conversation. It is especially so when speaking of one's own organization or neighborhood. Groups with many members who are marginalized because of their race, class, criminal record, or immigration status will often say that "everyone" there is oppressed or part of the "working poor"—even if that is not the case. Likewise, groups with members who are primarily middle or upper income will assert that they are representative of their larger community— even if their neighborhood is socioeconomically diverse. People find creative ways to avoid saying "Black" or "White," "wealthy" or "lower income," "blue collar" or "professional." Even "poor neighborhood" can be a difficult phrase to say out loud, especially in diverse company. For groups that address inequality head-on, however, the vocabulary related to privilege and oppression comes more easily. If you attend a meeting of FIGHT, it just might be pointed out that you are White, or a woman, or lack a high school education.

How people speak of inequality reflects the priority given to it. The more euphemisms we heard, the less likely race, class, gender, poverty, and privilege were to be on the agenda. This is not surprising. However, *not* having inequality in mind seems to have a pernicious side effect: inequality is not considered in seeking other goals. In pursuing activities such as historical zoning, citizen-city meet-and-greets, and tree planting, groups that do not deliberately focus on addressing inequality regularly employ tactics that inadvertently target privileged groups and exclude marginalized populations. For example, advertisements that appear only in English exclude a large Latino population. Likewise, Facebook posts only reach social media users. We also note that often groups recognize their claims or ideals of inclusivity are not actualized, but take little action to rectify this imbalance. An Oceanside Neighbors leader acknowledges his organization is gentrified but has few plans to change;

an Engage activist agrees that the group's activities reach only a select population but argues this is justified because they have to start where their influence is greatest; and a Parkside Coalition director reminisces about discontinued programs that successfully attracted the participation of a more diverse swath of the neighborhood. Even when inequality and unequal participation are acknowledged, as they are in each of these examples, taking action to correct them is often extremely difficult.

This sort of attention (or inattention) to inequality becomes part of how groups are perceived by other organizations. For groups that explicitly aim to fight poverty, the idea of collaborating with organizations *not* oriented around social justice issues incites concerns of being co-opted or duped. These other groups, in turn, refuse opportunities to work with people focused on addressing inequality because their tactics are too contentious, the activists are too "angry."

Without a doubt, civil society faces challenges and has shortcomings beyond those described in this chapter. However, the blind spots that surfaced most dramatically in our fieldwork and analysis were *not paying attention* to inequality and *not working* to combat it. Perhaps these aspects of civic culture captivated our attention because our research was conducted in such a dramatic moment. Perhaps it is also because we have an affinity for equality, and believe it is good for individual people's lives, for society, and for democratic health.[4] But these blind spots were outstanding enough that we believe they speak for themselves.

These blind spots certainly do not arise because Americans prefer, desire, or actively promote increasing inequality. No activists told us that they did not care about poverty, or that equality and social justice are passé. Nor did any of the three groups of civic imaginations explicitly discount marginalized groups. It is not that people are unable or unwilling to imagine a more equitable world, but simply that their imaginations at times do not expand to include what is not on the agenda. Questions like "Who will we include?" and "How will we let them know they are invited?" and "How will we make them feel welcome?" can grace the conversation of *any* group—whether focused explicitly on inequality or not—but these questions must be deliberately posed.

Ignoring inequality—or exacerbating it with oblivious organizing—is *not* inevitable. Community builders and problem solvers need not abandon their passions, or, indeed, their civic imaginations, in order to work for a more just and equitable world. Solidarity and community building play crucial roles in campaigns that target inequality by bringing together members of impacted communities and their allies. And civic innovation, technology, and business-like solutions have the potential to broaden participation, rectify economic inequalities, and provide data to document injustice. But in order to meet this potential, these efforts need to be accompanied

---

4. We are not alone in our attention to inequality. As we noted in the preface to this book, the need to pay attention to and organize around inequality gained national attention in the months following our research, as the Occupy Wall Street movement provided accessible language and broadly resonant tactics for challenging inequality. The "99 percent" became common parlance, and one can now "occupy" just about anything.

by thoughtful attention to inequality, the naming of privilege, and a willingness to engage groups whose tactics are different than their own.

These arguments speak to broader questions about the relationships between inequality, democracy, and working for political change. Does it matter if not all activists choose to address inequality head-on? What harm is done if groups use euphemisms instead of talking directly about racial, class, and gender privileges, or if some people write off groups that use contentious tactics? How can all civic imaginations be expressed in ways that (at best) address inequality and (at least) do not reify it? We turn to these questions in the concluding chapter.

Chapter 7

Making a Difference in American Political Life

The activists whose stories fill these pages are committed to the public good and are working in creative ways to pursue their visions of a better society. They share a widespread sense that the political system is broken, yet a hesitant hopefulness about the future of democracy. Most self-identify as "nonpolitical," even as they do the work of the democratic public; they nearly universally demand increased participation, transparency, accountability, and more direct relationships between citizens and the government; and everyone deeply cares about making their community a better place to live. The active citizens of America believe they can make a difference. Most obviously, we saw this in their moments of celebration. When the Rhode Island governor rescinded an executive order that a civic group felt was harmful to immigrants, group members proudly proclaimed that they were directly responsible for influencing public policy and improving the lives of immigrants. We also noted their hope for political change in times of disillusionment, when people voiced such sentiments as, "We were duped! We thought the government was listening, and it wasn't." To feel "duped" by government, one must first believe, or at least hope, that a functioning democratic process is possible.

In this chapter, we draw on the many stories from throughout the book to address the questions that motivated our research: Given Americans' skepticism about politics, how and why do they engage in civic life? How do Americans' ideas shape the way they diagnose political problems, imagine better futures, and take action for social change? What expressions of these civic imaginations are particularly salient in the contemporary moment? And how is inequality understood, framed, and discussed (or not) within the activist setting? Finally, if civic engagement can take many forms, what are the tradeoffs between different approaches to working for change?

We pay special attention to inequality, a theme woven throughout the book. As we have shown, the (often unintentional) exclusion of others is a shared blind

114

spot of many contemporary civic imaginations. In a moment marked by stark social inequalities, inequality is difficult to talk about directly and even harder to address. Given this context, how might it be possible to foster a democratic conversation that promotes greater equality? In other words, how can Americans truly make a difference when it comes to addressing inequality? We offer several suggestions for engaged citizens, activists, students, and scholars: first, that reflexivity is needed to identify the strengths and limitations of one's own imagination; second, that conflict can play an important role in civic life, especially around issues of inequality; and finally, that "going visiting" to others' imaginations allows individuals to better understand the perspectives of socially distant others.

EVERYDAY ENGAGEMENT

The parallel trends of cynicism about politics and engagement in American civic life, observable through quantitative survey data, provide an important starting point for queries about American political culture. Yet quantitative analyses in and of themselves do not say much about what these trends look like and why they take the forms that they do in activists' everyday lives. Our ethnography sheds light on how people understand their relations with their community and their politicians, and how people work to make positive changes in their cities and societies.

Shared Imaginations

Participating side by side with engaged citizens in Providence, we came to understand the meanings behind the puzzling pattern of skeptical engagement. People disavow everything having to do with politics and the political, creating a distinction between the polluted sphere of politics and the positive sphere of their own engagement. Rather than understanding their participation in public life as political, citizens see it as community-minded, civic, or neighborly. Because these realms are distinct from politics, they resolve the contradiction between being cynical about politics and hopeful about democracy. By redrawing boundaries between the civic and political spheres, people distance themselves from the political—and its negative connotations of corruption, self-interest, and conflict—and create positive, esteemed identities as engaged community members. Disavowing politics in this way allows people to engage in work they believe can generate positive change. We learned this by watching, listening to, and experiencing how people disavow, and by understanding the context of their disavowal enough to understand its intended outcome.

Americans' disavowal is a creative idiom for dealing with the disappointments of politics-as-is, and articulating the contours of a democracy they desire. One of the central facets of this imagined and improved democracy is community participation. In Providence, groups advocated for an engaged populace in a variety of ways. The leaders of Engage texted, tweeted, and posted real-time updates from city council meetings, hoping citizens would reciprocate the communication and participate in the debate via digital media. The neighborhood association Parkside Coalition gathered neighbors together to plant trees and celebrate holidays, hoping that the casual conversations facilitated in these settings would strengthen connections between neighbors and make it easier for people to organize together. The social justice organization Neighbors Driving Change provided education and information about issues central to their mission and offered opportunities to interact with public officials, hoping that feeling informed and connected would bring about a sense of empowerment to work for change.

Citizens also imagined a better democracy to include a government that listened to the problems and ideas of everyday people. Providence residents testified at public hearings and stood in long lines to participate in the mayor's "open hours." As a math teacher told the school board at a public hearing, "You're begging for solutions, yet you're not reaching out to those who are offering them." She provided her contact information and implored school board members to get in touch. Citizens also advocated for more and new opportunities for direct engagement. For example, citizen participation in city budgeting was a wildly popular idea that elicited activism from civic groups and engaged citizens of all kinds.

We also heard pleas for transparency and accountability—people wanted politicians to put into action the ideas, values, and priorities of their constituents. Some groups pursued accountability by hounding politicians to follow through with campaign promises, such as when Neighbors Driving Change pushed the new mayor to rescind an executive order on immigration. Others promoted new processes meant to facilitate transparency, like the mayor's "fiscal honesty tour." When the city released data on school enrollment and budgets and opened the conversation to the public, citizens flooded the public meetings, oftentimes after scrutinizing data and crunching their own numbers. They were determined to help the city identify the most cost-effective solutions.

Finally, we saw citizens inform themselves and each other about the political process, asserting that education was central to a functioning democracy. A group of "concerned parents" from the Parkside neighborhood released the following public statement to Mayor Taveras: "In order for ... collaboration to happen, [and] for that discussion to be fruitful, we need an educated citizenry, and by that, we mean a community that has all the facts that are at play in this current fiscal crisis. If we don't have the information you have, we are at a considerable disadvantage when it comes to finding meaningful, long-term solutions for our children's education." Other expressions were more subtle. For example, members of YAK worked directly with school department officials, including the superintendent, to improve education for Black youth, so that they, in turn, could use the political system to advocate for the Black community.

Americans are trying to rescue the basic tenets of democracy in this moment of distrust, cynicism, and skepticism about government. They assert, in diverse ways, "I care about my city," "I want to live in a place in which the state is responsive to residents," and "I want my community to be empowered to make decisions about our lives." In this way, they share a common language—one that articulates the desire for community, participation, transparency, accountability, and access to information and civic skills.

Three Distinct Grammars of Civic Life and Their Blind Spots

If democratic values are a common language in American civic life, it is a language marked by several different grammars—logics that underpin how people diagnose political problems, imagine possible futures, and understand the process of achieving those futures. We call these grammars "civic imaginations," and argue that they work as cognitive roadmaps, guiding political behavior. Although every person has her own unique civic imagination, three clusters of imaginations emerged in our fieldsites: first, aiming to fight structural sources of injustice; second, building community solidarity; and third, generating innovative, business-like solutions for solving social and political problems. These are not the only possible imaginations, and they are not fixed. In one day or even a single conversation, a person may draw on different logics for why she is involved, what she hopes to achieve, and how she thinks social change is best obtained. Here, we describe each such "family" of imaginations, identifying their ideas, their expressions (how they are acted upon and put into practice), and their blind spots.

First, civic imaginations focused on fighting power assert that there are structural explanations for local and individual outcomes. This perspective asserts that conflict with the status quo is necessary for political and social change. Individuals with this imagination tend to question the interests, motives, and knowledge of elites and to advocate for increased participation of marginalized populations. Policy goals are advanced when elites are forced to address structural inequality, traditional sources of power are challenged, and the interests of marginalized groups are promoted.

A popular expression of this imagination is social justice organizing, which explicitly aims to address inequalities by organizing people who are affected by and concerned about structural injustices, such as high rates of urban poverty or discrimination against immigrants. Like any expression of civic imagination, social justice organizing has its tradeoffs and blind spots, things it fails to see or chooses not to acknowledge. Social justice groups tend to employ contentious tactics and speak directly about inequality, which can alienate some potential participants. These groups often fear co-optation by collaborators and can thus limit their coalitions to a small circle of trusted organizations. In their efforts to include marginalized individuals, social justice organizations can overlook members' own privileges. In meetings, their emphasis on inclusion and acceptance can mean spending a lot of time catching people up to speed, rehashing old ideas, and allowing people to speak off topic.

In a second grammar of civic life, civic imaginations that focus on building solidarity understand that progress occurs when people come together as a community. In this way of thinking, community input is necessary for the government to make good decisions, policy making should be transparent down to the local level, and participation is inherently good. Citizens motivated by these ideas focus on involving and working with neighbors, bringing people together, and improving their local communities. They often go to great lengths to avoid conflict, which is considered impolite and counterproductive because it can disrupt a sense of solidarity.

We saw the solidarity imagination expressed most frequently at neighborhood associations, through activities like community-building events and neighborhood crime watch meetings. In these contexts, activists often fail to reach out to members of the community who are demographically different from the organization's extant members. This can lead to homogeneous group membership, exclusion of marginalized groups, and overstating the group's inclusivity, accessibility, and geographic representation. In these expressions, inequality and diversity are often euphemized, and commitments to multiculturalism and diversity are more rhetorical than practice-based. When these issues do rise to the surface, they are typically acknowledged and sometimes lamented, but rarely prioritized.

Finally, the third family of civic imaginations is focused on solving problems. Citizens coming from this perspective believe that communication, participation, and transparent processes lead to better outcomes. This perspective values novel and innovative ideas, prefers consensus building over conflict, and often sees technology as a desirable and exciting tool. People motivated by this imagination generally believe that experts who are formally trained and well versed on a subject provide the best ideas for policy and public action. This technocratic approach is applied to a variety of problems, the underlying logic being that improving processes will inevitably improve outcomes.

The problem-solving imagination was frequently expressed by the groups and citizens we call civic innovators. Innovators tend to focus on middle- and upper-class issues. In Providence, for example, their agenda ranged from mundane inconveniences (e.g., potholes) to economic austerity (e.g., renegotiating union contracts) to urban development (e.g., boosting the high-tech entrepreneurial sector). In a city where over a quarter of residents live below the poverty line, these likely do not reflect the problems most salient in poor and working-class neighborhoods. Innovators approach the immediate problems of political life without addressing larger, structural issues of power and inequality. This may in part explain their homogeneous membership. Their inability to recruit many participants from marginalized groups may also result from reliance for outreach on digital media and social networks, which have limited reach. Like solidarity builders, innovators often speak around inequalities or rationalize them away and prioritize expertise over anecdotes, tending to downplay lived experiences of oppression.

The Tendency to Exclude

When people express their civic imaginations in groups—no matter the focus of their imagination—they tend to fall victim to two blind spots. First, they find it hard to accurately describe the demographic makeup of their own groups. Whether understating or overstating their diversity, groups struggle to define themselves as they are. These misrepresentations are related to how organizations work to recruit and retain different types of members. Some groups claim to be all low-income or all directly impacted by the social problems the group aims to address, though their leaders include college-educated professionals. When groups *underreport* their diversity, they minimize the presence of privilege in their organization and accordingly target their outreach to marginalized groups. Other groups claim to represent a diverse constituency, though membership and input come from only a narrow and more privileged segment of that population. When groups *overreport* diversity, they minimize the extent to which their organizations are homogeneous, and, accordingly, their outreach tactics do not reach the full diversity of their target neighborhoods or constituencies. By not talking about, acknowledging, or considering the demographic makeup of their own groups, activists reduce their ability to be reflexive about the narrowness of their group membership.

A second commonly held blind spot, related to the first, is that groups struggle to include people who are unlike the majority of group members. Not surprisingly, given their unawareness of their own demographic membership, groups are often unable to acknowledge how their outreach tactics exclude certain populations or to rectify such habits. For example, Oceanside Neighbors often referred to "emailing the neighborhood" for input, consultation, and data collection, but their contact lists included few residents of non-White or poor areas of the neighborhood. Likewise, civic innovator groups often rely on digital media for outreach. Network-based outreach strategies, such as sharing news with Facebook friends, do not always reach far beyond one's peer group, and the digital divide—or unequal levels of access to technology—has real consequences.[1] These examples show that in practice, groups frequently target narrower segments than they claim.

Moreover, even if new people are invited to join, or invite themselves, civic organizations can make them feel like outsiders. Even subtle choices of language can be used to define a boundary around who "really" belongs. At one public event sponsored by Open Source that emphasized bringing together new ideas and broadening civic participation, an attendee said, "All of us here probably have degrees, so we know that to be successful within society we need some form of bachelor's degree." This statement would likely have made attendees without a college education feel unwelcome. In short, groups often claim inclusivity but can exclude through their discourses and actions.

Thus, while most groups, if asked, would state that they aim to include "everyone," they often exclude significant segments of the population by using technology that only reaches particular sectors of society, deploying exclusive language, or assuming cultural norms that resonate with a narrow audience. When groups are inadvertently exclusive, it limits their opportunities to draw on varied perspectives

---

1. Only 53 percent of individuals with annual income of $30,000 or less report using the Internet or email, while 95 percent of those making $75,000 or more use Internet or email (Pew Research Center 2012). See Pippa Norris's book *Digital Divide: Civic Engagement, Information Poverty, and the Internet Worldwide* (2001) for additional discussion.

and combine different resources. In this way, marginalizing discussions of diversity and unintentional exclusion can negatively influence the ability of civil society to work for change, particularly in regard to issues of inequality. If elites are less likely to raise the issues most salient to marginalized populations, inequality may not only be pushed to the side but also entrenched.

This tendency to exclude is closely aligned with a shared difficulty of many engaged citizens: whether and how to take on the issue of rising social inequalities in the United States. People have a difficult time talking about inequality and identifying ways to address it. Inequality is conspicuously omitted from groups' mission statements, overtly dismissed as too overwhelming to take on, and deemed, with silence, a topic too contentious to raise, especially in mixed company.

This struggle for equality extends beyond the activists we followed and permeates more than the groups we joined. As we talked to our own neighbors and friends, as we read the newspaper and followed candidates through elections, as we listened to the students in our classrooms, we tuned into a broader public conversation about democracy and inequality. The difficulties of inclusion that plagued the groups in our study are not unique; rather, they permeate American society. In light of these challenging conditions, how can engaged citizens and activists foster a democratic conversation that promotes greater equality? In the following sections, we offer some ideas.

CONFLICT AND THE DEMOCRATIC CONVERSATION

The notion that conflict has a role to play in civic life has been woven throughout the book. This is not surprising, as conflict lies at the intersection of inequality, civil society, and democracy. Arguments for greater equality challenge the distributional status quo at the societal level, as well as the sense of identity, opportunity, and self-determination in individuals' personal lives. Americans' aversion to conflict, however, stands in the way of building the cross-demographic, cross-imagination coalitions that could promote a more equal country.

Many Americans prefer politics to be organized around civil interactions, polite communication, and ordered participation. One of the reasons people disavow politics is to reject the contention and confrontation required of competing interests and disagreeing perspectives, as we described in Chapter 3. Conflict and its resulting discomfort and awkward interactions are especially unsavory for people with civic imaginations oriented around solidarity building and problem solving. For solidarity builders, conflict should be avoided because it disrupts the very sense of solidarity for which they are striving. For problem solvers, conflict should be avoided because problems are technical in nature, not ideological or systemic, and thus harmonious discussion will likely lead to an agreeable outcome for all.

Of the three grammars of civic imagination, only one accepts conflict as a necessary element in working for political change. For the activists who are oriented around fighting power, speaking directly about inequality and employing confrontational tactics are necessary in order to fight inequality. Yet the fact that many Americans do not talk about inequality directly means that those who do are going against the grain. In these contexts, their talk of inequality is seen as a disturbance. It insists that attention be paid to an issue many people would rather ignore, because it may challenge their worldviews or be an uncomfortable reminder that something is lacking in their visions for a better city or community. Thus, it is not surprising that those who talk directly about inequality are sometimes dismissed by other engaged citizens.

YAK's leader, Darnell, illustrates well the inherently contentious nature of talking about inequality, as well as how people who talk about inequality can sometimes be brushed aside. When Darnell appears in public life, he relentlessly voices issues of inequality. Commenting at public events, he often opens with a phrase such as, "There is a dynamic that no one wants to talk about ..." and then speaks about class and race. When Blacks are absent from a public space, he will say, "Look how unrepresented we are tonight." Darnell's comments are meant to be controversial, because this is a way of pushing people to think and talk directly about issues they normally prefer to avoid. "People ask me if I'm angry," he told us. "Goddamn right, I'm angry. When my people are living in this condition and I know there's something systemic about it, what kind of face am I supposed to put on? I'm not going to smile like this ..." he said, stretching an exaggerated smile across his face. We have heard Darnell described as a "strong presence," and others have used stronger words. An overly civil discourse tends to dismiss voices like Darnell's, inadvertently pushing inequality—and all of its related, complicated issues—aside.

Darnell's case also illustrates the importance of conflict for the broader conversation about inequality. Conflict has long been part and parcel to the ways that marginalized groups make claims for recognition and resources.[2] In drawing attention to unequal distribution of wealth, unequal opportunity, or unearned privilege, activists are asking citizens to grapple with realities in which they are deeply invested. At the societal level, it means challenging the notion of America as a meritocratic nation, a land of opportunity for all and rugged, bootstrapping individualism. On the individual level, the implied solutions of redistribution—of shifting privilege, power, and resources away from those who hold them—can be ideologically or personally unsettling. Challenging inequality is likely to cause conflict in that it necessitates identifying groups—the haves and the have-nots, the privileged and the oppressed—and asserting which groups deserve new privileges or heightened constraints. In contexts where polite agreement is prized, describing the demographic makeup of groups is difficult, and where redistribution is not part of the national conversation, it is no wonder that inequality has been pushed from the fore.

If the popular refrain that emerged from our fieldwork is that inequality is *too contentious to address*, we argue here that it is *too corrosive to ignore*. Addressing inequality will entail conflict—not of the "us versus them" sort, as some might

---

2. On this, see our lengthy discussion in Chapters 1 and 2 and also Žižek 1999.

worry—but as a productive part of the democratic process, as many political theorists have suggested.[3] Democracy necessarily entails a boisterous competition of ideas, and there is nothing prudent in holding out hope for consensus.

Confrontation is a small price to pay in the struggle for a society in which everyone's basic needs are met and people face more equal opportunities.

For those activists who address inequality head-on and insist on talking directly about race, class, oppression, and privilege, the challenge seems to be shouting loud enough to be heard but not so loudly as to be tuned out. Even if the inequalities that shape our nation should elicit emotional outrage, not everyone is prepared to get angry.

THE CONTRADICTIONS OF GROUP LIFE IN MAKING CHANGE

In the current moment of civic life, people steer clear of controversial topics, working harmoniously is highly valued, and civic groups often find it difficult to collaborate across ideological and stylistic divides. These challenges raise important questions: How is civic engagement constrained by contemporary public discourses around inequality? How can the democratic conversation be shifted in order to meaningfully address inequality? And how do civic imaginations create such possibilities?

Here, we examine the relationship between individual and collective imaginations. As we have shown, civic imaginations are shaped by individuals' social locations (such as their class, race, or gender), as well as their personal experiences and interactions, including participation in civic groups. These imaginations simultaneously guide an individual's civic actions and are guided by collective processes.

When individuals join groups, their actions can become more consequential. Indeed, it is often in and through group life that acting publicly becomes meaningful, and that larger-scale change can happen. Yet there is a downside to collective imagining. Groups have objectives and priorities, preferred tactics, and typical pathways of action—established customs, discourses, and boundaries. These norms delineate which ways of acting and thinking are acceptable or unacceptable. Thus, when like-minded individuals come together in civic groups, both their visions of a better future and the blind spots of these visions are made more durable. As these blind spots are reinforced, the group's collective imaginations of the world can narrow, especially when membership is relatively homogeneous.

A narrow understanding of the common good is one that does not account for all of its members. It dulls public conversations about the public good, and in this way compromises democracy. Too many public discussions are rote conversations: people repeat their views, they do not really listen, and they hear only their own positions. This failure to practice empathy in public life can reinforce a status quo in which exclusions are the norm, and can seriously impede the radical transformations that many engaged citizens seek.

---

3. On this, see Mouffe 2000; Hibbing and Theiss-Morse 2002.

Of course, alternate possibilities exist. Here, as Hannah Arendt (1978) writes, the need is to "train your imagination to go visiting." To "go visiting" is to deliberately use the imagination to try to understand the needs and interests of others. It is to envision how those who are different experience the world, and—perhaps most importantly—how they are affected by one's actions. If reinforcing blind spots can be thought of as "narrowing" one's thinking, this "enlarged" thinking expands the scope of our thoughts and actions and is thus particularly important for tackling intractable and overwhelming problems. If Americans are to address inequality, their imagination of the other needs to broaden; they must engage with people whose life experiences differ from their own.

When do people feel compelled to go visiting in this way, and how can enlarged thinking occur? Here, the civic imagination is key. The civic imagination, by its nature, entails thinking about what is not reality, about what is outside of one's own experience. Thus, the imaginative power of the individual to recognize, step into, and understand another's world draws on the same capacity to imagine and work toward a better social, civic, and political world that people employ in their civic imaginations. Individuals can move beyond reliance on the patterns of thought that are reinforced by group thinking by spending time with others who are very different from them, by listening carefully to others' voices, and by experiencing others' ways of life. It is up to individuals to have the courage to push to understand others' civic imaginations, to let themselves be uncomfortable, and to directly confront others with their strongly held principles, in the spirit of genuine debate.

In civic life, opportunities to go visiting are not difficult to find, but seizing them can be a challenge. In Chapter 6, we told the story of how social justice groups, civic innovators, and neighborhood associations came together at a forum to discuss implementing a participatory budgeting initiative. A shared goal and the opportunity to sit in the same room provided a perfect moment for these diverse groups to try to talk to each other. Yet instead of sharing ideas about what participatory budgeting could yield, or how to make it happen, they suspected each other of co-optation and looked down on each other's ways of engaging. Imagine if these activists had been willing to speak directly with each other about what participatory budgeting meant to them and how best to achieve it. This likely would have involved conflicting ideas, and perhaps confrontation and impolite conversation between groups, but perhaps they could have found common ground. Would this have led to transformative change? Could it have, in a small way, eased the inequalities that mark Providence? No one can say. Without a doubt, however, it was a missed opportunity for members of civil society to go visiting, to enlarge their imaginations.

SEEING ONE'S OWN LIMITATIONS

Seeing from others' points of view is only one aspect of overcoming blind spots in the civic imagination. Enlarged thought also requires an inward-looking and reflexive examination of one's own activism, beliefs about social change and the status quo, and interactions with other engaged citizens. As we have described throughout the book, conscious and unconscious choices and the consequences of those choices—tradeoffs and blind spots, as we call them—accompany people's expressions of their civic imaginations. Some groups choose not to prioritize bilingual outreach, which limits the demographic makeup of participants at their events. Other groups choose loud, contentious tactics, at the price of alienating some people. We found that groups often underestimate the consequences of these tradeoffs, which at times go directly against their intended and stated goals. Blind spots and their consequences are not inevitable, and tradeoffs need not be so stark. Here we show how being reflexive might help people in each family of imaginations to enlarge thought and go visiting to better understand people with different perspectives.

Problem solvers hold one of the most important keys to working for social and political change: fresh ideas about how citizens can connect more directly and more frequently with the state. Although these methods often privilege elite expertise over the knowledge of ordinary people, this does not necessarily have to be the case. A problem solver can make a point to recruit, listen to, and include the ideas put forth by marginalized populations and nonexperts, without compromising her belief that technology and new innovations can address social problems. Recognizing that lived experience is an irreplaceable type of expertise might allow problem solvers to address less visible perspectives and find unexpected common ground with "different" types of groups.

Community builders have found ways to bring together like-minded neighbors with similar interests and backgrounds and to leverage these relationships to solve the problems they have in common. Even though their outreach strategies and cultural habits may create environments where only a narrow segment of the population is included, this does not have to be the case. Community builders can make a point to look for diversity and inequality in their communities and their events, and then they can consider how their choices might contribute to this inclusion or exclusion. Small changes—in meeting times and locations, outreach methods, and multilingual offerings, for example—might help organizations meet their goals of serving an entire neighborhood, embracing diversity, or offering a space that welcomes everyone.

Activists who fight against power shine light on issues of social justice and the complex systems that underpin them. Their highly visible activities and bold accusations of who or what is to blame generate attention, but this sometimes comes at the cost of alienating people who are not comfortable using combative language or confrontational tactics. Without compromising their priorities or theories of social change, these activists can make their social action more welcoming, hospitable, and accepting of people who prefer more institutionalized approaches—like petitions, electoral campaigning, and policy research.

Being reflexive about one's own civic imagination is important not only for actively engaged citizens in Providence and elsewhere but also for students, researchers, and readers thinking about civic life.

We hope readers and students will consider what their civic imaginations owe to their social locations and lived experiences, and what they might have in common—or not—with the characters highlighted in this book. The notion of civic imagination can help make sense of diverse patterns of discourse and engagement, and how these are connected to social location, personal experiences, and group dynamics. The act of reflecting on one's own imagination promotes a deeper understanding of how ideas about social change have consequences. How one thinks about one's self, community, and work have implications for how one attempts to make a difference in political life—which problems to work on (or ignore), how to engage one's community, and which populations are empowered or marginalized as a result. In particular, we hope that those who are in the midst of defining their own paths of activism will consider how to avoid or mitigate the behaviors that can prevent broad participation, cross-cultural collaboration, or coalition building and that unwittingly perpetuate inequality.

We hope to have provided a model for researchers, scholars, and journalists studying American civic life to do so through collective, interdisciplinary ethnographies; to investigate seemingly unlike organizations, objects, or themes in the same study; and to develop qualitative and ethnographic explanations for documented trends or quantitative puzzles. This book provides one example of approaching diverse fieldsites with an equal openness to distinct ideas about making a difference in American political life. Behind the scenes, we have also attempted to go visiting in the worlds of the civic leaders with whom we worked—actively putting ourselves in the shoes of those individuals who people these pages. By sending multiple researchers to the same event, writing collaboratively, and working across disciplines, we have challenged each other's assumptions about what we experience in the field and how to make sense of these experiences in light of our own civic imaginations.

A particular focus of this book has been on the ability of civil society to meaningfully address inequality. To this end, we hope engaged citizens, students, activists, and researchers alike will take an interest in considering the forms and consequences of their own imaginations as they relate to issues of inequality. The limits of imaginations are both identifiable and rectifiable—but addressing them is not enough. The practices of going visiting in others' worlds and embracing the (often uncomfortable) conflict that comes from working with others are also part of enhancing the collective capacity to take on the most intractable problems of our time.

MAKING A DIFFERENCE BY CHANGING THE DEMOCRATIC CONVERSATION

America's active citizens are working hard to envision and create a better tomorrow. Civic imaginations generate optimistic visions of the future and guide the everyday actions that try to make those futures possible. Yet the desire for change and a plan to achieve it are not, on their own, sufficient. Americans are disappointed in their political system. Inequality is rampant, oppressive, and growing. And people often put great energy into participation, transparency, accountability, and citizen-led change, but in spite of their efforts, meaningful change toward equality—even in one's own community—is often unrealized or in short supply.

Yet the public conversation about inequality, civil society, and democratic promise can be improved. Concerned citizens can make a difference by promoting a democratic conversation that regularly and openly addresses inequality. The public discussions and debates that sustain democracy require more reflection on the limits of our imaginations, more empathy and understanding about what others experience, and the patience and will to work through conflicts that arise when political issues are on the table. Such change is possible.

Of course, changing the terms of the conversation alone is unlikely to lead to a more equal world, and, as we have noted, making a difference in political life also requires a shift in the policies and structures that actively cause or passively reinforce inequalities. Yet we focus on the public conversation because we believe it is there that meaningful social change begins. For this reason, we close with a simple reflection, as relevant for each one of us as it is for any of our readers: How can we, individually and in the groups through which we engage, contribute to a democratic conversation that changes our society and promotes equality? How can we, in our thinking, as well as in our words and deeds, create a democracy that works with and for all of its citizens? Therein lies the power of the civic imagination.

Methodological Appendix A

How Many Scholars Does It Take to Answer a Question?

ANSWER: FIVE!

The five of us, four eager graduate students and one faculty member excited about doing research in a new way, officially gathered for the first time in May 2010 in a classroom at Brown University in Providence, Rhode Island. Alissa and Stephanie prepared to take notes on the whiteboard in the front of the room, Elizabeth and Peter opened their computers to digitally document our discussion, and Gianpaolo began explaining the origins of the research we were about to undertake and some of his ideas for *how* we could go about undertaking this research.

> I see this as a one-year group ethnography on the post-political and civic reform. It seems like a good second project for everyone. We'll do research together for a year and then write together for a year.... The collaborative nature means that this is not an RA [research assistant] project. It means we are equal partners. I don't see it as having different sites where we each research a different place. It's something that we will write together. We don't have a lot of models for this, but my colleagues who have done this sort of thing say this collective process is a good one.

We immediately started exchanging ideas about the people and groups we could follow, outlined how we would "map the field" of civic engagement in Providence, and talked about the scholarly literature that we would want to engage. Our experiment in fully collective research and writing had begun.

Our methodological approach, "multi-sited collective ethnography," can best be described as one part mundane logistics, one part uncomfortable reflexive moments, five parts scholarly inquiry, and ten parts epic teamwork. This appendix narrates the epistemological decisions and serendipitous events that made up our research trajectory. We draw on detailed meeting notes and email correspondence, as well as personal reflections and group memories of our research. It is an effort to fully disclose our process, opening the black box of the ethnography we conducted. By showing the messiness and false starts that are so central to the craft of social science, but so often absent from final, published products, we aim to make the implicit explicit, defining our unique approach within its humble origins.

To this end, we identify and discuss the elements of this approach that "worked," as well as those aspects we have come to consider tradeoffs or shortcomings. We share some painfully intricate details that scholars interested in replicating or adapting our methodology will find useful, but we also imagine this appendix may resonate with a more general audience interested in epistemology, ethnography, or collective research. We also reflect on ourselves as a team of privileged, liberal, Ivy League–affiliated researchers studying issues of immigration, racial discrimination, economic inequality, urban development, and politics. To conclude, we offer both recommendations and our very best wishes to researchers who adopt or adapt our methodology to answer their own questions. The second appendix, "Life of 'Project,'" is written not by us but by Tatiana Andia, an ethnographer who studied our group and process in this context.

FINDING OUR PEOPLE

Our cast of characters consists of four PhD students and one senior faculty at Brown University. The professor (Gianpaolo Baiocchi) and two of the graduate students (Alissa Cordner and Peter Taylor Klein) were in the Department of Sociology, and the other students were in the Department of Anthropology (Stephanie Savell) and the Department of Political Science (Elizabeth A. Bennett). Each of us has a background in activism or social justice, but our experiences are diverse: Gianpaolo has been intimately involved in urban issues and participatory budgeting, Elizabeth in international development and trade relations, Alissa in environmental advocacy, Peter in conflict mediation and violence among youth, and Stephanie in social entrepreneurship. We took on *The Civic Imagination* as a collective "side project," research supposedly second in priority to our own areas of investigation, but also as a life experience—a communal inquiry into scholarship, neighborly relations, and what it means to be a committed and engaged member of one's community.

In spring 2010, an "un-protest" organized by the "un-partisan" group we call Engage caught Gianpaolo's attention (we talk about this in the beginning of Chapter 5). The language of "un"-everything was eye-catching, but what struck him was the group's approach to increasing participation in local politics: the rejection of "politics" and "partisanship" was remarkably different from the discourse of FIGHT, another Providence organization also working to increase public participation in city politics but through different tactics and with different end goals. Gianpaolo was intrigued by two socially distinct groups setting the same objective—improving public access to and participation in the political process—but choosing dramatically different paths toward reaching it. He began to formulate research questions: How do these groups understand civic life? How do they develop an aspirational, imagined civic community?

A few weeks later, in a meeting about the graduate Qualitative Methods course they were co-teaching,[1] Alissa and Peter talked with Gianpaolo about developing a collaborative ethnographic project in Providence. Alissa and Peter were interested in gaining experience with ethnographic methods and learning more about Brown's host community, and Gianpaolo was keen to investigate the questions raised by Engage and FIGHT. Gianpaolo circulated a three-page memo about the potential of "new" forms of civic engagement, about how they compared to "traditional" activism, and how their work resonated with scholars' claim that we are living in a "post-political" era. This memo became the seedling for *The Civic Imagination.* Casual conversation, shared research interests, and a history of enjoying each other's company brought Elizabeth and Stephanie into the collaboration, and the quintet was born.

MORE SALAD THAN MELTING POT

Immediately, our team defined itself as collective and interdisciplinary. Having recently had a positive experience with collective writing and editing (Alvarez et al. forthcoming), Gianpaolo was enthusiastic about extending the model to be a fully collective research and writing process. He set the tone by insisting we discard the traditional cross-rank relationship of "principal investigator and research assistants," and share decisions and responsibilities equally. Our team's equitable relations were reinforced by the fact that Gianpaolo was not the provider of funding. Over time and in practice, however, we did not achieve this goal of full parity. The differences in academic position were evident in that the students conducted more of the fieldwork, while Gianpaolo had the responsibility of training students in interview methods, guiding the negotiation of a book contract, liaising with Brown's Institutional Review Board,[2] and providing office space and professional connections. Despite the occasionally unequal distribution of responsibilities, we constantly worked toward parity, and in the end, the project was more egalitarian than any other faculty-student collaborations we had experienced or heard about.

If the "collective" aspect of our multi-sited collective ethnography was evident in the beginning, it only became more central over time. In March of the research

---

1. Alissa, Peter, and Gianpaolo describe this co-teaching experience in their article "Co-Designing and Co-Teaching Graduate Qualitative Methods: An Innovative Ethnographic Workshop Model" (Cordner, Klein, and Baiocchi 2012).

2. Institutional Review Boards approve and review all research activities involving human participants. These boards weigh the risks and benefits of participation to help protect the health and best interests of research participants. For information, see the Office for Human Research Protections, which is part of the US Department of Health and Human Services (http://www.hhs.gov/ohrp).

year, we named our collectivity "Project" with the capital *P* of a proper noun, loosely inspired by Latour's *Aramis* (1996), a book that depicts an object (a personal rapid transit system) as having a voice and agency, or an idea that is larger than the sum of its parts.[3] Project was credited for our written output; Project had relationships in our fieldsites; and Project demanded hours of attention. When one privileged his or her principal line of research over Project, it was noted that Project "felt neglected." Project made sure that no one took credit for brilliant pages of writing or felt inadequate for missing a deadline. Project refused to keep score of who had completed which tasks, or which ideas belonged to whom. Project had five heads, but only one mind, and we would often comment that this mind was more than the sum of its parts.

AN INTERDISCIPLINARY SEARCH FOR CIVIC IMAGINATION IN THE FIELD

Project's first task was fieldsite selection. We aimed to "map the field" by identifying all of the groups in Providence that explicitly worked to "make the city a better place to live." We started by listing groups and individuals we knew to be "active" in the city's civic scene. Individually or in pairs, the team met with these actors to learn about their individual trajectories in Providence activism, the objective of their work, tactics employed, funding, perspective on the 2010 political races, and a description and explanation of "what is wrong with Providence," and how these problems could be addressed. We completed each interview by asking, "Who else wants to make Providence a better place? With whom should we meet?" We combined this snowball sampling with Internet-based queries, a reading list about Providence's history, and regular consumption of Providence-based media. To track current events, each researcher was responsible for monitoring an online news venue, and archiving and sharing potentially relevant stories.

After a few months of mapping the civic landscape in Providence, we selected fieldsites, a task each of us identified as a particularly challenging element of working across disciplines. The field of potential sites was broad and diverse, and included youth empowerment organizations, communities of faith, ethnic clubs, neighborhood associations, partisan drinking groups, and grassroots networks. How would we decide which groups to study? Site selection brought out the disciplinary biases of each researcher. We differed on how to connect theory and evidence, on the purpose of a research question, and on standards for "good research." We debated the issue of representative sampling, how to and whether we even should categorize groups in Providence, and in which sites we would have the best access (and how that should affect our selection process). Ontological differences were exacerbated by (real or imagined) pressure from a depressed academic job market, which pushed

---

3. Although Aramis died before it was born (Latour 1996), Project went on to become the book you have in your hands.

the four graduate students to worry about how Project would be received by future hiring committees.

The team labored for weeks to develop and employ a site selection process. Gianpaolo asserted that we should be careful and somewhat deliberate in our site selection, but that "we'll get good info from wherever we are—[we] can't really go wrong." For some, this approach raised anxieties and inspired alternative proposals. Elizabeth presented a two-by-two table contrasting traditional and innovative organizations with organizations that worked toward social justice or giving voice; Stephanie suggested we identify categories and choose one group per category; and Alissa worried that any typology would fail to capture the differences and commonalities among groups. Our methodological impasse was gentle—for example, Gianpaolo responded to Elizabeth's two-by-two scheme by suggesting a less rigid system of plotting organizations on two axes—but nonetheless conflicted. The issues of representative sampling, typologies, and access were revisited over and over throughout the process. There were numerous ways we could typologize these groups—they were issue-based, place-based, and identity-based; they were conservative, reactionary, and innovative; they were well-established or remarkably young; they worked locally, nationally, or internationally; they were gentrifiers and anti-gentrifiers. Identifying the sources of conflict helped us to build consensus on fieldsite selection. Stephanie noted that she had been pushing against any preconceptions in our project because, as an anthropologist, she uses *field-based* participant observation; all the while, Gianpaolo, as a sociologist, was using *theory-based* participant observation. Alissa brought in the sociological "middle-ground," suggesting that participant observation connect to both theory and the field—the need to narrow what we're looking for while being open to what emerges. In contrast, Elizabeth noted that, as a political scientist, she was frustrated because case selection ought to be *informed by a research question* whose answers would contribute to existing theory.

In the end, we decided that typologizing in advance of intensive fieldwork could introduce bias, and that we would adopt a symmetrically open approach to all groups, instead of looking for evidence that supported our presupposed categories. Finally, in September 2010, we agreed on the seven fieldsites introduced in Chapter 2. As is often the case in ethnography, our final decision was based on a combination of the practical, the empirical, and the theoretical: we selected groups to which we already had access or anticipated success in negotiating access, and which were active enough to offer a variety of opportunities for fieldwork; we chose groups that were particularly interesting; and we tried to cover the field in a way that would likely lead us to answers about our research questions. We acknowledged that it was impossible to talk to everyone and study every group, and decided to be attentive to how people in our fieldsites talked about the whole of Providence civil society and, as we commented in our meeting notes, "how they think about who is included. Our fieldsites don't need to reflect everyone in Providence but have to represent what we claim to be talking about."

In part, our decisions were influenced by the methodological interventions of actor- network theory, which directs social scientists to follow the actors, interrogate structures, and approach research symmetrically (e.g., Callon 1986; Latour 1987). In particular, the principle of symmetry, which we describe in Chapter 2, inspired us to select cases that are not typically studied together, and then apply a uniform and evenly agnostic framework. Cases that would not typically be studied together include social justice organizations led by former convicts and Marxists, neighborhood associations run by middle-class homeowners, and passion-projects founded by Ivy League business school graduates and sponsored by local elites. This symmetrical approach is unique for three reasons. First, ethnographers have traditionally been more likely to "study down," despite long-standing calls for "studying up" and "studying sideways" (Nader 1974; Hannerz 2006). In other words, researchers have tended to study marginalized populations rather than elites or the middle class. Second, rarer still are studies that *simultaneously* study up, down, and sideways. We selected cases that would span this spectrum of social groups. In the end, we felt we were often studying sideways in that our team had much in common with many of the people and groups we studied: we lived in the same neighborhoods, we attended some of the same types of schools, and we had similar work experiences before entering academia. Finally, our symmetrical treatment of diverse sites leaves open the possibility of comparative studies, but does not predetermine how groups are similar or different, or what the important similarities or differences will be.

Of course, the arduous process of fieldsite selection was no antidote for self-doubt. In the months that followed, we questioned our decision to only study organized groups. Was it correct to ignore the civic imaginations of the truly disenchanted, the marginally involved, or the everyday "good citizen" who eschewed organized engagement? Alternatively, we worried that some sites were not organized enough to be considered groups, or that the groups' memberships overlapped too much. We were concerned about missing demographic groups or substantive issues not taken up in any of our fieldsites, a concern that rekindled old debates about representing the field. In these moments, we regained self-assurance in our site selections for two reasons. First, we found ourselves able to follow and understand news, meetings, and informal conversations about civic life in Providence: we knew the key actors, were familiar with organizations, could appreciate the conflicts, and often caught the meanings of inside jokes or doublespeak. Second, our fieldnotes were speaking to the research questions in interesting, helpful, and challenging ways. To be sure, data were speaking to theory. The process of fieldsite selection had two results: the obvious—choosing fieldsites—and the unintended, but equally important, effect of understanding each other's epistemological and disciplinary positions.

DIVIDE AND CONQUER! (OR NOT)

As we developed our methodological approach to working with seven fieldsites, we drew from a few of the (relatively rare) examples of collective ethnography. This method had been carried out in two ways: first, multiple researchers studying a single fieldsite; and second, multiple researchers each studying a distinct fieldsite, to compare those sites according to preestablished similarities and differences. Ethnography of the first sort traditionally involved husband-wife teams, but other scholars have taken up this approach. For example, sociologist Javier Auyero and anthropology student Debora Swistun co-researched and co-wrote *Flammable* (2009), an ethnography of a polluted Argentinean neighborhood. Another example is the team of six researchers in Finland who carried out collective ethnographic studies in the mid-1990s on secondary school and gender (Tuula et al. 2006). Reuben May and Mary Pattillo-McCoy (2000), whose participation in a larger ethnographic project most often involved distinct fieldsites but occasionally involved joint fieldsite visits, reflect on those moments when they attended the same event to highlight the benefits and challenges of group ethnography. We found fewer examples of collective research of the second variety—in which multiple researchers independently study the same social phenomenon across multiple, discrete sites. A team of six anthropologists headed by Jennifer Hirsch (2009) conducted a multi-sited comparative ethnography on marriage, secrets, and infidelity across five different countries. Another example—one closer to us thematically—is *Local Democracy under Siege*, a book researched and written by a team of faculty and graduate students that studied patterns of civic and political engagement across the United States (Holland et al. 2007). Our methodology is indebted to both versions of collective ethnography, and to each of these studies, but ultimately pushes into uncharted territory.

Project's diversity of backgrounds and disciplinary training provided a unique opportunity for methodological innovation—to view each of seven sites through five lenses. Thus, the goal became for *each of the researchers* to know and feel comfortable at *all of the fieldsites*. Whenever possible, two or more researchers would attend one event and write shared fieldnotes. While this was simple in theory, it proved difficult in practice. We succeeded in that each organization's leaders knew each of the researchers by name, each researcher was able to find meeting locations, and each of us was familiar with the norms, stories, activities, and quirks of each organizations. However, each of us felt more comfortable with some organizations than others, and over time, each organization identified one or two point people among the five of us. That person would receive organizing phone calls and emails, and would be inquired about if another researcher attended an event at the site. We realized that although we could aim to treat seven sites symmetrically, we could not expect seven or more group leaders to treat five researchers equally. Additionally, some sites were more active than others, or moved in different ways. For example, Neighbors Driving Change had several meetings at the same location each week, while Engage became primarily an online presence, and YAK often announced events by phone only hours in advance. Our research sites often flowed (or clashed!) together in city events. For example, when Providence mayor Taveras proposed closing several public schools, subsequent public hearings and organizing meetings brought several fieldsites into a single space (see Chapter 4 on civic imaginations and the school closure situation), but not always on the same side of the issue (for another example, see Chapter 6 on participatory budgeting).

Our multi-sited collective ethnography provided three main benefits. First, researchers gained cross-site perspective, allowing them to place site-specific observations in a broader context. For example, the school closing issue was described and explained to us by innovators with an antiunion orientation, parents interested in sending their children to neighborhood schools, social justice activists concerned about educational equality across the city, and an outspoken antiracism organizer with a strong structural approach. The diversity in their reactions to the same event helped us to probe our concept of civic imagination early on in our research project. A second benefit of a collective approach was that our sites were each observed through five lenses, informed by five different life experiences. For example, Elizabeth identified elements of liberation theology and Base Christian Communities—familiar to her from years of working with grassroots movements in Mexico—in Neighbors Driving Change. Gianpaolo alluded to the World Social Forum in his conversations with FIGHT. Similarly, Stephanie was better positioned to understand the language of civic innovators, whose businesslike rhetoric was reminiscent of her time working for Ashoka, a nonprofit organization that supports social entrepreneurs around the world. The civic innovators' "Government 2.0" language at Engage was completely foreign to Alissa, but was common parlance to Stephanie. These differing reactions among researchers allowed them to unpack their own biases, and the team helped each other to critique what they initially accepted, and find empathy for what otherwise elicited skepticism or even disdain.

Lastly, this type of collective approach addresses the critique that ethnography as a research methodology can be very subjective. The lone ethnographer's view of the world is informed by personal baggage, personality, past experiences, and a host of other factors that inevitably influence the research he or she is doing. Five lenses on the same actors, events, and phenomena help overcome or at least mitigate the biases created by these factors by providing a sort of "checks and balances" system. We were able to talk about the same events from different perspectives, wrestle with what we observed, and debate what we thought actors meant by what they said or did. The symmetric, collective approach to a fieldsite honors but is not paralyzed by the ontological position that "there is neither one truth, nor one reality, nor one stable social world to observe" (May and Pattillo-McCoy 2000, 65).

GIVING AND TAKING: ACCESS, RULES, ROLES, AND RECIPROCITY

Early on in our fieldwork, we met with leaders from each group to explain the general nature of our interest, discuss our five-researcher approach, and request the opportunity to attend meetings, participate in events, and observe and learn as researchers. In the spirit of reciprocity, we asked how we could help each organization meet its objectives. Our offer to volunteer was accepted by each organization, and we found ourselves serving in myriad ways: taking notes at membership meetings, staffing reception tables at events, doing data entry, marching and rallying, running errands, researching policy documents, and drafting grants. Some of the less conventional ways we returned time and energy to our fieldsites included cleaning up pumpkin guts splattered from a trebuchet while wearing a cow costume; selecting words for and competing in a teen Scrabble competition; and going door to door in low-income neighborhoods to educate residents about foreclosure alternatives. We declined any requests to serve as leaders because we were concerned about impacting the fieldsites. We wanted to observe and participate, but not to direct (Lichterman 1996). For the year of research, we also declined to provide public comments about hot city issues on the behalf of organizations, because we were concerned about being associated with one group or one political position.

Our acts of "reciprocity" not only reduced our guilt about Project's consumption of organizations' and individuals' time and resources but also built rapport and provided unique insight into civic imaginations. For example, one of our fieldsites requested that we distribute fliers advertising their upcoming meeting. Although the organization claimed to represent the interests of a whole neighborhood, we were instructed to prioritize the distribution of fliers to the areas around board members' homes, and only pass out the invitations to other, less affluent, areas if time and resources remained. The concept of representation became something that we focused on when studying this group.

TEN HANDS, FIVE LAPTOPS, ONE DATASET

From May 2010 to June 2011, we attended over 150 meetings or events, and generated over 500 pages of detailed fieldnotes. We recorded notes at fieldsites in whatever way appropriate—most often handwriting in a notebook, but sometimes typing on a laptop, jotting on a napkin, or simply making a mental note. The fieldnotes included a general narrative of who said and did what at the events we attended, with special attention to several topics, including who was there, attendees' relationships to each other, what norms guided interactions, what happened when norms were broken, how we or others (especially newcomers) were included or excluded and by whom, how physical space was used, what seemed important to leaders, how decisions were made, what language was appropriate, where boundaries were drawn, how groups differentiated themselves from the other groups we studied, what claims of representation were made, how some things were (or were not) "political," how motives for action were described, how civic problems were discussed and explained, and what role was played by Brown University and its students.

Right after a fieldsite visit, a researcher would type up detailed fieldnotes in a Word document describing the experience [and adding personal reflections or thoughts in brackets]. We each wrote in a designated text color: Gianpaolo in red, Elizabeth in green, Alissa in purple, Peter in orange, and Stephanie in blue. When multiple researchers attended the same event they produced a joint fieldnote, with the "primary" writer creating a full record and the "secondary" adding additional descriptions [and bracketed reflections]. This allowed us to disaggregate description from comment, and to connect data to researcher. Project's digital data management system was developed by trial and error, but in the end provided a reliable, intuitively organized dataset. Fieldnotes were titled "date_organization_event name_researcher initials" and filed in the organization's folder. The five researchers shared a Dropbox folder to facilitate online file sharing and syncing (www.dropbox.com). We also collected data on the context in which our groups were operating by continuing to monitor local news and blogs, spending time at popular hangouts, and "friending" organizations and individuals on Facebook. We circulated relevant stories to each other by email; filed hard copies of fliers and handouts in our shared office; and archived electronic copies of emails, news stories, and documents in Dropbox.

The conclusion of our fieldwork year presented two tasks: choosing pseudonyms and analyzing data. Although we had used groups' and individuals' real names in our discussions and fieldnotes, we decided to substitute real names with pseudonyms in our published writings to protect confidentiality. We recognize that certain individuals or organizations may be readily identifiable to Providence insiders and to the people themselves. Certainly, this added to an already strong sense of responsibility to our research subjects. The more difficult task was developing a method to review our collected data. Remaining true to our collective process, four of the researchers spent a weekend on the coast of Maine creating a coding scheme of twenty-three codes, ranging from issues (e.g., immigration) to concepts (e.g., disavowal) to potentially useful fieldnotes for writing (e.g., group history). We divided our data evenly among researchers, with each of us reading and coding one fourth of the fieldnotes. After this initial pass, we each read another quarter of the fieldnotes so that in the end, each fieldnote was coded by two of us and each of us had read half of the data. At the end of this intensive reading and coding retreat, we discussed what stood out to us, what surprised us, and how this coding would help us move forward as we developed conceptual and theoretical ideas about our research. [We hope these details are helpful to readers!]

CONNECTING THEORY AND EVIDENCE

While Project had a strong theoretical foundation, it also saved space for theoretical discovery. Project's theoretical trajectory was based on Gianpaolo's early interest in how the Providence case challenged or exemplified scholars' assertions about the post-political era (e.g., Žižek 1999; Rancière 1995) and on our collective interest in the literatures on civic engagement (e.g., Skocpol 2004; Alexander 2006), actually existing civil society (e.g., Eliasoph and Lichterman 2003), and social movements (e.g., McAdam, Tilly, and Tarrow 2001). We also embraced some of the methodological innovations of actor-network theory, such as following the individuals we were working with and taking them seriously, avoiding taking concepts of "politics" or "engagement" for granted, resisting using a particular predisposed framework or metanarrative to understand what we were seeing, and acknowledging that political projects require coordination and assembly. However, we rejected the notion that the world is "flat" (Latour 2005, 172), insisting on recognizing that power does matter, even if we need to interrogate "power" as a concept for what it does for people, situations, and scholars. Project could not ignore structure—in Providence, it was evident that people have varying levels of access to decision-makers, different understandings of the role of racism and class oppression in their daily lives, and different beliefs regarding the role of the state and thus the type of political change they wanted to support.

To facilitate the process of linking our fieldwork to theory, our weekly meetings rotated among three activities: (1) discussing fieldnotes and fieldsites; (2) sharing memos on readings and conversing about theory; and (3) drafting thematic analytical memos linking the theory and data. The goal of this rotation was to identify concepts and questions in the literature that resonated with our fieldwork and to target our fieldwork observations to gather data related to theory. This practice was heavily influenced by social scientists who provide guidance on the practice of going back and forth between theory and method, including Michael Burawoy's ethnography workshops (e.g., 1991) and his "extended case method" (1998), Robert Alford's construction of arguments (1998), Howard Becker's "tricks" of social science research (1998), and Arthur Stinchcombe's work on the relationship between concepts and data (2005). For example, in the fall of 2010 we read literature on American sociology of culture and civil society, including selections from Lichterman's *The Search for Political Community* (1996), Bellah et al.'s *Habits of the Heart* (2008 [1985]), Eliasoph's *Avoiding Politics* (1998), and a methodological chapter by Lichterman on "Seeing Structure Happen" (2002). Each researcher wrote a memo summarizing and discussing the readings, and commenting on how our observations seemed to support or challenge them. As a result, five concepts—boundaries, customs, interests, vocabularies, and outcomes—became the objects of special attention during the early stages of fieldwork. We continued reading about these concepts (e.g., Lamont 2001) and added codes in brackets to our fieldnotes for easy searching (e.g., [CUSTOMS]). Over time, we realized that these concepts and the existing literature could not explain everything we were experiencing in the field, so we repeated a similar process with additional concepts, including interests, political disavowal, and inequality. The iteration between theory (literature) and fieldwork led to spirited conversations among the five of us as we developed the concepts and arguments now included in this book.

WE FOUND WE HAD SOMETHING TO SAY ...
BUT HOW TO WRITE IT DOWN?

Project was committed to collective writing—not just collective fieldwork—from early on. Notes from a meeting in May 2010 contain this telling mandate: "Once you write a chunk, it's not yours. You write and then the group works on it together. Line by line." But without a doubt, writing and theorizing together was exponentially more difficult than researching as a group. Ernesto Ganuza, a Spanish sociologist with experience in collective writing (e.g., Ganuza et al. 2010), came to a Project work session to provide reflections on our process. He highlighted the importance of agreeing to move through impasses after a certain period of deliberation, even in absence of consensus. "As long as you keep on moving," he advised, "that's more important than full consensus." It was sage advice, but we often ignored it. Writing with ten hands is slow and frustrating, and often led our group in circles and to dead ends. However, the redeeming aspect of collective authorship is that the ideas produced together were consistently better than what any one of us had brought to the table individually.

The process of learning to write together commenced with modest goals. Sometimes we all wrote memos on a single question or theme, and then talked about our work and made notes about what we could collectively conclude. For example, when our disavowal concept began to emerge, we each wrote a general memo on what it meant, where we saw it, how it interacted with what we had read, and what questions our fieldsites might be able to answer about it. Together, we debated, compared, discarded, and synthesized the pool of ideas, producing a sloppy collective list of ideas about disavowal. Another early activity was a one-paragraph proposal for a panel at a regional academic conference. We graduated to several conference papers, (unsuccessful) funding applications, and a book proposal. A difficult and tedious learning experience was an attempt to move the conference paper about disavowal to a journal article. We divided the paper into sections, and wrote, cut, pasted, and produced a horrible paper that repeated vignettes, never came to a point, used terms inconsistently, and read terribly. It took us over a year to identify its problems, solve them, and submit it to a journal, but through this process we adopted a new approach. We passed the article from one person to another, each researcher taking on a task that was enjoyed and was important before giving it to the next writer. This process paid off: as this book went to press, our article "Disavowing Politics: Civic Engagement in an Era of Political Skepticism" was forthcoming in the *American Journal of Sociology* (Bennett, Cordner, Klein, Savell, and Baiocchi forthcoming).

As we mastered (or at least managed) the process of writing an article, another opportunity and challenge presented itself: writing a book. In August 2011, after circulating a collectively authored book proposal, we signed a contract with Paradigm Publishers in Boulder, Colorado. Our overambitious goal was to produce the manuscript—and two articles—within a year, finishing by August 2012. Since each researcher was moving away from Providence or traveling for extended periods of time, we commenced our "writing year" with a three-day retreat in Las Vegas, where we had convened for the American Sociological Association Annual Meeting. We developed concepts, worked on arguments, outlined each chapter in great detail, and assigned tasks due at our midterm retreat in January 2012. Our approach was modeled after our article-writing method. We assigned two researchers to each of the four chapters due in January, and anticipated that the subsequent chapters could be written in a similar fashion by June. All of these drafts would be discussed among the larger group, and revised by someone outside of the pair of authors.

It should not have surprised us that our writing year compounded extant challenges and brought new ones. With authors scattered across continents and time zones, our meetings relied on stable Internet connections, availability of quiet work spaces, and flexibility to schedule meetings at odd times of the day. Our meetings became less frequent, technological difficulties with phones and Internet service slowed conversation, and the demands of our primary research projects detracted from time available for Project. We sorely missed the in-person meetings that allowed for thought-provoking conversations and relatively rapid group development of ideas. When we reconvened for a weekend in Providence in January 2012, we were abysmally behind schedule, and still lacked a well-developed main argument. As it turned out, collective theorizing and writing is even slower and more frustrating across time and space than it is in person. We clarified our conceptual and theoretical arguments, and reaffirmed our commitment to collective writing, convinced that the benefits would outweigh the drawback of snail-paced progress. In 2012 we continued along the arduous path of collective work—chapters written in pairs, a group discussion to critique substance, and circulation to others to revise. We also pushed back our deadline for completing the book. Twice.

By the fall of 2012, our final deadline of March 1, 2013, was in sight, and we faced more challenges, new and old. In an exaggerated iteration of our logistical problems, we found ourselves holding meetings over three continents, four countries, and five different time zones. Fieldwork, job searches, and other projects became even more demanding. Technology continued to interfere. And other problems related to writing such a lengthy manuscript presented themselves and demanded attention. We had different writing styles. We disagreed on how to use fieldnotes. We arrived at different theoretical conclusions, applied and defined concepts inconsistently, and made contradicting arguments. Whether it was the way a quote was used or how a concept was developed, each of us found ourselves disagreeing with elements of the book.

It was in this context that two of our most important lessons emerged: First, just write. Second, let go. We developed a pattern of reaching consensus in discussion, then discovering differences in reading the prose developed from group conversation. Hashed out on paper where we could dissect and debate each other's arguments, we saw internal inconsistencies, weak connections between theory and data, and incomplete arguments, but we also learned to value writing as a way forward. Developing ideas together was fun and fruitful, but it was not until those ideas were drafted that we were able to tear them apart, debate the options, and rebuild based on group consensus. By writing, we moved forward. The pressure of late 2012 and early 2013 taught us the second important lesson about collective writing: letting go. Each of us, while spearheading a particular chapter, would inevitably draft arguments and make points that excited us, or that we found particularly insightful. When shared with the group, however, these points were often debated, and sometimes dismissed in favor of an alternative. We each faced a difficult balance between feeling ownership over the writing, on the one hand, and deferring to group consensus, on the other. Phrases like, "That was not my starting point, but I can see why you want to move in that direction, and I can be OK with that. Please don't take it as far as . . ." became commonplace, and easier to articulate and to hear over time. What we published is not what any of us would have written on our own, but it is something we all stand behind.

By January 2013, we had drafted all but the introduction and conclusion. Collectively, the chapters presented a new problem: our method had led to a book that read like a series of articles. With the pressure of time growing unbearable, we held near-daily meetings over Skype. We went through the chapters one by one, and everyone commented on each chapter. We addressed everything from overarching arguments ("What is the difference between what is imagined and what already exists?") to stylistic details ("'fieldnotes' is one word, not two"). Individuals and pairs were assigned to chapters, using the comments and notes from our group meetings to revise. These frequent calls reinvigorated the group, as did encouragement and constructively articulated criticisms from our reviewers. We were inspired to (finally!) write the introduction and conclusion, and debate, rewrite, and revise the manuscript as a whole.

To write collectively, we found, is to write fieldnotes together, think together, draft sloppy memos together, create arguments together, outline together, select poignant vignettes together, and craft prose together. It worked best when the group created a detailed outline; two people wrote a first draft; the three remaining authors circulated the draft for comments; the whole team discussed, debated, refined, rehashed, and reenvisioned; and one of us who had not created the first draft finalized revisions. *That*, in our experience, *is how collective writing gets done!*

FEEDBACK AND REFLEXIVITY

Throughout the research and writing processes, we elicited feedback about our work from social science colleagues in several ways. We organized conference panels and presented at professional association meetings such as the Eastern Sociological Society and the American Sociological Association. We also consulted experienced ethnographers and researchers who have participated in collective research to provide suggestions regarding our methodological approach. As we wrote the book, we shared chapters with nearly a dozen scholars around the country, asking for honest comments and critique. We also sought advice and reactions to our work in some less conventional ways. For example, we invited five academics in Providence to be on a "Friends of Project Board" to review our early work and provide feedback in the spring of 2011. They read about our project's theoretical scaffolding and methodology, and spent hours over Cuban food and red wine reflecting on everything from the post-political to power dynamics of the Brown-Providence relationship. In another group discussion of our work, we shared working drafts of chapters as part of a political ethnography workshop at the University of Georgia. These interactions provided both moments of validation and critique. Colleagues reminded us that no method is perfect, praised our commitment to reciprocity, reiterated the importance of our research questions, and expressed respect for the ability to work collectively—especially across professional rank and discipline. They also offered pointed analysis and challenges to our work, which we hope we have addressed in ways that have improved the clarity of our arguments.

In addition to the productive critique of our theoretical and conceptual work, a frequent challenge put forth by our academic community was about the need to be reflexive in our ethnographic practice given our social location as five Ivy League–affiliated mostly White folks from educated families.[4] We frequently discussed the question of reflexivity—awareness that the *researcher* matters for the research process and product. Together we had read feminists and reflexive sociologists (e.g., Wacquant 1989; Bohman 1999; DeVault 1999) and took to heart the notion that the researcher is not an "invisible, anonymous voice of authority" but a real, historical individual with "concrete, specific desires and interests" and that his or her beliefs and behaviors are part of the empirical evidence used in advancing claims (Harding 1987, 9).

Brown University has an enormous and often messy footprint in Providence. On the one hand, Brown students often eagerly participate in the city's life by volunteering at its nonprofits, organizing fund-raising efforts, and using organizations as research sites. In fact, the president of Brown estimated in 2012 that the university will provide over $50 million in voluntary contributions over twenty years (Simmons 2012). This means that Brown's presence is highly visible and often acknowledged as a desirable contribution to the community. Not surprisingly, a number of the actors in our fieldsites were Brown students and alumni. But on the other hand, Brown is chastised as a land-grabber and catalyst of gentrification. When Mayor Angel Taveras took office in 2010, he shocked Providence residents with news of deep, serious budgetary problems. In the fiscal crisis that followed, he announced that several public schools would close, and the conflict we document in Chapter 4 ensued. Community activists framed Brown and other tax-exempt institutions as sources of the city's financial difficulties, highlighting the contrast between the university's wealth and the city's poverty, and stressing the injustice of town-gown relations.

At our fieldsites, we learned about (and in some cases were pointedly reminded of) other student researchers who had "parachuted" in, completed their agenda, and departed without a contribution to their host. Unable to shed our affiliation with—and real connection to—Brown's baggage, our solution was a commitment to reciprocity and clear communication with organizations about our purpose and timeline. We were also conscious of the fact that all of us were privileged by our Whiteness, by the current and prospective benefits associated with Brown, and by the good fortune of health and healthy appearances. We found ourselves highlighting different aspects of our identity in different forums; Stephanie's previous affiliation with Ashoka or Elizabeth's protest at the World Trade Organization, for example, were social currency in some circles but not others. Likewise, we found ourselves dressing differently, using different language, and taking on different habits of punctuality at various sites. We

---

4. Gianpaolo is Brazilian, identifies himself as Latino, and speaks Spanish as well as Portuguese. Brazilians in the United States occupy an ambiguous place in relationship to the broader Latino identity (Beserra 2005), an issue compounded by many Brazilians' unease with the category, especially in locations with the presence of other Lusophone groups, like Rhode Island (Marrow 2003). In his case, also, the privilege (or stigma) associated with being "Brown faculty" was often an overwhelming marker.

struggled with these multiple identities and, most of all, with what we missed in the field because of who we were in the context of the field.

We also talked about how "epistemic privilege" (DeVault 1999, 44) varied among our group. At a fieldsite that focused on structural injustice, we realized that the experience of men and women researchers was very different, something that came to be important in how we understood the leaders' civic imaginations. At another site, the ability to speak or understand Spanish influenced researchers' observations. Likewise, our own backgrounds in activism and social change biased our observations of others' civic imaginations. Protesting, using market-based solutions, and risking arrest stirred up different associations within each of us. For example, Alissa had developed a visceral discomfort with canvassing and aggressive leadership development after working for a poorly run environmental organization. Elizabeth felt at home with the leftist slogans and references to American imperialism of one group—they reminded her of the organization she had worked for in Mexico for two years—but was critical of the "market-based solutions" other groups touted because of her dissertation research studying the greenwashing of fair trade. Similarly, Gianpaolo's prior involvement with the Right to the City movement and participatory budgeting made him empathetic to the struggle of pushing for citizen control of city budgets. Our weekly meetings about fieldsites often served as a forum for reflexive musings, and we gently helped each other to understand and work with our own lenses.

Another part of our reflexive practice was to include the actors from our fieldsites in the process of analysis. We wanted to be accountable to those affected by the methods and findings of our research, and we wanted to leverage forms of epistemic privilege that eluded Project—the knowledge that can only come by occupying the spaces that we could not access (Bohman 1999, 465). At the end of our research year, in June 2011, we requested a meeting with leaders at each of our fieldsites, where we summarized our thinking on disavowal and the civic imagination. We were clear that the purpose of these meetings was eliciting data, not correcting our findings or "fixing" our interpretations. The feedback was enlightening. One social justice leader responded to a question about disengagement by saying, "It's not an issue of apathy; it's an issue of hopelessness and not believing in the power of collective action to facilitate change." Another civic innovator told us, "Civic engagement does not produce the added value."

Perhaps the most original innovation in feedback and reflexivity was to accept a request from Tatiana Andia, a student ethnographer, to conduct an ethnography of Project. "Project's Ethnographer," as we called her, joined our weekly team meetings, reviewed our group meeting notes, and attended gatherings. Her reflections can be read in Methodological Appendix B.

MULTI-SITED COLLECTIVE ETHNOGRAPHY: THE GOOD, THE BAD, AND A FEW SUGGESTIONS

The sections above describe the process of muddling through by trial and error, rethinking and revising, and planning and scrapping to develop a methodology that we now neatly package and present as multi-sited collective ethnography. In this method, investigation takes place at *multiple* fieldsites that are approached symmetrically, and the research team works *collectively*. These attributes stand in contrast to typical ethnographic methods in three ways: (1) typically, ethnography is conducted at a single fieldsite or perhaps a pair of sites, but our approach examines multiple sites; (2) multi-sited ethnographies usually begin with a comparative design based on assumptions about the similarities and differences across cases, but our approach studies cases that differ on several dimensions without prefabricated expectations for comparative analysis; and (3) research teams generally divide fieldsites and individually author chapters, whereas the *collective* approach requires sites and writing to be shared. Like any method, multi-sited collective ethnography is an appropriate method for some research questions and contexts but not others. This section suggests when this method may be appropriate for social science research and examines some of the benefits and shortcomings of the approach.

The decision to employ multi-sited collective ethnography depends on the research team, the fieldsites, and the theoretical framework. Most obviously, during the data collection phase, all researchers must be located near the fieldsites, which must be located in the same general location to allow regular attendance at all sites by all researchers. In the writing phase, the team must either be able to meet deadlines remotely or arrange for regular meetings and multiday work retreats. We ourselves missed internal and external deadlines and heard several collective-writing horror stories from colleagues in which geographically separated writers were unable to prioritize the project, either dragging it out over a decade or killing it completely. This method is also most suitable for a team that is diverse in a way that is conceptually meaningful to the project. In our case, we each had been "civically engaged" in different ways before studying civic engagement, and our varied disciplinary training, life experience, and distinct areas of expertise led to different manners of thinking critically. Additionally, diversity in skills (e.g., foreign language competency) among group members can help ensure access to varied fieldsites, as it did in our research. We also recommend convening researchers whose philosophies of science are capable of coming to methodological consensus.

This method may not be appropriate for fieldsites in which individuals are sharing sensitive information, or where exceptionally strong personal rapport is required, as information will be shared among researchers, and each researcher will spend only a portion of his or her fieldwork time at each site. For example, in studying a domestic violence facility for teen women, it would likely not be appropriate for a researcher to expect to build rapport in twice-monthly visits, or for actors at the fieldsite to accept that their stories will be recorded and shared with four other researchers. It was very helpful for us to study the interaction among fieldsites that occurred at public events, such as the presentation about participatory budgeting at Brown we discuss in Chapter 6. Thus, a field involving public debates and discussions may be particularly suited to this method. As discussed in the section about fieldsite selection, it is difficult to disaggregate the notion of multiple fieldsites from the concept of representative sampling. This method may thus be less suitable than random sampling survey methods for some research questions. However, we found our multi-sited symmetrical approach to be particularly useful for drawing similarities across groups typically not studied together.

Volumes have been authored about the challenges of ethnography, and we do not aim to repeat them. However, there are several difficulties that are particular to—or more prominent in—multi-sited collective ethnography, even in the context of an ideal team, suitable sites, and appropriate theoretical grounding. First, despite our intentions, we felt sympathies and antipathies about our various fieldsites, and reinforced them as a group with inside jokes and under-the-breath comments. This challenged our ability to treat groups symmetrically. The method is also incredibly time intensive, and we struggled to draw boundaries between what field experiences were important and which were not. We also faced difficult group dynamics, especially about creating priorities under time constraints (e.g., all researchers coding every fieldnote versus all researchers coding half of the fieldnotes, to save time for discussion) and how to approach writing and argument development (create an outline of an argument, fill it with data, and turn it into prose versus loosely organizing thoughts by musing in writing, and seeing the argument after you have written). We also face the downside that none of us can reference Project's output as our own—a chapter will not serve as a writing sample on the job market, and all credit is divided by five, resulting in a plethora of "Baiocchi et al." authorships. Our imagined solution to this problem (rotating lead authorship and the production of four distinct articles in addition to the book) was difficult to implement.

Despite these challenges, the method served us well. As discussed throughout this appendix, we employed different lenses, drew on different skill sets and demographics to increase access, and could attend five times as many events (including those held simultaneously!). In writing, our interdisciplinary background has prevented us from overuse of disciplinary jargon and the assumption of common theoretical background, making the output (we hope) accessible to a wider readership. While no method will be universally successful, we can reasonably expect that any collective ethnography team that uses the symmetrical, multi-sited approach will also enjoy these benefits. What we *cannot* say with any certainty, however, is whether you will also experience five heads becoming one mind. We credit Project for making that happen. Project convinced us that sometimes, it really does take five social scientists to answer a question.

Methodological Appendix B

Life of "Project"

Tatiana Andia

You know ... when you do participatory things ... or group things ... things really do take a life of their own.

—Gianpaolo Baiocchi

INTRODUCING PROJECT

A group of people working on an ethnographic project about politics in Providence, Rhode Island, gets together every week to discuss their research. At the moment they are working on the notion of "disavowal"—the idea that while civic organizations reject or disavow politics, usually seeing it as contaminated, they actually actively participate in politics themselves. On this particular afternoon the work seems really challenging. The collective conceptualization process is further complicated by the fact that there are five people in the group, that they want to "do justice to the field," that they want to publish something soon, and that they all have to balance the time they invest into this process with all of their other commitments.

I present here an ethnographic picture of the group. I attended their meetings for several weeks as an observer, had access to their meeting notes, and interviewed all the group members for this research. In addition, I also participated in many of their other informal activities, like having drinks with a subset of them at the Graduate Student Bar. In time, I became more familiar with the notions of "disavowal," "civic imagination," "ambiguities," and the difference between "politics" and "political." But since you can read the product of their work in this book, I don't summarize their arguments here.

Instead, in this ethnography of ethnography, I focus on something else that happened in those weekly meetings and other gatherings, apart from discussions about civic groups' forms of political engagement. I am referring here to the

145

formation of a group: its name is Project. To get to know Project, I decided to follow the actors themselves and listen to their accounts. As Latour would suggest, I tried to "learn from them what the collective existence [became] in their hands, [and] which methods they elaborated to make it fit together" (Latour 2005, 12). I was invited by the group to publish these fieldnotes and reflections as an appendix to the book that was the end result, as an additional lens on the process itself. With the exception of the one identifying detail noted below, and minor feedback on language and style, no one in the group had any substantive impact on the contents of this appendix.

It is important to warn, however, that what I will present here is an incomplete picture of Project in at least two ways: First, I did not observe Project's members while they were observing others, but only when they brought back their data and processed it indoors—that is, I participated with the group and observed most of what happened in their fourth-floor lab, but I have only a partial idea of how the inputs for the production of their facts were collected. Second, I have added my own interpretation to the actors' explanations, and in the process I have decided to emphasize the aspects of Project's experience that seemed important to me but that may not be perceived as important by members of the group.

My main argument is that Project is a case of meaning-making (Wedeen 2008, 2009) and boundary-making (Gieryn 1983; Lamont and Molnar 2002) that places both ethnography and collective participatory interdisciplinary work at the center of a subaltern way to go about social research. Moreover, I argue that meaning-making and boundary-making are two sides of the same coin: the meaning-making practices are also boundary-work.

Meaning-making practices are the observable ways in which people make sense of their world, and boundary-work includes the "kinds of typification systems, or inferences concerning similarities and differences, that groups mobilize to define who they are" (Lamont and Molnar 2002, 171). Moreover, boundary-work is an instrument for professional distinction that allows a group to define who they are through contrast to what they are not—to expand, monopolize, and protect their autonomy over an academic territory (Gieryn 1983, 791–792). Based on these definitions I argue that Project's sense of "groupness" comes from some iterable practices (rituals) that (re)produce the idea that Project, unlike most social science work, is a participatory enterprise for knowledge production.

Through participatory rhetoric and practices, Project became both a way of producing social science research that was carefully crafted as distinct from conventional scholarship and, at the same time, a lens through which its members could see and understand their world. Collective political ethnography, with all its ups and downs, is both an academic territory owned by Project and a way to give meaning to Project's and its members' academic lives. However, Project's rhetoric and participatory lifestyle were in contradiction with the zealous maintenance of boundaries as to who can participate in Project. Just as Gieryn describes science, Project is at the same time democratic (everyone in the group is equally listened to and informants are not put into boxes) and elitist (only its members and selected "experts" can comment on what they do) (Gieryn 1983, 792).

In this short piece I want to accomplish two basic goals: (1) illustrate how Project performed participation; and (2) argue why this can be considered boundary-work.

PERFORMING PARTICIPATION

I first met Project on a Friday afternoon. I bumped into Stephanie, one of the members of the group, in the restroom, and she told me that she was very happy about my doing an ethnography about Project. I looked at her, puzzled. I didn't know what she was talking about.

She quickly realized she had made a mistake. She grabbed her mouth like trying to stop any other words from coming out, and she then said, "Ohh ... Gianpaolo hasn't told you?... He told us and we agreed that it would be nice for you to do it ... but I am sure he is going to tell you ... so act surprised." In fact, I later was told that the five of them as a group had agreed that I could work on an ethnography about Project. Only later did it become evident to me that "agreeing as a group" was a recurring practice within Project.

I encountered this "agreeing as a group" practice in many forms. Project agreed as a group on who should go to which fieldsite on a particular week, following availability and pertinence criteria; how to move forward after a three-hour meeting; what individual tasks each of the members should carry out in a given week; and how they should relate to the outsiders:

> Suddenly, they turn to discussing about whether they should work for one of their organizations. Apparently, the person in charge of this particular organization (XX) had asked them to attend some events and do some work.[1] This person is coming today after the meeting and they need to have an answer by then.
>
> Elizabeth argues that it is not a good idea because they don't share their politics. Alissa then clarifies that Project's name won't appear. Elizabeth says that this could be contaminating the field unnecessarily, and that they don't owe them and that this won't grant them better access either.
>
> I feel that the rhythm of today's meeting is slower.
>
> Gianpaolo remembers that they said they were going to try to be more symmetrical and agnostic, although he doesn't like XX either.
>
> Peter argues that is important to do what they ask for the purpose of the research, but nobody seems to see the point. Alissa, Elizabeth and Stephanie argue that working for them won't help them understand anything better and it will be a pain!

---

1. The nature of the work requested was struck from the fieldnotes in order to preserve anonymity of the group in question.

Peter insists that, in between, they will get the criteria the organization uses to decide what to tweet and so on. Stephanie looks at Peter while he talks and starts nodding. She seems to be changing her mind and says that maybe they could use this to make some experiments reporting things that XX would reject and seeing what happens.

Then Stephanie brings up a transparency issue: "I feel we should probably be honest about how we feel about working for them."

Alissa is also changing her mind. She says that perhaps they should figure out what this person does and how she does it; like follow her. Immediately Gianpaolo picks up and says, smiling: "Yes! We have to follow the actors!" A collective laugh invades the room and Peter starts making fun of Alissa saying that this is precisely what she does, she disavows and then she just does it!

They keep reflecting about what they like and dislike about this organization, and conclude that it depends on the topic. Some things that they do are just fine.

Stephanie says that maybe Peter should be the one engaging with them, since he has posed it in such a nice way.

Gianpaolo just confirms by reaffirming that he dislikes them emotionally but he can see how they have to respect them. Elizabeth also agrees and says: "Yes, you guys bring great points that I haven't thought about before."

Twenty minutes have passed and XX's representative arrives. The meeting is over. (Fieldnotes 4/18/2011)

On this occasion, even though some members of the group continued to be hesitant about the work idea, an agreement was reached and communicated as a monolithic and consensual decision to the person on the outside of Project—in this case, the representative of XX organization. Hence, "agreeing as a group" is not just a demanding practice whereby Project decides on different issues based on a deliberative democratic logic and that distinguishes it from many other academic collaborative efforts. "Agreeing as a group" is also a way of demarcating what only Project members know and can access, from what people on the outside perceive.

Another episode may illustrate this point further:

Stephanie has to leave early and right after she leaves Project starts discussing my access. Alissa is sitting next to me. She turns around a bit so that her torso would face me. She looks at me in the eye; she usually looks at everybody in the eye and almost perfectly divides the time of her speech evenly, so that everybody's eyes would get the same amount of attention.

She argues that she doesn't have any problem with me coming to their meetings, but that she would not feel ok with me going to private meetings with their groups. Everybody nods in agreement, so we decide that I would only attend public events. I asked that they point me to those ones when they occur [I never attended any]. Then, Alissa says that they had decided not to grant me access to their fieldnotes, and that they still have to discuss further if I should be able to see their meeting minutes. I stand up for myself saying that regarding those minutes we can have a different approach in which I can discuss my findings with them, so that I don't misinterpret anything, and in order for them to be able to filter any sensible content. The conversation is in that way postponed.

Finally, we talk about the focus of my ethnography, and Alissa again says that she won't feel comfortable with me focusing on their relationships with their groups. I say that that is not my interest considering that I don't feel I could gather enough data to do that. I quickly and very preliminarily hint that I could focus on the collaborative process or on the politics involved.... That last sentence created a strange silence (or maybe it was just my impression)....

Gianpaolo touches the table with both hands and says, "I am fine with whatever you decide to do." Peter nods. (Fieldnotes 04/06/2011)

Up to that point, it seemed that an incomplete agreement, in which only some members of the group fully agreed to something, could prosper. However, a couple of weeks later, something else happened, which reassured me that the practice of "agreeing as a group" could take more than one round, but it would be adhered to.

Peter wrote to me today after the interview he gave me. The email contained a draft of the agreement Project wants me to sign before they can share their meeting notes with me. The agreement reads as follows:

Memorandum of Agreement

The ethnographer will be granted access to meeting notes and memos that were generated for internal purposes. She may not publish the contents of these documents or findings based on these documents without the permission of all five authors: Gianpaolo Baiocchi, Elizabeth Bennett, Alissa Cordner, Peter Klein, and Stephanie Savell.

This agreement is not meant to restrict scholarly inquiry, reflexive practice, dissemination of findings, or critical feedback to the authors. It is intended to prevent wholesale slander based on misinterpretation or distortion of our research process.

I exchanged emails with Elizabeth immediately afterward. This was meant to be communicated to me as a "Project preference" despite the fact that not everybody felt equally strongly about it. (Fieldnotes 5/6/2011)

In this and many other instances, deliberation continued until Project had a preference, even if its preference contradicted Project's founding principles. Project was ethnographic and participatory, and yet refused to be ethnographically participated in.

"Agreeing as a group" goes also beyond quotidian decision making and of course beyond deciding what type of access to grant to the ethnographer or how to control the product of her research. It is also the way in which they go about producing knowledge.

Knowledge production happens in several places, but the "agreeing as a group" about concepts tends to happen mostly in Project's office. The first time I came into the office it shocked me that it indeed seemed like a collective office: It has no desk, but a big table in the center of the room, although there is one little table with a computer. Unlike any other office with a desk, here the computer was facing the door so that everybody sitting at the table could see the screen.

The office is full of pictures. There is a board and next to it there is a timetable made of a sequence of letter papers simulating a vertical calendar. At that time the last date on the calendar was somewhere in June, but those dates have gradually been pushed forward as they adapt to the incredibly slow process of reaching enough agreement to collectively write a paper.

The pace of the process has affected the morale of the group more than once; as Elizabeth said, "I am surprised about how overwhelming and slow this process is." But, no matter how tired or discouraged, they would never violate the "agreeing as a group" principle. This is possible only because the frustration is transitory and is usually followed by two types of moments:

- A *moment of realization*, such as when after reading everybody else's memos Elizabeth said, "It's not as disjointed as I thought it would be," and she laid out how they were individually influenced by what they thought collectively in the former meeting and then they took it away with them and it came out in a way that ultimately made their memos fit really nicely together.
- An *aha moment*, which is a moment of breakthrough, in which in the midst of the discussion they all see the same thing and a bunch of "this is great," "this is really productive," and "this is neat" are released and float for a while around the room.

Gianpaolo interrupts saying that he has a thought. He has been thinking about the difference between politics and political.

"Political is what the literature on post-political talks about, but this doesn't always match politics.... So in the schools' case for example, there is disavowal of politics but not of the political. They want to tax the rich but they despise politics." [This is referring to the fact that the post-political literature assumes that people won't engage, or will avoid fundamental conflict about inequality.]

Gianpaolo says: "As far as I know nobody has done this before"—i.e., talking about this distinction in the way they could. "We should discuss this to figure it out collectively."

Alissa says that she understands it as ideas = ideal type = the political = civic imagination. And that practices = politics.

Gianpaolo is taking notes. His notes are very scattered; he writes very few words like they were dots in the middle of the page and then he circles the more important ones. He uses a Moleskine notebook and a blue Lamy fountain pen.

Peter has a really bad back pain so he has a blue heat bag on his lower back under his t-shirt. He says: "I feel this whole politics versus political thing makes everything more muddy instead of clearer to me."

In the meantime Elizabeth was drawing, so Gianpaolo asks her what she had been doing there and she shows her drawing to everyone to help clarify the politics-political matter.

Stephanie says: "I'm with Peter. I don't see it as meaningful."

I was sitting next to Gianpaolo so I could see his foot moving a lot, but particularly rapidly at some moments. Like when Alissa asked if he had arranged the interviews as he promised he would do [but he didn't]. It seems as if he moves his foot faster when there is some disagreement in the group . . . like a sign of positive anxiety.

Peter argues that maybe the best thing would be to go back to the data and let the data speak. Maybe it is too soon to start doing two by twos and fix the categories.

Gianpaolo goes back to his point about why this distinction is this important. The point is that they are not talking about how people avoid the inequality conversation . . . and then Elizabeth and Alissa nod in agreement and say, "We are talking about more than this type of disavowal."

They finally settle the dispute . . . their disavowal is different from the post-political one where people disavow only the political, which in turns leads to neoliberalism.

Gianpaolo says, "And in reality you can see both. . . . This is what is great about Project."

Alissa leaves to bring some water. When she comes back she asks, "Did I miss something seminal?"

Elizabeth then says that this notion of "politics vs. political" is about the object and not the language. . . . Alissa says, "This is nice!" (Fieldnotes 4/11/2011)

However, "agreeing as a group" is not only about revelation moments; it also requires consistent work to keep at bay theoretical affinities that are not shared by all. This has been particularly evident in the case of Latour, because many of the group members would like to have him as a main methodological guide in this process, but since not all of them share that position, Latour just needs to be bracketed and kept as a periodic joke.

As Peter explained to me one day while making fun of the whole Latour issue, apparently Project was kind of obsessed with Latour, and after some of the members took a course about it, some sort of Latour Club was created from which Peter felt excluded, given that he couldn't take that course. Alissa did take the course, but she feels differently about it.

ALISSA: Being surrounded by people who are talking about Latour all the time, when I have a strong disavowal of Latour, it's made me think much more carefully about what I actually believe, and why I feel strongly about the things that I do.

TATIANA: So that disavowal about Latour . . . so you didn't take that course. . . .

ALISSA: The whatever it was . . . the Latour class . . . last fall.

TATIANA: So it was just that when you read it you were not convinced.

ALISSA: Yeah! The more I read ... the more I read the more I felt like ... I mean there are certainly virtues of it. There's really interesting things about Latour and from my understanding of how science and technology studies evolved from the '70s, '80s, and '90s, sure he was very refreshing and needed.... Some of his ideas like the idea of translation or the idea of looking at practices is great ... it's really great.... But a Latourian perspective misses so much ... and you can't ... you can't see everything if you're only looking at things close up.... You can definitely see interesting things but you can't explain, you can't elaborate out from the one lab or the one controversy that you are looking [at].... And I don't think social science is good just for explaining. I think that there are serious problems and inequalities in the world that all of us care about, that is why I want to do research and not because I'm interested in how people organize their test tubes but ... where do they get their money and why are they all White men, and things like that ... and he can't explain stuff like that.... So the more I read the more I felt like he was kind of a like a right-wing talk show host ... you know ... speaking so passionately, and using generalizations and using compelling anecdotes but just not ... not explaining the world that I see. (Interview 6/16/2011)

Collectively deciding or "agreeing as a group" about everything, from the tiniest detail to the most substantive decision, is definitely one of Project's main characteristics. As described above, Project members did not actually agree about many things, but they did value the extenuating deliberations and the partial consensus that was reached after them. The deliberative logic then is a procedural logic that created some boundary-work in the sense that Project's members knew that this respectful valuing of everybody's position and collectively deciding distinguished them from any other group. As Alissa said clearly to me in an interview,

I think when you have five people all thinking about the same thing, it can sort of twist and turn in unexpected directions, ... and it's been neat to see that you can have five people with very ... different theoretical and different empirical perspectives on things, and sort of end up aligning when you spend so much time discussing an issue.... That's been neat.... It's been a very good exercise for me in group process ... because (*laughs*) we all work really differently.... I think Elizabeth and I work more like each other and Peter and Stephanie work more like each other, but there are differences between all four of us and how we work ... and I've got myself, not into trouble, but I've ended up in places where I thought I understood that we were doing one thing and others thought that we were doing different things and so we end up not in the same place.... I think because ... in other projects that I've collaborated on there is normally one person who is maybe in charge or taking the lead in a given project ... and in this one I think we are all pretty careful not to feel like anyone is stepping on anyone else's toes and so it's hard to not have a leader in some of these projects.

I think that we are all the type of people that like to get things done, and so we are extra delicate to not infringe on other people's creative lives and thought processes and none of us wants to be bossy about where we think the project should go and so then we end up.... I think because of that, because we are all very aware that we all have our own thoughts and our own brains and everything, we end up not moving forward as quickly as we could if someone was taking more control ... but if someone was taking more control it wouldn't be the same dynamic. (Interview 6/16/2011)

Of course, Project is distinct from many other groups in that they deliberate, and end up making some decisions with which all of them are at least partially comfortable, but this deliberative procedural logic is not the only thing that gives meaning to Project or distinguishes it from other academic groups doing some boundary-work. This deliberative democratic logic is only complete when articulated with the other participatory practices.

Project "agrees as a group" because it challenges hierarchies, both in terms of academic stature and in terms of gender dynamics within the group, and—though less successfully—between academics and practitioners in its relationship with the outside world. For example, almost obsessively, Project rejects the idea of "putting people into boxes."

Alissa says that civic imagination and disavowal are connected; they could happen at the same time.

Elizabeth concludes that this is a great case for not matching each disavowal with a civic imagination.... One could have three types of disavowal paired with just one civic imagination.

Stephanie says that people don't articulate all their disavowals.

Alissa says ... "What is unique about our approach: we don't put people into boxes; but we take multiple versions and explain them." ... Elizabeth adds, "We are able to make connections that other people can't." (Fieldnotes 4/27/2011)

Project also "agrees as a group" because it crosses disciplinary boundaries, which are far more difficult to identify than social scientists may want to believe—in Elizabeth's words, "It's hard to tell what's disciplinary and what's personality." Finally, agreeing as a group is at all possible because all Project members are in solidarity with each other and are deeply committed to Project, not only in terms of work but also in terms of keeping professional and other types of anxieties at bay. Project cannot be contaminated.

TATIANA: Do you think transparency is a really valuable thing within Project ... so you think everybody is being very transparent? Are you?

ELIZABETH: Transparency within the five of us? Or more like when we are representing Project in front of other people?

TATIANA: Among you.

ELIZABETH: I think ... (*silence*) I think transparency is important.... I am thinking about transparency as being forthcoming about what is going on and very candid ... and I don't think it's something that we've done very well, because we are really nice to each other? And I think it's a priority to maintain good relationships and we haven't had any major blow-out yet, so I don't think we are comfortable calling each other out on things that are really difficult. . . . So it would've been nice sometimes if we've said things like you need to get here on time or you didn't do this thing or (*silence*) . . . I really feel like you haven't read this. (Interview 5/19/2011)

CONCLUDING REMARKS: GUARDING THE BOUNDARY

Political ethnographers have delimited their professional territory as one in which the researchers look at politics as it unfolds in the small world of everyday interaction between ordinary people (Lichterman 2005b; Baiocchi and Connor 2008). Thus, political ethnographers look at "politics under a microscope" (Auyero 2006). But, within the boundaries of political ethnography, Project does something else. As I described, Project erected yet another boundary, one that methodologically distinguishes them from their political ethnography peers. Project decided to look at politics under the microscope through participatory decision making, and in the process they owned and guarded that particular professional territory.

References

Adams, Maurianne, Warren J. Blumenfeld, Carmelita Castañeda, Heather W. Hackman, Madeline L. Peters, and Ximena Zúñiga, eds. 2000. *Readings for Diversity and Social Justice: An Anthology on Racism, Antisemitism, Sexism, Heterosexism, Ableism, and Classism.* New York: Routledge.

Alexander, Jeffrey. 2006. *The Civil Sphere.* New York: Oxford University Press.

Alford, Robert. 1998. *The Craft of Inquiry: Theories, Methods, Inference.* New York: Oxford University Press.

Almond, Gabriel, and Sidney Verba. 1963. *The Civic Culture.* New Jersey: Princeton University Press.

Alvarez, Sonia, Gianpaolo Baiocchi, Agustín Lao Montes, Jeffrey Rubin, and Millie Thayer. Forthcoming. *Interrogating the Civil Society Agenda: Social Movements, Civic Participation, and Democratic Innovation.* Durham, NC: Duke University Press.

American Community Survey. 2011. "2006–2010 American Community Survey 5-Year Estimates: Poverty Status in the Past 12 Months." Accessed February 2, 2012. http://factfinder2.census.gov.

ANES (American National Election Studies). 2010. "Guide to Public Opinion and Electoral Behavior." Accessed March 12, 2013. http://www.electionstudies.org/nesguide/gd-index.htm#5.

Ansolabehere, Stephen, and Shanto Iyengar. 1995. *Going Negative: How Political Advertising Shrinks and Polarizes the Electorate.* New York: Free Press.

Appadurai, Arjun. 2004. "The Capacity to Aspire: Culture and the Terms of Recognition." In *Culture and Public Action,* edited by Vijayendra Rao and Michael Walton, 59–84. Palo Alto, CA: Stanford University Press.

Arendt, Hannah. 1978. *The Life of the Mind.* Edited by Mary McCarthy. New York: Harcourt Brace Jovanovich.

———. 1992. *Lectures on Kant's Political Philosophy.* Edited by Ronald Beiner. Chicago: University of Chicago Press.

———. 1994. *Essays in Understanding: 1930–1954.* Edited by Jerome Kohn. New York: Harcourt Brace.

Auyero, Javier. 2006. "Introductory Note to 'Politics under the Microscope: Special Issue on Political Ethnography I.'" *Qualitative Sociology* 29 (3): 257–259.

Auyero, Javier, and Debora Swistun. 2008. "The Social Production of Toxic Uncertainty." *American Sociological Review* 73 (3): 357–379.

———. 2009. *Flammable.* New York: Oxford University Press.

Baiocchi, Gianpaolo. 2005. *Militants and Citizens: Local Democracy on a Global Stage in Porto Alegre*. Palo Alto, CA: Stanford University Press.

Baiocchi, Gianpaolo, and Brian Connor. 2008. "The Ethnos in the Polis: Political Ethnographies in Sociology." *Sociology Compass* 1 (3): 139–155.

Baiocchi, Gianpaolo, and Lisa Corrado. 2010. "The Politics of Habitus: Publics, Blackness, and Community Activism in Salvador, Brazil." *Qualitative Sociology* 33 (3): 369–388.

Baiocchi, Gianpaolo, Patrick Heller, and Marcelo Silva. 2011. *Bootstrapping Democracy: Transforming Local Governance and Civil Society in Brazil*. Palo Alto, CA: Stanford University Press.

Barry, Francis S. 2009. *The Scandal of Reform: Grand Failures of New York's Political Crusaders and the Death of Nonpartisanship*. New Brunswick, NJ: Rutgers University.

Bass, Alan. 2000. *Difference and Disavowal: The Trauma of Eros*. Palo Alto, CA: Stanford University Press.

Becker, Howard. 1998. *Tricks of the Trade: How to Think about Your Research While You're Doing It*. Chicago: University of Chicago Press.

Bellah, Robert, Richard Madsen, William Sullivan, Ann Swindler, and Steven Tipton. 2008 [1985]. *Habits of the Heart: Individualism and Commitment in American Life*. Berkeley: University of California Press.

Bennett, Elizabeth. 2012. "Global Social Movements in Global Governance." *Globalizations* 9 (6): 799–813.

Bennett, Elizabeth A., Alissa Cordner, Peter Taylor Klein, Stephanie Savell, and Gianpaolo Baiocchi. Forthcoming. "Disavowing Politics: Civic Engagement in an Era of Political Skepticism." *American Journal of Sociology*.

Bennett, Stephen. 1997. "Why Young Americans Hate Politics, and What We Should Do about It." *Political Science and Politics* 30 (1): 47–53.

Beramendi, Pablo, and Christopher Anderson. 2008. *Income Inequality and Democratic Representation*. New York: Russell Sage Foundation.

Berger, Ben. 2009. "Political Theory, Political Science and the End of Civic Engagement." *Perspectives on Politics* 7 (2): 335–350.

Berman, Evan M. 1997. "Dealing with Cynical Citizens." *Public Administration Review* 57 (2): 105–112.

Berry, Jeffrey M. 1999. *The New Liberalism and the Rising Power of Citizen Groups*. Washington, DC: Brookings Institution Press.

Beserra, Bernadete. 2005. "From Brazilians to Latinos? Racialization and Latinidad in the Making of Brazilian Carnival in Los Angeles." *Latino Studies* 3 (1): 53–75.

Bishop, Matthew, and Michael Green. 2008. *Philanthrocapitalism: How Giving Can Save the World*. New York: Bloomsbury Press.

Bleich, Sara, Marian Jarlenski, Caryn Bell, and Thomas LaVeist. 2012. "Health Inequalities: Trends, Progress, and Policy." *Annual Review of Public Health* 33: 7–40.

Bohman, James. 1999. "Theories, Practices, and Pluralism: A Pragmatic Interpretation of Critical Social Science." *Philosophy of the Social Sciences* 29 (4): 459–480.

Boltanski, Luc. 2011. *On Critique: A Sociology of Emancipation*. Cambridge: Polity Press.

Boltanski, Luc, and Eve Chiapello. 2005. *The New Spirit of Capitalism*. London: Verso.

Boltanski, Luc, and Laurent Thévenot. 2006. *On Justification: The Economies of Worth*. Translated by Catherine Porter. Princeton, NJ: Princeton University Press. Originally published as *De La Justificacion: Les Économies de la Grandeur*. Paris: Editiones Gallimard, 1991.

Bonilla-Silva, Eduardo. 2010. *Racism without Racists: Color-Blind Racism and the Persistence of Racial Inequality in the United States.* Boulder, CO: Rowman & Littlefield.

Booth, John A., and Mitchell A. Seligson. 2009. *The Legitimacy Puzzle in Latin America.* New York: Cambridge University Press.

Bourdieu, Pierre. 1990. *The Logic of Practice.* Palo Alto, CA: Stanford University Press.

———. 1994. "Structures, Habitus, Power: Basis for a Theory of Symbolic Power." In *Culture/Power/History: A Reader in Contemporary Social Theory,* edited by Nicholas B. Dirks, Geoff Eley, and Sherry B. Ortner, 155–199. Princeton: Princeton University Press.

———. 1996. *The Rules of Art: Genesis and Structure of the Literary Field.* Palo Alto, CA: Stanford University Press.

Bourdieu, Pierre, and Richard Nice. 1980. "The Production of Belief: Contribution to an Economy of Symbolic Goods." *Media, Culture & Society* 2: 261–293.

Boyle, Mary-Ellen, and Ira Silver. 2005. "Poverty, Partnerships, and Privilege: Elite Institutions." *City & Community* 4 (3): 233–253.

Bradley, Ian C. 2007. *Enlightened Entrepreneurs: Business Ethics in Victorian Britain.* Oxford: Lion.

Buechler, Steven M. 1995. "New Social Movement Theories." *Sociological Quarterly* 36 (3): 441–464.

Burawoy, Michael. 1998. "The Extended Case Method." *Sociological Theory* 16 (1): 4–33.

Burawoy, Michael, Alice Burton, Ann Arnett Ferguson, Kathryn J. Fox, Joshua Gamson, Nadine Gartrell, Leslie Hurst, Charles Kurzman, Leslie Salzinger, Josepha Schiffman, and Shiori Ui. 1991. *Ethnography Unbound: Power and Resistance in the Modern Metropolis.* Berkeley: University of California Press.

Butler, Judith. 2011. "Composite Remarks." Washington Square Park, New York City, October 23. Accessed February 6, 2013. http://occupywriters.com/works/by-judith-butler.

Cain, Bruce, Russell J. Dalton, and Susan Scarrow, eds. 2003. *Democracy Transformed? The Expansion of Political Access in Advanced Industrialized Democracies.* Oxford: Oxford University Press.

Calhoun, Craig. 1998. "The Public Good as a Social and Cultural Project." In *Private Action and the Public Good,* edited by W. Powell and E. Clemens, 20–35. New Haven, CT: Yale University Press.

Callon, Michel. 1986. "Some Elements of a Sociology of Translation: Domestication of the Scallops and the Fishermen of St. Brieuc Bay." In *Power, Action and Belief: A New Sociology of Knowledge,* edited by John Law, 196–233. London: Routledge and Kegan Paul.

Capella, Joseph, and Kathleen Jamieson. 1997. *Spiral of Cynicism: The Press and the Public Good.* New York: Oxford University Press.

Castells, Manuel. 2012. *Networks of Outrage and Hope: Social Movements in the Internet Age.* Cambridge: Polity Press.

Castoriadis, Cornelius. 1994. "Radical Imagination and the Social Instituting Imaginary." In *Rethinking Imagination: Culture and Creativity,* edited by Gillian Robinson and John Rundell, 136–154. London: Routledge.

———. 1998. *The Imaginary Institution of Society.* Translated by Kathleen Blamey. Cambridge, MA: MIT Press. Originally published as *L'instituion imaginaire de la société.* Paris: Éditions du Seuil, 1975.

Center for Information and Research on Civic Learning and Engagement (CIRCLE). 2011. "Survey Measures of Civic Engagement." Accessed June 27, 2013. http://www.civicyouth.org/tools-for-practice/survey-measures-of-civic-engagement.

Chakravartty, Paula, and Denise Ferreira da Silva. 2012. "Accumulation, Dispossession, and Debt: The Racial Logic of Global Capitalism—An Introduction." *American Quarterly* 64 (3): 361–385.

Chaloupka, William. 1999. *Everybody Knows: Cynicism in America*. Minneapolis: University of Minnesota Press.

CityCamp. 2012. Accessed April 24, 2012. http://citycamp.govfresh.com.

City of Providence. 2009. "Creative Providence: A Cultural Plan for the Creative Sector." Accessed August 29, 2012. http://www.providenceri.gov/efile/47.

Clarke, Julia. 2002. "A New Kind of Symmetry: Actor-Network Theories and the New Literacy Studies." *Studies in the Education of Adults* 34 (2): 107–122.

CNCS (Corporation for National and Community Service). 2006. "Volunteer Growth in America: A Review of Trends since 1974." Accessed February 24, 2012. http://www.nationalservice.gov/about/role_impact/performance_research.asp #VOLGROWTH.

———. 2012. "Volunteering and Civic Life in America 2012." Washington, DC. Accessed January 15, 2013. http://www.volunteeringinamerica.gov/assets/resources /FactSheetFinal.pdf.

Cohen, Stanley. 2001. *States of Denial: Knowing about Atrocities and Suffering*. Cambridge: Blackwell Publishers.

Cordner, Alissa, Peter T. Klein, and Gianpaolo Baiocchi. 2012. "Co-Designing and Co-Teaching Graduate Qualitative Methods: An Innovative Ethnographic Workshop Model." *Teaching Sociology* 40: 215–226.

Craig, Stephen C. 1993. *The Malevolent Leaders: Popular Discontent in America*. Boulder, CO: Westview Press.

Dalton, Russell J. 2004. *Democratic Challenges, Democratic Choices: The Erosion of Political Support in Advanced Industrial Democracies*. New York: Oxford University Press.

DeVault, Marjorie. 1999. *Liberating Methods: Feminism and Social Research*. Philadelphia: Temple University Press.

Dewey, John. 1954. *The Public and Its Problems*. Denver: Swallow.

Douglas, Mary. 2002 [1966]. *Purity and Danger: An Analysis of Concepts of Pollution and Taboo*. London: Psychology Press.

Du Bois, W. E. B. 1999 [1903]. *The Souls of Black Folk*. Edited by Henry Louis Gates Jr. and Terri Hume Oliver. New York: W. W. Norton.

Duggan, Lisa. 2003. *The Twilight of Equality? Neoliberalism, Cultural Politics, and the Attack on Democracy*. Boston: Beacon Press.

Durkheim, Émile. 1964. *The Division of Labor in Society*. New York: Free Press of Glencoe.

Edgell, Paul, Joseph Gerteis, and Douglas Hartmann. 2006. "Atheists as 'Other': Moral Boundaries and Cultural Membership in American Society." *American Sociological Review* 71 (2): 211–234.

Eggers, William. 2007. *Government 2.0: Using Technology to Improve Education, Cut Red Tape, Reduce Gridlock, and Enhance Democracy*. Boulder, CO: Rowman & Littlefield.

Eliasoph, Nina. 1997. "'Close to Home': The Work of Avoiding Politics." *Theory and Society* 26 (5): 605–647.

———. 1998. *Avoiding Politics: How Americans Produce Apathy in Everyday Life*. New York: Cambridge University Press.

———. 2009. "Top-Down Civic Projects Are Not Grassroots Associations: How the Differences Matter in Everyday Life." *VOLUNTAS: International Journal of Voluntary and Nonprofit Organizations* 20 (3): 291–308.

———. 2011. *Making Volunteers: Civic Life After Welfare's End*. Princeton: Princeton University Press.

Eliasoph, Nina, and Paul Lichterman. 2003. "Culture in Interaction." *American Journal of Sociology* 108 (4): 735–794.

Emirbayer, Mustafa, and Ann Mische. 1998. "What Is Agency?" *American Journal of Sociology* 103 (4): 962–1023.

Etzione, Amitai. 1996. *The New Golden Rule: Community and Morality in a Democratic Society*. New York: Basic Books.

Fine, Gary. 2010. "The Sociology of the Local: Action and Its Publics." *Sociological Theory* 28 (4): 355–376.

Fischer, Mary J. 2003. "The Relative Importance of Income and Race in Determining Residential Outcomes in US Urban Areas, 1970–2000." *Urban Affairs Review* 38: 669–696.

Fitzpatrick, Ed. 2010. "Voters Seem to Say Out with the Old, in with the New." *Providence Journal*, September 27.

Flores, Glenn. 2010. "Racial and Ethnic Disparities in the Health and Health Care of Children." *Pediatrics* 125 (4): e979–e1020.

Florida, Richard. 2003. "Cities and the Creative Class." *City & Community* 2 (1): 3–19.

Foucault, Michel, Paul Rabinow, and James D. Faubion. 1997. *The Essential Works of Michel Foucault, 1954–1984*. New York: New Press.

Freud, Sigmund. 1959. "Splitting of the Ego in the Process of Defense." In *Collected Chapters: Volume 5, Miscellaneous Chapters, 1888–1938*. New York: Basic Books.

Friedman, Michael. 1998. "On the Sociology of Scientific Knowledge and Its Philosophical Agenda." *Studies in the History and Philosophy of Science* 29: 239–271.

Frye, Margaret. 2012. "Bright Futures in Malawi's New Dawn: Educational Aspirations as Assertions of Identity." *American Journal of Sociology* 117 (6): 1565–1624.

Fuller, Paul, and Tim McCorry. 2011. "Governing the Neighborhood—Governing the Self." Unpublished manuscript.

Ganuza, Ernest, Lucrecia Olivari, Pablo Paño, Luz Buitrago, and Concha Lorenzana. 2010. *La Democracia en Acción: Una Visión Desde las Metodologías Participativas*. Madrid: Antigona.

Gemerchak, Christopher. 2004. "Fetishism and Bad Faith: A Freudian Rebuttal to Sartre." *Janus Head* 7 (2): 248–269.

Gibson, David R. 2011. "Speaking of the Future: Contentious Narration during the Cuban Missile Crisis." *Qualitative Sociology* 34 (4): 503–522.

Gieryn, Thomas F. 1983. "Boundary-Work and the Demarcation of Science from Non-Science: Strains and Interests in Professional Ideologies of Scientists." *American Sociological Review* 48 (6): 781–795.

Giugni, Marco G. 1998. "Was It Worth the Effort? The Outcomes and Consequences of Social Movements." *Annual Review of Sociology* 24: 371–393.

Glaeser, Andreas. 2011. *Political Epistemics: The Secret Police, the Opposition, and the End of East German Socialism*. Chicago: University of Chicago Press.

Goffman, Erving. 1961. *Encounters: Two Studies in the Sociology of Interaction*. Indianapolis: Bobbs-Merrill.

Goldfarb, Jeffrey. 1991. *The Cynical Society*. Chicago: University of Chicago Press.

Goodnough, Abby. 2011. "Mayor Trics to Reassure Providence Teachers as Furor Grows over Firing Notices." *New York Times*, February 25. Accessed February 20, 2013. http://www.nytimes.com/2011/02/26/us/26providence.html?_r=0.

Gramsci, Antonio. 1971. *Selections from the Prison Notebooks of Antonio Gramsci.* Translated and edited by Quintin Hoare and Geoffrey Nowell-Smith. New York: International Publishers.

Gutmann, Matthew. 2002. *The Romance of Democracy: Compliant Defiance in Contemporary Mexico.* Berkeley: University of California Press.

Habermas, Jürgen. 1989 [1962]. *The Structural Transformation of the Public Sphere: An Inquiry into a Category of Bourgeois Society.* Cambridge: Polity Press.

Hannerz, Ulf. 2006. "Studying Down, Up, Sideways, Through, Backwards, Forwards, Away and at Home: Reflections on the Field Worries of an Expansive Discipline." In *Locating the Field: Space, Place, and Context in Anthropology,* edited by Simon Michael Coleman and Peter Collins. Oxford: Berg.

Harding, Sandra. 1987. "Introduction: Is There a Feminist Method?" In *Feminism and Methodology,* edited by Sandra Harding, 1–14. Bloomington: Indiana University Press.

Hart, Stephen. 2001. *Cultural Dilemmas of Progressive Politics: Styles of Engagement among Grassroots Activists.* Chicago: University of Chicago Press.

Hayes, Michael T. 1986. "The New Group Universe." In *Interest Group Politics,* edited by Allan Cigler and Burdett Loomis, 133–145. Washington, DC: CQ Press.

Herbert, Steve. 2005. "The Trapdoor of Community." *Annals of the Association of American Geographers* 95 (4): 850–865.

HERI (Higher Education Research Institute). 1999. "The American Freshman: National Norms for Fall 1999." Accessed March 15, 2013. http://www.heri.ucla.edu/PDFs /pubs/TFS/Norms/Monographs/TheAmericanFreshman1999.pdf.

Hibbing, John, and Elizabeth Theiss-Morse. 2002. *Stealth Democracy: Americans' Beliefs about How Government Should Work.* Cambridge: Cambridge University Press.

Hirsch, Jennifer, Holly Wardlow, Daniel Smith, Harriet Phinney, Shanti Parikh, and Constance Nathanson. 2009. *The Secret: Love, Marriage, and HIV.* Nashville, TN: Vanderbilt University Press.

Hochschild, Jennifer, and Nathan Scovronick. 2003. *The American Dream and the Public Schools.* Oxford: Oxford University Press.

Holland, Dorothy, Donald Nonini, Catherine Lutz, Lesley Bartlett, Marla Frederick-McGlathery, Thaddeus Guldbrandsen, and Enrique Murillo Jr. 2007. *Local Democracy under Siege: Activism, Public Interests, and Private Politics.* New York: New York University Press.

Ilcan, Suzan, and Tanya Basok. 2004. "Community Government: Voluntary Agencies, Social Justice, and the Responsibilization of Citizens." *Citizenship Studies* 8 (2): 129–144.

Inglehart, Ronald. 1988. "The Renaissance of Political Culture." *American Political Science Review* 82 (4): 1203–1230.

———. 1990. *Culture Shift in Advanced Industrial Society.* Princeton: Princeton University Press.

Itzigsohn, Jose. 2009. *Encountering American Faultlines.* New York: Russell Sage Foundation Publications.

Jackson, Robert A., Jeffery J. Mondak, and Robert Huckfeldt. 2009. "Examining the Possible Corrosive Impact of Negative Advertising on Citizens' Attitudes toward Politics." *Political Research Quarterly* 62 (1): 55–69.

Jacobs, Ronald N. 2000. *Race, Media, and the Crisis of Civil Society from Watts to Rodney King.* Cambridge: Cambridge University Press.

Jerzyk, Matthew. 2009. "Gentrification's Third Way: An Analysis of Housing Policy and Gentrification in Providence." *Harvard Law and Policy Review* 3: 413–429.

Joas, Hans. 1996. *The Creativity of Action*. Translated by Jeremy Gaines and Paul Keast. Chicago: University of Chicago Press.

Kahn, Richard, and Douglas Kellner. 2004. "New Media and Internet Activism: From the 'Battle of Seattle' to Blogging." *New Media and Society* 6 (1): 87–95.

Keane, John. 2009. *The Life and Death of Democracy*. New York: W. W. Norton.

King, Martin Luther, Jr. 1963. "Letter from Birmingham Jail." Accessed March 20, 2013. http://mlk-kpp01.stanford.edu/index.php/encyclopedia/encyclopedia/enc_letter_from_birmingham_jail_1963.

Klein, Melanie, and Juliet Mitchell. 1986. *The Selected Melanie Klein*. New York: Free Press.

Lamont, Michele. 2001. "Symbolic Boundaries." In *International Encyclopedia of the Social and Behavioral Sciences*, edited by Neil Smelser and Paul Baltes, 15341–15347. Amsterdam: Elsevier.

Lamont, Michele, and Virag Molnar. 2002. "The Study of Boundaries in the Social Sciences." *Annual Review of Sociology* 28: 167–195.

Latour, Bruno. 1987. *Science in Action: How to Follow Scientists and Engineers through Society*. Cambridge, MA: Harvard University Press.

———. 1996. *Aramis, or the Love of Technology*. Cambridge, MA: Harvard University Press.

———. 2005. *Reassembling the Social: An Introduction to Actor-Network-Theory*. Oxford: Oxford University Press.

Lee, Caroline W. 2007. "Is There a Place for Private Conversation in Public Dialogue? Comparing Stakeholder Assessments of Informal Communication in Collaborative Regional Planning." *American Journal of Sociology* 113 (1): 41–96.

———. 2013. *Down Market Democracy: How Talk Got Tough When Times Got Tight*. Oxford: Oxford University Press.

Lee, Caroline W., Michael McQuarrie, and Edward T. Walker. Forthcoming. "Introduction." In *Democratizing Inequalities: Pitfalls and Unrealized Promises of the New Public Participation*, edited by Caroline W. Lee, Michael McQuarrie, and Edward T. Walker. Under review.

Lichterman, Paul. 1996. *The Search for Political Community: American Activists Reinventing Commitment*. Cambridge: Cambridge University Press.

———. 2002. "Seeing Structure Happen: Theory-Driven Participant Observation." In *Methods of Social Movement Research*, edited by Bert Klandermans and Suzanne Staggenborg, 118–145. Minneapolis: University of Minnesota Press.

———. 2005a. *Elusive Togetherness: Church Groups Trying to Bridge America's Divisions*. Princeton: Princeton University Press.

———. 2005b. "Risking Inconvenience: Observations on Ethnography." *Political Sociology: States, Power, and Societies* 11: 1–3.

———. 2008. "Religion and the Construction of Civic Identity." *American Sociological Review* 73 (1): 83–104.

Lichterman, Paul, and Daniel Cefaï. 2006. "The Idea of Political Culture." In *The Oxford Handbook of Contextual Political Studies*, edited by Robert Goodin and Charles Tilly, 392–424. New York: Oxford.

Logan, John, and Charles Zhang. 2010. "Global Neighborhoods: New Pathways to Diversity and Separation." *American Journal of Sociology* 115 (4): 1069–1109.

Macedo, Stephen. 2005. *Democracy at Risk: How Political Choices Undermine Citizen Participation, and What We Can Do about It*. Washington, DC: Brookings Institution Press.

Macgregor, Lyn C. 2010. *Habits of the Heartland: Small-Town Life in Modern America*. Ithaca, NY: Cornell University Press.

Magee, Neal E. 2004. "Remembering to Forget: Theological Tropologies of Confession and Disavowal." PhD diss., Syracuse University.

Mair, Johanna, and Ignasi Marti. 2004. "Social Entrepreneurship: What Are We Talking About? A Framework for Future Research." IESE Research Paper, D/546, IESE Business School. Accessed January 11, 2013. http://ideas.repec.org/s/ebg/iesewp.html.

Marinetto, Michael. 2003. "Who Wants to Be an Active Citizen? The Politics and Practice of Community Involvement." *Sociology* 37 (1): 103–120.

Marrow, Helen. 2003. "To Be or Not to Be (Hispanic or Latino): Brazilian Racial and Ethnic Identity in the United States." *Ethnicities* 3 (4): 427–464.

Marx, Karl, Friedrich Engels, and E. J. Hobsbawm. 1998 [1848]. *The Communist Manifesto: A Modern Edition*. London: Verso.

May, Reuben Buford, and Mary Pattillo-McCoy. 2000. "Do You See What I See? Examining a Collaborative Ethnography." *Qualitative Inquiry* 6 (1): 65–87.

McAdam, Doug, Charles Tilly, and Sidney Tarrow. 2001. *Dynamics of Contention*. Cambridge: Cambridge University Press.

McCain, John. 2008. Speech at the Greater Columbus Convention Center. Columbus, OH. Printed in the *New York Times*. Accessed March 6, 2013. http://www.nytimes.com/2008/05/15/us/politics/15text-mccain.html?pagewanted=all&_r=0.

McQuarrie, Michael. 2013. "No Contest: Participatory Technologies and the Transformation of Urban Authority." *Popular Culture* 25 (1 69): 143–175.

Milkman, Ruth, Stephanie Luce, and Penny Lewis. 2013. *Changing the Subject: A Bottom-Up Account of Occupy Wall Street in New York City*. The Murphy Institute, CUNY. Accessed January 31, 2013. http://www.law.harvard.edu/programs/lwp/papers/Changing_the_Subject.pdf.

Miller, Melissa K. 2010. "Membership Has Its Privileges: How Voluntary Groups Exacerbate the Participatory Bias." *Political Research Quarterly* 63 (2): 356–372.

Mills, C. Wright. 1959. *The Sociological Imagination*. New York: Oxford University Press.

Mische, Ann. 2009. "Projects and Possibilities: Researching Futures in Action." *Sociological Forum* 24 (3): 694–704.

Motte, Mark T., and Laurence A. Weil. 2000. "Of Railroads and Regime Shifts: Downtown Renewal in Providence, Rhode Island." *Cities* 17 (1): 7–18.

Mouffe, Chantal. 2000. *The Democratic Paradox*. London: Verso.

———. 2005. *On the Political*. New York: Routledge.

Myers, Samuel L., Jr. 1997. "Why Diversity Is a Smoke Screen for Affirmative Action." *Change* 29 (4): 24–32.

Nader, Laura. 1974. "Up the Anthropologist—Perspectives Gained from Studying Up." In *Reinventing Anthropology*, edited by Dell Hymes, 284–311. New York: Pantheon Books.

NBC. 2009. "Firefighters Picket US Mayors Conference." June 10. Accessed January 26, 2013. http://www2.turnto10.com/news/2009/jun/10/mayor_union_chief_remain_divided_on_contract-ar-47795.

Norgaard, K. M. 2006. "People Want to Protect Themselves a Little Bit: Emotions, Denial, and Social Movement Nonparticipation." *Sociological Inquiry* 76 (3): 372–396.

Norris, Pippa. 2001. *Digital Divide: Civic Engagement, Information Poverty, and the Internet Worldwide*. New York: Cambridge University Press.

———. 2011. *Democratic Deficit: Critical Citizens Revisited*. Cambridge: Cambridge University Press.

Norton, Quinn. 2012. "A Eulogy for #Occupy." *Wired*. December 12, 2012. Available at http://www.wired.com/opinion/2012/12/a-eulogy-for-occupy/all.

Nye, Joseph S., Jr., Philip D. Zelikow, and David C. King, eds. 1997. *Why People Don't Trust Government*. Cambridge, MA: Harvard University Press.

NYT/CBS (*New York Times*/CBS News Poll). 2011. "Americans' Approval of Congress Drops to Single Digits." October 25. Accessed March 15, 2013. http://www.nytimes.com/interactive/2011/10/25/us/politics/approval-of-congress-drops-to-single-digits.html?_r=0.

Obama, Barack H. 2008. Speech at the Democratic National Convention. Denver, CO. Accessed March 6, 2013. https://itunes.apple.com/us/podcast/2008-democratic-national-convention/id289667306.

OECD (Organisation for Economic Co-operation and Development). 2012. Income Distribution—Inequality—Country Tables. OECD StatExtract. Accessed December 4, 2012. http://stats.oecd.org/Index.aspx?QueryId=26068.

Offe, Claus. 2006. "Political Disaffection as an Outcome of Institutional Practices? Some Post-Tocquevillean Speculations." In *Political Disaffection in Contemporary Democracies*, edited by Mariano Torcal and J. R. Montero, 23–45. London: Routledge.

Ong, Aihwa. 2006. *Neoliberalism as Exception: Mutations in Citizenship and Sovereignty*. Durham, NC: Duke University Press.

Pacewicz, Josh. 2010. "Partisans and Partners: The Politics of the Post-Industrial Economy." PhD diss., University of Chicago.

Paley, Julia. 2002. "Toward an Anthropology of Democracy." *Annual Review of Anthropology* 31 (1): 469–496.

Pattillo-McCoy, Mary. 1999. *Black Picket Fences: Privilege and Peril among the Black Middle Class*. Chicago: University of Chicago Press.

Peck, Jamie. 2005. "Struggling with the Creative Class." *International Journal of Urban and Regional Research* 29 (4): 740–770.

———. 2012. "Austerity Urbanism: American Cities under Extreme Economy." *City* 16 (6): 626–655.

Perrin, Andrew. 2005. "Political Microcultures: Linking Civic Life and Democratic Discourse." *Social Forces* 84 (2): 1049–1082.

———. 2006. *Citizen Speak: The Democratic Imagination in American Life*. Chicago: University of Chicago Press.

Perrotta, John A. 1977. "Machine Influence on a Community Action Program: The Case of Providence, Rhode Island." *Polity* 9 (4): 481–502.

Pew Research Center. 2010. "The People and Their Government: Distrust, Discontent, Anger and Partisan Rancor." Washington, DC: Pew Research Center. Accessed March 1, 2012. http://www.people-press.org/2010/04/18/distrust-discontent-anger-and-partisan-rancor.

———. 2012. "Degrees of Access." Analysis based on the Pew Internet and American Life Survey, May 2008. Accessed December 12, 2012. http://www.slideshare.net/PewInternet/degrees-of-access-may-2008-data?type=powerpoint.

Pharr, Susan, and Robert Putnam, eds. 2000. *Disaffected Democracies: What's Troubling the Trilateral Countries?* Princeton, NJ: Princeton University Press.

Pichardo, Nelson. 1997. "New Social Movements: A Critical Review." *Annual Review of Sociology* 23: 411–430.

Piven, Frances Fox, and Richard A. Cloward. 1997. *The Breaking of the American Social Compact*. New York: New Press.

Polletta, Francesca. 2006. *It Was Like a Fever: Storytelling in Protest and Politics*. Chicago: University of Chicago Press.

———. 2013. "Participatory Democracy in the New Millennium." *Contemporary Sociology: A Journal of Reviews* 42 (1): 40–50.

Postero, Nancy Grey. 2007. *Now We Are Citizens: Indigenous Politics in Postmulticultural Bolivia*. Palo Alto, CA: Stanford University Press.

Providence Journal. 2010. "Hundreds Line Up for Jobs at Westerly's Ocean House." March 16. Accessed February 18, 2013. http://news.providencejournal.com/breaking-news /2010/03/hundreds-line-up-for-jobs-at-w.html.

Przeworski, Adam, and Henry Teune. 1970. *The Logic of Comparative Social Inquiry*. New York: John Wiley & Sons.

Public Policy Polling. 2013. "Congress Less Popular Than Cockroaches, Traffic Jams." January 8. Accessed January 12, 2013. http://www.publicpolicypolling.com/pdf/2011 /PPP_Release_Natl_010813_.pdf.

Purdy, Jedediah. 1999. *For Common Things: Irony, Trust, and Commitment in America Today*. New York: Vintage Books.

Putnam, Robert. 1993. *Making Democracy Work: Civic Traditions in Modern Italy*. Princeton, NJ: Princeton University Press.

———. 1996. "Robert Putnam Responds." *American Prospect* 25 (March–April): 26–28.

———. 2000. *Bowling Alone: The Collapse and Revival of American Community*. New York: Simon & Schuster.

Quillian, Lincoln. 2012. "Segregation and Poverty Concentration: The Role of Three Seg-regations." *American Sociological Review* 77 (3): 354–379.

Rancière, Jacques. 1995. *On the Shores of Politics*. London: Verso.

———. 2012. *The Intellectual and His People*. London: Verso.

Rappleye, Charles. 2006. *Sons of Providence*. New York: Simon & Schuster.

RealtyTrac. 2011. "Record 2.9 Million U.S. Properties Receive Foreclosure Filings in 2010 Despite 30-Month Low in December." January 12. Accessed February 22, 2013. http://www.realtytrac.com/content/press-releases.

Reardon, Sean, and Kendra Bischoff. 2011. "Growth in the Residential Segregation of Families by Income 1970–2009." US 2010 Project. Accessed January 15, 2013. http://www .s4.brown.edu/us2010/Data/Report/report111111.pdf.

Rhode Island Community Food Bank. 2010. "Status Report on Hunger in Rhode Island 2010." Accessed February 18, 2013. http://rifoodbank.org/Portals/0/Uploads /Documents/Public/Publications/StatusReport_2010.pdf.

Rhode Island State Board of Elections. "2008 General Election." Accessed March 1, 2012. http://www.elections.ri.gov/elections/results/2008/general_election /statewidesummary .php.

Riemer, Francis J. 2001. *Working at the Margins: Moving off Welfare in America*. Albany: State University of New York.

Rose, Nikolas. 1999. "Inventiveness in Politics." *Economy and Society* 28 (3): 467–493.

Ross, Marc. 1997. "Culture and Identity in Comparative Political Analysis." In *Comparative Politics: Rationality, Culture, and Structure*, edited by Marc I. Lichbach and Alan Zuckerman, 42–80. New York: Cambridge University Press.

Saez, Emmanuel. 2012. "Striking It Richer: The Evolution of Top Incomes in the United States." *Pathways Magazine*, Winter 2008, 6–7. Updated with 2009 and 2010 esti-mates on March 2, 2012. Accessed January 11, 2013. elsa.berkeley.edu/~saez/saez -UStopincomes-2010.pdf.

Sassen, Saskia. 2001. *The Global City: New York, Tokyo, and London*. Princeton, NJ: Princeton University Press.

Schinkel, Willem. 2007. "Sociological Discourse of the Relational: The Cases of Bourdieu and Latour." *Sociological Review* 55 (4): 707–729.

Schlozman, Kay, Benjamin Page, Sidney Verba, and Morris Fiorina. 2004. "Inequalities of Political Voice." Report for American Political Science Association Task Force on Inequality and American Democracy. Accessed January 11, 2013. https://www.apsanet.org/imgtest/voicememo.pdf.

Schudson, Michael. 1998. *The Good Citizen: A History of American Civic Life*. New York: Free Press.

———. 2006. "New Technologies and Not-So-New Democracies." *Tidsskriftet Politik* 9 (2): 6–14.

Schutz, Alfred. 1959. "Tiresias, or Our Knowledge of Future Events." *Social Research* 26: 71–89.

Scott, James. 1985. *Weapons of the Weak: Everyday Forms of Peasant Resistance*. New Haven, CT: Yale University Press.

———. 1990. *Domination and the Arts of Resistance*. New Haven, CT: Yale University Press.

Sedgwick, Eve Kosofsky. 2003. *Touching Feeling: Affect, Pedagogy, Performativity*. Durham, NC: Duke University Press.

———. 2007. "Melanie Klein and the Difference Affect Makes." *South Atlantic Quarterly* 106 (3): 625–642.

SeeClickFix. 2013. "SeeClickFix" homepage. Accessed January 22, 2013. http://seeclickfix.com.

Sherman, Arloc, and Chad Stone. 2010. "Income Gaps between Very Rich and Everyone Else More Than Tripled in Last Three Decades." Center on Budget and Policy Priorities. Washington, DC.

Silber, Ilana F. 2003. "Pragmatic Sociology as Cultural Sociology: Beyond Repertoire Theory?" *European Journal of Social Theory* 6 (4): 427–449.

Silver, Hilary. 2009. *Southside: The Fall and Rise of an Inner-City Neighborhood*. Rhode Island Public Broadcasting System. February 14, 2009.

Simmons, Ruth. 2012. "Update on City Discussions." January 13, 2012. Letter to the Brown University Community.

Sirianni, Carmen, and Lewis Friedland. 2001. *Civic Innovation in America: Community Empowerment, Public Policy, and the Movement for Civic Renewal*. Berkeley: University of California Press.

Skocpol, Theda. 2004. "Voice and Inequality: The Transformation of American Civic Democracy." *Perspectives on Politics* 2 (1): 1–18.

Sloterdijk, Peter. 1987. *Critique of Cynical Reason*. Minneapolis: University of Minnesota Press.

Smilde, David. 2006. *Reason to Believe: Cultural Agency in Latin American Evangelicalism*. Berkeley: University of California Press.

Smith, David Horton. 1992. "National Nonprofit, Voluntary Associations: Some Parameters." *Nonprofit and Voluntary Sector Quarterly* 21 (Spring): 81–94.

Snow, David, and Leon Anderson. 1987. "Identity Work among the Homeless." *American Journal of Sociology* 92 (6): 1336–1371.

Stanton, Mike. 2003. *The Prince of Providence: The True Story of Buddy Cianci, America's Most Notorious Mayor, Some Wiseguys, and the Feds*. New York: Random House.

Sterne, Evelyn S. 2003. *Ballots and Bibles: Ethnic Politics and the Catholic Church in Providence*. Ithaca, NY: Cornell University Press.

Stiglitz, Joseph. 2012. *The Price of Inequality: How Today's Divided Society Endangers Our Future.* New York: W. W. Norton.

Stinchcombe, Arthur. 2005. *The Logic of Social Research.* Chicago: University of Chicago Press.

Stivers, Richard. 1994. *The Culture of Cynicism: American Morality in Decline.* Oxford: Blackwell.

Tapscott, Don, Anthony D. Williams, and Dan Herman. 2008. *Government 2.0: Transforming Government and Governance for the Twenty-First Century.* Houston: New Paradigm Publishing.

Tarrow, Sidney. 1994. *Power in Movement: Social Movements, Collective Action, and Politics.* Cambridge: Cambridge University Press.

Taveras, Angel. 2010. "Angel Taveras Will Be the Jobs Mayor That Providence Needs." *Providence Journal,* August 31.

———. 2012. "Peaceful End to Occupy Movement's Burnside Park Encampment Distinguishes Providence Nationally." City of Providence website. Accessed February 6, 2013. http://providenceri.com/print/mayor/peaceful-end-to-occupy-movements -burnside-park.

Tax Foundation. 2013. "U.S. Federal Individual Income Tax Rates History, 1913–2013 (Nominal and Inflation-Adjusted Brackets)." Accessed March 16, 2013. http:// taxfoundation.org/sites/taxfoundation.org/files/docs/fed_rates_history_nominal _1913_2013_0.pdf

Taylor, Paul, Rakesh Kochhar, Richard Fry, Gabriel Velasco, and Seth Motel. 2011. "Wealth Gaps Rise to Record Highs between Whites, Blacks and Hispanics." Washington, DC: Pew Social & Demographic Trends. Accessed January 11, 2013. http://www .pewsocialtrends.org/files/2011/07/SDT-Wealth-Report_7-26-11_FINAL.pdf.

Thévenot, Laurent. 2001. "Pragmatic Regimes Governing the Engagement with the World." In *The Practice Turn in Contemporary Theory,* edited by Theodore Schatzki, Karin Knorr-Cetina, and Eike Von Savigny, 56–73. New York: Routledge.

Thrift, Nigel. 2005. *Knowing Capitalism.* London: Sage Publications.

de Tocqueville, Alexis. 2003 [1840]. *Democracy in America: And Two Essays on America.* New York: Penguin Classics.

Tolchin, Susan J. 1996. *The Angry American: How Voter Rage Is Changing the Nation.* Boulder, CO: Westview Press.

Tolich, Martin. 2004. "Internal Confidentiality: When Confidentiality Assurances Fail Relational Informants." *Qualitative Sociology* 27 (1): 101–106.

Tucker, Eric. 2011. "RI Gov. Chafee Rescinds Immigration Order." Associated Press, January 5. Accessed June 29, 2012. http://www.boston.com/news/local/rhode_island /articles/2011/01/05/ri_gov_chafee_to_rescind_immigration_order.

Tucker, Kenneth H., Jr. 2005. "From the Imaginary to Subjectivation: Castoriadis and Touraine on the Performative Public Sphere." *Thesis Eleven* 83 (November): 42–60.

Tuula, Gordon, Pirkko Hynninen, Elina Lahelma, Tuija Metso, Tarja Palmu, and Tarja Tolonen. 2006. "Collective Ethnography, Joint Experiences and Individual Pathways." *Nordisk Pedagogik* 26: 3–15.

Unger, Roberto Mangabeira. 1975. *Knowledge and Politics.* New York: Free Press.

US Bureau of Labor Statistics. 2012. "Fastest Growing Occupations." Accessed February 6, 2013. http://www.bls.gov/emp/ep_table_103.htm.

———. 2013. "Employment Status of the Civilian Noninstitutional Population, 1942 to Date." Accessed February 22, 2013. http://www.bls.gov/cps/#tables.

US Census Bureau. 2011a. "2010 Census. Race and Hispanic or Latino Origin: 2010 Census Summary File 1." Accessed February 28, 2012. http://factfinder2.census.gov.

———. 2011b. "Population Estimates: Rhode Island, All Incorporated Places, 2000–2009." Accessed February 21, 2012. http://www.census.gov/popest/data/cities/totals/2009 /SUB-EST2009-4.html.

———. 2012. "Table 397. Participation in Elections for President and U.S. Representatives: 1932 to 2010." Accessed January 21, 2013. www.census.gov/compendia/statab/2012 /tables/12s0397.xls.

———. 2013. "2010 Census Interactive Population Search." Accessed March 7, 2013. http:// www.census.gov/2010census/popmap.

US Department of Agriculture. 2013. "Supplemental Nutrition Assistance Program." February 8. Accessed February 22, 2013. http://www.fns.usda.gov/pd/SNAPsummary.htm.

US Department of Health and Human Services. 2011. "Information on Poverty and Income Statistics: A Summary of 2011." September 13. Accessed February 22, 2013. http:// aspe.hhs.gov/poverty/11/ib.shtml#sec1.

———. 2013. "Office for Human Research Protections." Accessed March 13, 2013. http:// www.hhs.gov/ohrp.

Uslaner, Eric, and Mitchell Brown. 2005. "Inequality, Trust, and Civic Engagement." *American Politics Research* 33 (6): 868–894.

Verba, Sidney, Kay Lehman Schlozman, and Henry Brady. 1995. *Voice and Equality: Civic Volunteerism in American Politics.* Cambridge: Harvard University Press.

Wacquant, Loic J. D. 1989. "Towards a Reflexive Sociology: A Workshop with Pierre Bourdieu." *Sociological Theory* 7 (1): 26–63.

Wagner-Pacifici, Robin. 2009. "When Futures Meet the Present." *Sociological Forum* 24 (3): 705–709.

Walker, Edward T. 2009. "Privatizing Participation: Civic Change and the Organizational Dynamics of Grassroots Lobbying Firms." *American Sociological Review* 74 (1): 83–105.

Wallace, David. 2000. "The Otherness of Castoriadis." *Topia: Canadian Journal of Cultural Studies* 3 (Spring): 110–115.

Wedeen, Lisa. 2007. "The Politics of Deliberation: Qat Chews as Public Spheres in Yemen." *Public Culture* 19 (1): 59–84.

———. 2008. *Peripheral Visions: Publics, Power, and Performance in Yemen.* Chicago: University of Chicago Press.

———. 2009. "Ethnography as Interpretive Enterprise." In *Political Ethnography: What Immersion Contributes to the Study of Power,* edited by Edward Schatz, 75–94. Chicago: University of Chicago Press.

Wilkinson, Richard, and Kate Picket. 2010. *The Spirit Level: Why Greater Equality Makes Societies Stronger.* New York: Bloomsbury Press.

Williamson, Vanessa, Theda Skocpol, and John Coggin. 2011. "The Tea Party and the Remaking of Republican Conservatism." *Perspectives on Politics* 9 (1): 25–43.

Wittgenstein, Ludwig. 1966. *Ludwig Wittgenstein: Lectures and Conversations on Aesthetics, Psychology, and Religious Belief,* edited by Cyril Barrett. Oxford: Basil Blackwell.

Wood, Richard L. 2002. *Faith in Action: Religion, Race, and Democratic Organizing in America.* Chicago: University of Chicago Press.

WPRI. 2009. "Protesters Picket US Mayors Conference: Firefighters, Grassroots Campaigns Target Mayor." June 12. Accessed March 6, 2013. http://www.wpri.com/dpp/news /local_news/local_wpri_providence_hundreds_firefighters_picket_us_conference _of_mayors_20090612_nek.

Wuthnow, Robert. 1994. *Sharing the Journey: Support Groups and America's New Quest for Community.* New York: Free Press.

———. 2002. *Loose Connections: Joining Together in America's Fragmented Communities.* Cambridge, MA: Harvard University Press.

Zinn, Howard. 2011. *Howard Zinn on History,* second edition. New York: Seven Stories Press.

Žižek, Slavoj. 1999. *The Ticklish Subject: The Absent Centre of Political Ontology.* London: Verso.

Zukin, Cliff, Scott Keeter, Molly Andolina, Krista Jenkins, and Michael Z. Delli Carpini. 2006. *A New Engagement? Political Participation, Civil Life, and the Changing American Citizen.* New York: Oxford University Press.

Index

activism. *See* civic engagement

actor-network theory, 28, 130, 130n3, 131–132, 136. *See also* Latour, Bruno

agency, 58n4, 66. *See also* structure-agency issue

Alexander, Jeffrey, 64

anthropology of democracy, 26

ambiguities, 42, 43–49

angry activists. *See* conflict

Appadurai, Arjun, 66–67

Arab Spring, vi, 13

Arendt, Hannah, 20–22, 75, 123

associational life. *See* civic engagement

Bellah, Robert, 11, 25, 25n8, 39, 54, 137

blind spots. *See* civic imagination

Boltanski, Luc, 24, 28, 58, 94. *See also* pragmatism

boundaries, 42–43, 54, 72–73, 89–90, 105–108, 118–119; between civic groups, 108–110, 119–120; class and, 91–92, 94, 106; in ethnographic research, 146, 154; Spanish language and, 71–72, 92

Bourdieu, Pierre, 29n17, 40n2, 61

Brown University, ix, 82, 84, 141. *See also* universities

business language. *See* civic innovation

Castoriadis, Cornelius, 20–22

civic culture. *See* political culture

civic engagement: definitions of, 6–7, 54; despite skepticism, 43–5, 114–117;

forms of, 2, 6–7, 12–13, 39, 55; measurement of, 6–7; reasons for, 13, 41, 75; trends in America, 7, 39–40, 54; types of groups, 32–33. *See also* group culture *and* democracy

civic imagination: definition, 3, 15, 20, 21, 55–58, 75, 117–118, 125–126; democracy and, 54–55, 125–126; disavowal and, 43–51, 115–117; examples of, 66–69, 97–99; expressions, 79, 99, 128; role of groups, 69, 115–117, 122–123; tradeoffs and blindspots, 3, 4, 69–75, 110–113, 124–125; trends, 14n20; varieties of, 4, 56, 59–65, 117–118. *See also* power-oriented civic imaginations, problem-solving civic imaginations, *and* solidarity-oriented civic imaginations

civic innovation: as an elite social movement, 83–84; blindspots of, 16, 88–95; business language and, 81, 84–85, 94; civic imaginations and, 65, 79, 85–88, 93; definition of, 16, 34, 78–79, 81–82, 93; examples of, 34–35, 62, 77–78, 80–81, 84

civic innovators. *See* civic innovation

civic groups. *See* civic engagement *and* group culture

civic participation. *See* civic engagement

civil society, 5, 25, 84n5; inequality and, 110–113. *See also* civic engagement

class. *See* inequality

About the Authors

Gianpaolo Baiocchi directs the Urban Democracy Lab at the Gallatin School of Individualized Studies at NYU, where he is Director of Civic Engagement and Associate Professor of Individualized Studies and Sociology. He researches and writes on cities, civil society, critical theory, and ethnographic methods. His other current work, with Ernesto Ganuza, is an ethnographic account of the travel of ideas about citizen participation.

Elizabeth A. Bennett is Research Associate and Associate Director of Strategic Partnerships at the Center for Fair and Alternative Trade at Colorado State University and a PhD candidate in political science at Brown University. Her dissertation examines how North-South inequality is challenged or further entrenched by social enterprises, global social movements, and international nongovernmental organizations. Her research agenda includes private global governance, fair trade, ethical supply chain management, and food politics. Bennett is the author of several chapters and articles, including the first history of fair trade labeling.

Alissa Cordner is Assistant Professor of Sociology at Whitman College. She received her PhD in sociology from Brown University in 2013. Her research focuses on environmental sociology, the sociology of risk, environmental health and ethics, and public engagement in science and policy making. She is working on a book manuscript about the intersection of science, regulation, activism, and industry decision making related to environmental health risks and consumer exposure to chemicals.

Peter Taylor Klein is a PhD candidate in sociology at Brown University. His research focuses on the intersection of political processes and associational life, development discourses, and environmental conflicts. His dissertation uses an ethnographic lens to examine local contestations around the construction of the Belo Monte hydroelectric facility in the Brazilian Amazon, analyzing civil society demands and state responses in the context of a rapidly changing social and environmental landscape.

Stephanie Savell is a PhD candidate in anthropology at Brown University. She studies everyday violence, public security, and rights-based activism in marginalized urban areas. Her dissertation examines a militarized policing program and its consequences for the poor in Rio de Janeiro's favelas, as the city prepares to host the 2014 World Cup and 2016 Olympics. Stephanie works to bridge scholarship and practice through various projects, partnerships, and engagements in the United States and Brazil.

CPSIA information can be obtained
at www.ICGtesting.com
Printed in the USA
FSOW04n1145211215
14557FS